# 100

Colorful Granny Squares
To Crochet

# 100

## Colorful Granny Squares
## To Crochet

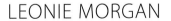

LEONIE MORGAN

St. Martin's Griffin
New York

Library of Congress Cataloging-in-Publication
Data Available Upon Request

ISBN: 978-1-250-02512-8

First St. Martin's Press Edition: February 2013

QUAR.CAFG

Conceived, designed, and produced by
Quarto Publishing plc
The Old Brewery
6 Blundell Street
London N7 9BH

Senior editor: Katie Crous
Copy editor: Liz Jones
Art director: Caroline Guest
Art editor: Jackie Palmer
Designer: Julie Francis
Chart illustrations: Kuo Kang Chen
Photography: (squares) Phil Wilkins;
    (projects) Nicki Dowey, Simon Pask
Creative director: Moira Clinch
Publisher: Paul Carslake

Color separation by
PICA Digital Pte Ltd, Singapore
Printed in China by
1010 Printing International Ltd

10 9 8 7 6 5

# Contents

# Foreword

I have always had an interest in crafts, but it's crochet that has really hooked me and become a wonderful obsession. Originally inspired by my Mum's granny blanket, I rummaged in books and taught myself. I soon began to write my own patterns, being drawn to granny squares in particular because of their portability and versatility—they can be used to make coasters and pot holders, bags and purses, scarves and shawls, pillows and throws, and so on. I still find a magical delight and satisfaction in turning a ball of yarn into a snuggly scarf or cozy throw.

Through trial and error, I have learned that using bright, vibrant colors in my work creates the most satisfying results. Crochet enables you to take such colors and turn them into something homely and warm. An afghan in riotous colors isn't garish—it's gorgeous! I hope the colors used in this book will provide inspiration and help you to explore.

In the following pages I share my love of crochet, color, texture, and design. Beginners will be encouraged to get off the mark and make their very first granny square, and the more experienced among you should find plenty to enhance your skills. Use the designs as a base to creating your own stunning and unique projects, mixing styles and techniques while using vibrant and scrumptious colors.

So wherever you are, pick up a ball of yarn and get crocheting—you can be assured that somewhere in the world, I'm doing the same thing. Happy Hooking!

# About This Book

This book is an eye-catching resource of multiple blocks and projects for you to crochet. As well as the 100-plus designs, there is information on yarn requirements, crochet tools, and techniques.

## Chapter 1: Tools and Techniques, pages 8–33
These pages feature everything you need to know to get started, from a summary of the different yarns available to advice on how to get the most from working with color. An illustrated, comprehensive, and concise guide helps you work both the basic crochet stitches and the more advanced stitches used in the book. Finishing techniques—such as joining and embellishing—are also covered.

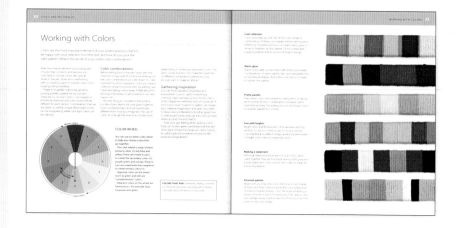

## Chapter 2: Block and Stitch Designs, pages 34–141

At the heart of this book are the 100-plus square designs: 45 main designs, each accompanied by one color variation and one stitch variation; five with inspirational projects; and five size variations. The color and stitch variations make it easy for you to mix and match within the guiding design, or, as you gain confidence, try combining different styles of squares to make truly unique projects.

Photos of all three variations show the end result.

Alternating colors in the charts indicate each round/row. A third color would indicate surface crochet.

Use the estimated yarn requirements for making a baby blanket, lap blanket, or bed throw to give you an idea of total cost for a project.

The main design

Skill level gives a rough guide to difficulty.

Written pattern takes you through round by round.

Variations help you make alternative squares that tie in with the main design.

Yardage estimates for each color provide a useful shopping guide.

The written pattern, chart, and yardage are given for the core square design of each project.

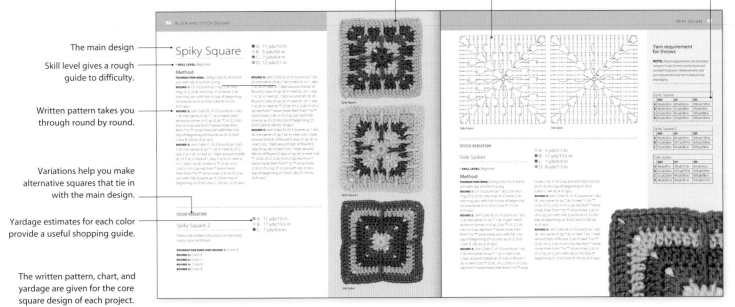

Project notes guide you through how to make the photographed piece; or use all the information on these pages as inspiration for making your own version.

The main photo shows you how the blocks can be joined together to make a beautiful project.

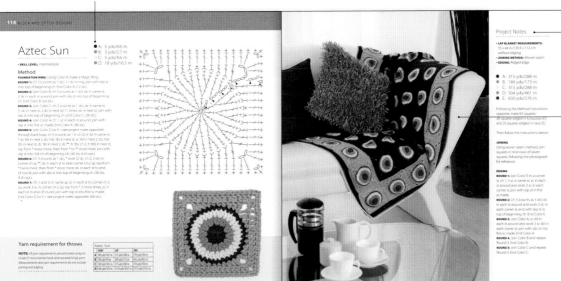

CHAPTER 1

# Tools and Techniques

# Materials and Notions

When you walk into a yarn store, you'll find yourself bombarded with gorgeous yarns in scrumptious colors, differing weights, and all types of textures. The choice available is exciting and a little perplexing to begin with, and the same can be true for the hooks and accessories. Use the guide below to find out exactly what you need to get started.

## Yarns

Suitable yarns for crochet range from very fine cotton to bulky wool and come in a range of different fibers and fiber combinations. As a general rule, yarns that have a smooth texture and a medium or high twist are the easiest to work with. For making afghans, a medium-weight yarn is probably best, as it works up quickly, has good drape and stitch definition, and provides a warm and cozy afghan. All the blocks and projects in this book have been worked in worsted-weight yarn.

Another thing to consider while standing in front of all that yarn is the fiber content and the kind of drape that you would like to achieve in your project.

Before purchasing enough yarn to complete a project, it's a good idea to buy just one ball. Make a test block, wash it following the instructions on the ball band, block it to shape, and see whether you are comfortable using the yarn and whether it turns out how you'd intended.

## Wool

Wool is an excellent choice for afghans. It is a resilient fiber that feels good to crochet and has great stitch definition. If you are making a project that you would like to hand down to future generations and it is within your budget, wool is the fiber to use. Do find out whether or not the wool can be machine washed.

## Acrylic

Acrylic yarn is a perfect choice for beginners and popular with crochet enthusiasts. It's great for practicing stitches and techniques and testing color combinations. Acrylic yarns come in a huge array of colors and it is an affordable choice for your first project. Although acrylic can pill and lose its shape eventually, it does have the benefit of being machine-washable, making it a good choice for items that may require frequent washing.

## Combination yarns

A yarn comprised of both wool and synthetic fiber is a dependable choice. Picking something that has a small percentage of synthetic fiber (for example nylon or acrylic) makes a nice yarn to work with and launder while still retaining the advantages of wool.

## Cotton and cotton mixes

Cotton can present more of a challenge for beginners. It can be a little stiff to work with, but the stitches are crisp and neat. A cotton mix is usually softer to work with, yet still retains crisp, neat stitch definition. Afghans crocheted with cotton or a cotton mix are durable and cool, so are perfect for summer.

## Novelty yarns

Although novelty yarns are tactile and enticing, they are not easy to work with. You can use a splash of novelty yarn to add some interest but on the whole they are tricky to use, and also hide the stitches.

## Crochet hooks

Hooks come in different sizes and materials. The material a hook is made from can affect your gauge. To start out, it's best to use aluminum hooks, as they have a pointed head and well-defined throat and work well with most yarns. Bamboo hooks are also pleasing to work with, but can be slippery with some yarns. Plastic hooks can be squeaky with synthetic yarns. You can also purchase hooks with soft-grip or wooden handles, which are great to work with, particularly if crochet becomes an obsession.

### What size?

You may find that using the recommended hook size for a particular yarn or pattern isn't satisfactory, and your work may be too tight or too loose. Try different hook sizes until you are happy with the completed block. Ultimately, you want to use a hook and yarn weight that you are comfortable with—yarn/hook recommendations are not set in stone.

**YARN LABELS:** *Not all yarn labels give a recommended hook size. Use the recommended knitting-needle size as a guide, or a hook one or two sizes bigger.*

## Notions

Although all you need to get started is a hook and some yarn, it's handy to have the following items in your work bag.

### Needles

Yarn or tapestry needles are used for sewing seams and weaving in yarn tails. Choose needles with blunt ends to avoid splitting stitches. Yarn needles have different-sized eyes, so choose one that will easily accommodate the weight of yarn you will be using.

### Pins

Use rustproof, glass-headed pins for wet and steam blocking squares. Quilter's pins or safety pins are useful for holding blocks in place when joining.

### Stitch markers

Split-ring markers are handy for keeping track of the first stitch of a row, particularly when starting out. Also, use them to hold the working loop when you put your work down for the night. Use for marking and counting when working edging patterns.

### Scissors

Use a pair of small, sharp embroidery scissors.

### Ruler and measuring tape

A rigid ruler is best for measuring gauge and block size. A sturdy measuring tape or dressmaking measuring tape with imperial and metric measurements is good for taking larger measurements.

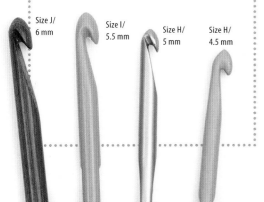

Size J/ 6 mm

Size I/ 5.5 mm

Size H/ 5 mm

Size H/ 4.5 mm

# Stitches and Techniques

All crochet stitches are based on a loop pulled through another loop by a hook. There are only a few simple stitches to master, each of a different length. Crochet can be worked in rows, beginning with a foundation chain, or in rounds, working outward from a foundation ring of chain stitches. Practice making chains and working the basic stitches before moving on to more challenging techniques.

## Holding the hook and yarn

The most common way of holding the hook is shown below, but if this doesn't feel comfortable to you, try grasping the flat section of the hook between your thumb and forefinger as if you were holding a knife.

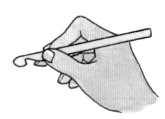

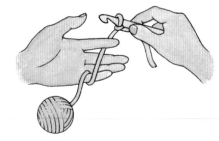

1 Holding the hook like a pen is the most widely used method. Center the tips of your right thumb and forefinger over the flat section of the hook.

2 To control the supply and keep an even gauge on the yarn, loop the short end of the yarn over your left forefinger, and take the yarn coming from the ball loosely around the little finger on the same hand. Use the middle finger on the same hand to help hold the work. If you are left-handed, hold the hook in your left hand and the yarn in your right.

## Making a slip knot

1 Loop the yarn as shown, insert the hook into the loop, catch the yarn with the hook, and pull it through to make a loop over the hook.

2 Gently pull the yarn to tighten the loop around the hook and complete the slip knot.

## Foundation chain

The foundation chain is the equivalent of casting on in knitting, and it is important to make sure that you have made the required number of chains for the pattern you are going to work. Count each V-shaped loop on the front of the chain as one chain stitch, except for the loop on the hook, which is not counted. When working the first row of stitches into the chain, insert the hook under one thread or two, depending on your preference.

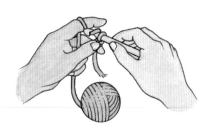

1 Holding the hook with the slip knot in your right hand and the yarn in your left, wrap the yarn over the hook. Draw the yarn through to make a new loop and complete the first chain stitch.

2 Repeat this step, drawing a new loop of yarn through the loop already on the hook until the chain is the required length. After every few stitches move up the thumb and finger that are grasping the chain to keep the gauge even.

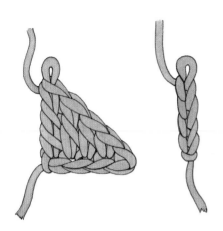

## Turning and starting chains

When working crochet in rows or rounds, you will need to work a specific number of extra chains at the beginning of each row or round. When the work is turned at the end of a straight row, the extra chains are called a turning chain, and when they are worked at the beginning of a round, they are called a starting chain.

The extra chains bring the hook up to the correct height for the stitch you will be working next. The turning or starting chain is counted as the first stitch of the row or round, except when working single crochet where the single turning chain is ignored. A chain may be longer than the number required for the stitch, and in that case counts as one stitch plus a number of chains. At the end of the row or round, the final stitch is usually worked into the turning chain worked on the previous row or round. The final stitch may be worked into the top chain of the turning or starting chain or into another specified stitch of the chain.

---

**Single crochet (sc):** *1 turning chain*
**Half double crochet (hdc):** *2 turning chains*
**Double crochet (dc):** *3 turning chains*
**Treble crochet (tr):** *4 turning chains*
**Double treble crochet (dtr):** *5 turning chains*

---

## Slip stitch (sl st)

Slip stitch is the shortest of all the crochet stitches and its main uses are joining stitches and carrying the hook and yarn from one place to another.

Insert the hook from front to back into the required stitch. Wrap the yarn over the hook and draw it through both the work and the loop on the hook. One loop remains on the hook and one slip stitch has been worked.

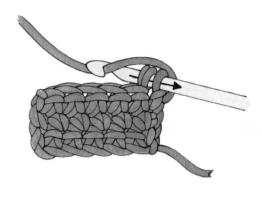

## Single crochet (sc)

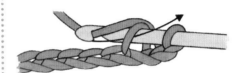

1 Begin with a foundation chain and insert the hook from front to back into the second chain from the hook. Wrap the yarn over the hook and draw it through the first loop, leaving two loops on the hook.

2 To complete the stitch, wrap the yarn over the hook and draw it through both loops on the hook, leaving one loop on the hook. Continue in this way, working one single crochet into each chain.

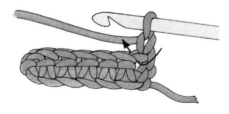

3 At the end of the row, turn, and work one chain for the turning chain (remember that this chain does not count as a stitch). Insert the hook into the first single crochet at the beginning of the row. Work a single crochet into each stitch of the previous row, working the final stitch into the last stitch of the row, but not into the turning chain.

## Half double crochet (hdc)

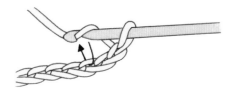

1 Begin with a foundation chain. Wrap the yarn over the hook and insert the hook into the third chain from the hook.

2 Draw the yarn through the chain, leaving three loops. Wrap the yarn over the hook and draw through all three loops on the hook, leaving one loop on the hook.

3 Continue along the row, working one half double crochet into each chain. At the end of the row, work two chains to turn. Miss the first stitch and work a half double crochet into each stitch made on the previous row. At the end of the row, work the last stitch into the top of the turning chain.

## Double crochet (dc)

1 Begin with a foundation chain, then wrap the yarn over the hook and insert the hook into the fourth chain from the hook.

2 Draw the yarn through the chain, leaving three loops on the hook. Wrap the yarn again and draw the yarn through the first two loops on the hook, leaving two loops on the hook.

3 Wrap the yarn over the hook, and draw the yarn through the two loops on the hook, leaving one loop on the hook. Repeat along the row. At the end of the row, work three chains to turn. Miss the first stitch and work a double crochet into each stitch. At the end of the row, work the last stitch into the top of the turning chain.

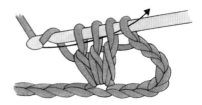

## Bobble (B)

A bobble is a group of between three and six double-crochet stitches worked into the same stitch and closed at the top. Bobbles are worked on wrong-side rows and they are usually surrounded by shorter stitches to throw them into high relief. When working bobbles in a contrasting color, use a separate length of yarn to make each bobble, carrying the main yarn under the bobble stitches or across the back of the bobble.

To make a three-stitch bobble, work three double crochet stitches into the same stitch, omitting the last stage of each stitch so the last loop of each one remains on the hook. You now have four loops on the hook. Wrap the yarn over the hook and draw it through the four loops to secure them and complete the bobble.

## Treble crochet (tr)

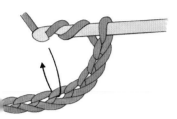

1 Begin with a foundation chain. Wrap the yarn over the hook twice and insert the hook into the fifth chain from the hook.

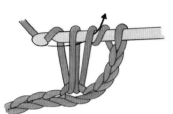

2 Draw the yarn through the chain, leaving four loops on the hook. Wrap the yarn again and draw the yarn through the first two loops on the hook, leaving three loops on the hook.

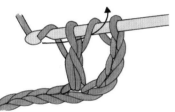

3 Wrap the yarn again and draw through the first two loops on the hook, leaving two loops on the hook.

4 Wrap the yarn again and draw through the two remaining loops, leaving one loop on the hook. Continue along the row, working one treble crochet stitch into each chain. At the end of the row, work four chains to turn. Miss the first stitch and work a treble crochet into each stitch made on the previous row. At the end of the row, work the last stitch into the top of the turning chain.

## Double treble crochet (dtr)

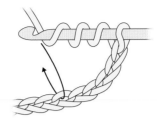

1 Begin with a foundation chain. Wrap the yarn over the hook three times and insert the hook into the sixth chain from the hook.

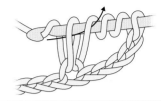

2 Draw the yarn through the chain, leaving five loops on the hook. Wrap the yarn again and draw it through the first two loops on the hook, leaving four loops on the hook.

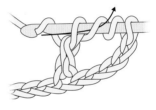

3 Wrap the yarn again and draw through the first two loops on the hook, leaving three loops on the hook.

4 Wrap the yarn again and draw through the first two loops on the hook, leaving two loops on the hook.

5 Wrap the yarn again and draw through the two remaining loops, leaving one loop on the hook.

## Cluster (Cl)

A cluster is made with a multiple of single, half double, double, or treble crochet stitches. The last loop of each stitch remains on the hook until they are worked together at the end. Count the turning or starting chains as the first stitch.

**1** To work a cluster of three double-crochet stitches, work the first stitch, omitting the last stage to leave two loops on the hook. Work the second and third stitch in the same way, leaving the last loop of each stitch on the hook. You now have four loops on the hook.

**2** Draw the yarn through all four loops to complete the cluster and secure the stitch.

## Puff stitch (PS)

A puff stitch is a cluster of half double crochet stitches worked in the same place (the number of stitches may vary). When working a beginning puff stitch, count the turning chain as the first stitch.

**1** Wrap the yarn over the hook, insert the hook where required, and draw a loop through (three loops on the hook). Repeat this step twice more, inserting the hook into the same stitch (seven loops on the hook).

**2** Wrap the yarn over the hook and draw it through all seven loops on the hook. Work an extra chain stitch at the top of the puff to complete the stitch.

## Working around posts

This technique creates raised stitches by inserting the hook around the post (stem) of the stitch below, from the front or the back.

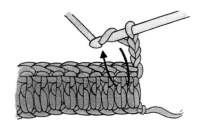

**Front post double crochet (FPdc)**
Wrap the yarn over the hook from back to front, insert the hook from the front to the back at right of the next stitch, then bring it to the front at the left of the same stitch. Complete the stitch in the usual way.

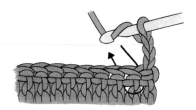

**Back post double crochet (BPdc)**
Wrap the yarn over the hook, insert the hook from the back to the front at right of the next stitch, then take it back again at the left of the same stitch. Complete the stitch in the usual way.

## Popcorn (PC)

A popcorn is a group of double-crochet stitches (the number may vary) sharing the same base stitch, which is folded and closed at the top so the popcorn is raised from the background stitches.

**1** To make a popcorn with four stitches, work a group of four double-crochet stitches into the same place.

**2** Take the hook out of the working loop and insert it under both loops of the first double crochet in the group. Pick up the working loop with the hook and draw it through to fold the group of stitches and close it at the top.

## Spike stitch (Ss)

Spike stitches are made by inserting the hook one or more rows below the previous row, either directly below the next stitch or to the left or right.

To work a single-crochet spike stitch, insert the hook as directed by the pattern, wrap the yarn over the hook and draw through, lengthen the loop to the height of the working row, then complete the stitch.

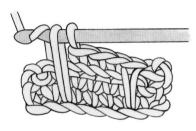

## Decreases

One or two stitches can be decreased by working two or three incomplete stitches together, and the method is the same for single, half double, double, and treble crochet stitches.

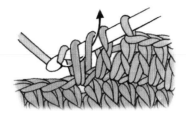

**1** Leave the first stitch incomplete so there are two loops on the hook, then work another incomplete stitch so you have three loops on the hook.

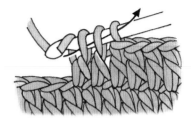

**2** Wrap the yarn and draw through all three loops to finish the decrease. Two stitches can be decreased in the same way by working three stitches together. When working in double crochet, this decrease is called dc3tog.

## Making a Magic Ring

A Magic Ring can be used in place of a Foundation Ring for crocheting in the round. The benefit of this method is that after pulling the yarn tail to draw the stitches together there is no hole at the center of your work.

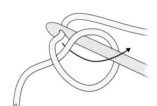

**1** Wind the yarn around your finger once, leaving the yarn tail on the left and the working yarn on the right.

**2** Insert your hook under the strands of the ring and draw through a loop of the working yarn.

**3** Now work the number of starting chains required in the pattern.

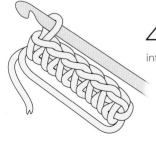

**4** Continue in the same manner as for working into a foundation ring.

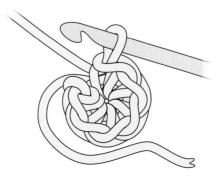

**5** When the first round is complete, pull tightly on the yarn tail to close the Magic Ring.

## Working in rounds

Blocks worked in rounds are worked outward from a central ring of chains, called a Foundation Ring, or from a Magic Ring (see page 17).

### Making a Foundation Ring

Work a short length of foundation chain as specified in the pattern. Join the chains into a ring by working a slip stitch into the first stitch of the foundation chain.

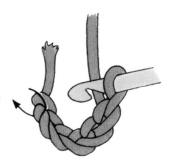

## Joining a new color when working in the round

When the pattern states "Join Color B," this is done in the same place the old yarn ended, usually at the start of a round. To join a new color, insert the hook in the work as instructed, draw up a loop of the new color leaving a tail about 4 in. (10 cm) long, and chain 1. Continue with new yarn.

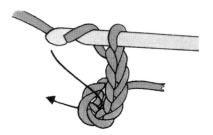

### Working into the ring

1 Work the number of starting chains specified in the pattern—three chains are shown here (counting as one double-crochet stitch). Inserting the hook into the space at the center of the ring each time, work the number of stitches specified in the pattern.

2 Count the stitches at the end of the round to check that you have worked the correct number. Join the first and last stitches of the round together by working a slip stitch into the top (or other specified stitch) of the starting chain.

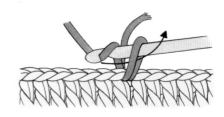

## Changing colors at the start or middle of a row

When working the last stitch of the old color, leave the stitch incomplete, wrap the new color around the hook, and finish the stitch.

1 Draw the new color through the last two loops of the stitch.

## Finishing off the final round—an alternative to slip stitch join

1 Cut the yarn, leaving a tail of about 4 in. (10 cm), and draw it through the last stitch. With right side facing, thread the tail in a yarn needle and take it under both loops of the stitch next to the starting chain.

2 Insert the needle into the center of the last stitch of the round. On the wrong side, pull the needle through to complete the stitch, adjust the length of the stitch to close the round, then weave in the tail on the wrong side and trim.

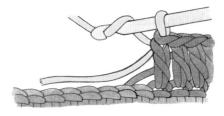

2 Continue working in the new color.

## Sewing in ends

For a block worked in rows, sew in ends diagonally on the wrong side. For a block worked in the round, sew in ends under stitches for a couple of inches. If the pattern doesn't allow this, sew under a few stitches, then up through the back of a stitch, and under a few more stitches on the next row.

## Tapestry crochet

Tapestry crochet is similar to colorwork crochet but is usually worked in single crochet and the carried strand is woven in.

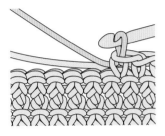

1 Work as for colorwork until the first color change, change color in the same way as for colorwork.

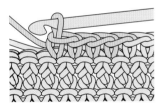

2 Continue following the pattern carrying the unused yarn along the top of the previous row and working over it.

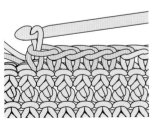

3 After the next color change, continue to carry the unused yarn in the same way.

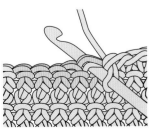

4 On the next, and all other rows, insert the hook under the carried yarn and into the stitch to lock the carried yarn in place.

## Surface crochet

Surface crochet is worked onto the crochet block when it is complete; the stitches used are usually chain stitch or single crochet and can be used to "draw" lines, swirls, and letters.

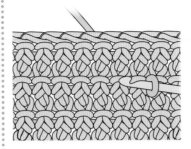

1 Holding the working yarn at the back of your work at all times, insert the hook from front to back through the fabric in a space between two stitches and pull through a loop.

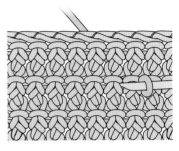

2 Insert hook from front to back in space between next two stitches.

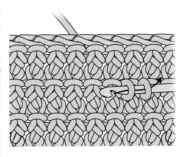

3 Pull up a loop.

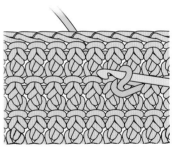

4 Pull loop through the loop on the hook to make a chain stitch.

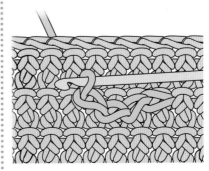

5 Continue in this way, working chain stitches to form a pattern. Secure yarn ends.

# Reading Patterns and Charts

With all those symbols, abbreviations, and charts, crochet can seem daunting and complex to begin with. A little explanation though, and all becomes clear.

Blocks can use a number of different stitches, so to make patterns quicker and easier to follow, abbreviations are used. Abbreviations and symbols may vary from one pattern publisher to another, so always check that you understand the system in use before commencing work.

## SYMBOLS

| Symbol | Stitch or term |
|---|---|
| * | Start of repeat |
| ** | End of last repeat |
| [ ] | Repeat the instructions within the brackets the stated number of times |
| ( ) | Can either be explanatory (counts as 1 dc) or can be read as a group of stitches worked into the same stitch or space (dc, ch2, dc) |
| ➤ | An arrowhead indicates the beginning of a row or round |

## Arrangements of symbols

**Symbols joined at top**
A group of symbols may be joined at the top, indicating that these stitches should be worked together at the top, as in cluster stitches, and for decreasing the number of stitches (i.e. sc3tog).

**Symbols joined at base**
Symbols joined at the base should all be worked into the same stitch below.

**Symbols joined at top and base**
Sometimes a group of stitches are joined at both top and bottom, making a puff, bobble, or popcorn.

**Symbols on a curve**
Sometimes symbols are drawn at an angle, depending on the construction of the stitch pattern.

**Distorted symbols**
Some symbols may be lengthened, curved, or spiked, to indicate where the hook is inserted below.

## ABBREVIATIONS

| Symbol | Stitch or term | Abbreviation |
|---|---|---|
| ○ | Chain | ch |
| ● | Slip stitch | sl st |
| + | Single crochet | sc |
| T | Half double crochet | hdc |
| Ŧ | Double crochet | dc |
| Ŧ | Treble crochet | tr |
| Ŧ | Double treble crochet | dtr |
| Ⱥ | Cluster | Cl |
| e.g. bobble of 5 doubles | Bobble | B |
| e.g. puff of 4 half doubles | Puff stitch | PS |
| e.g. popcorn of 5 doubles | Popcorn | PC |
| e.g. single in back loop | Back loop | bl |
| e.g. half double in front loop | Front loop | fl |
| | Back post | BP |
| | Front post | FP |
| | Chain space | ch sp |
| | Together | tog |
| | Through back loop | tbl |
| | Yarn over | yo |
| | Beginning | beg |
| | Repeat | rep |
| | Right side | RS |
| | Wrong side | WS |

Some patterns include special abbreviations, which are explained on the instructions pages.

## Reading charts

Each design in this book is accompanied by a chart, which should be read together with the written instructions. Once you are used to the symbols they are quick and easy to follow. All charts are read from the right side.

### Charts in rows

• Wrong-side rows are numbered at the left, and read from left to right.
• Right-side rows are numbered at the right, and read from right to left.
• Rows are numbered or indicated by an arrow.

### Surface crochet

Surface crochet is marked on the charts in a different color and is worked after the block has been completed.

### Colorwork/tapestry crochet charts in rows

Colorwork charts are read in the same way as charts in rows, but each square represents a stitch (usually sc). When changing color, follow the instructions for joining a new color (see page 18). If the color change is for a large area, you can end the unused color. If the color change is for a few stitches, carry the unused color under the new stitches. When working the next row, insert the hook under the loops of the stitch and under the carried thread. This helps to hide the carried yarn in tapestry crochet work.

### Charts in rounds

These charts begin at the center, and each round is read counterclockwise, in the same direction as working. The beginning of each round is indicated by an arrow. Some charts have been stretched to show all the stitches.

# Gauge

It's important to crochet a test square before you start your project to establish gauge.

No two people will crochet to the exact same gauge, even when working with identical yarn and hooks. Gauge can be affected by the type of hook you use, the type of yarn you choose, how you hold the hook, and how the yarn feeds through your fingers. Beginners tend to have a tight gauge, so may benefit from using a larger hook than the pattern recommends.

Always make a test swatch before you start your project. Your test swatch will allow you to compare your gauge with the pattern gauge and will give you a good idea of how the finished project will feel and drape. It's also useful for testing out color combinations. All of the blocks in this book have been worked in worsted-weight yarn and a size H (5 mm) crochet hook. To test your gauge, make a sample block in the yarn you intend to use following the pattern directions. The block should measure a little less than the finished size to allow for blocking. Block the sample square then measure again. If your block is larger, try making another block using a smaller hook. If your block is smaller, try making another block using a bigger hook. Also do this if the fabric feels too loose and floppy or too dense and rigid. Keep trying until you find a hook size that will give you the gauge, or until you are happy with the drape and feel of your block. Ultimately it's more important that you use a hook and yarn you are comfortable with than that you rigidly follow the pattern instructions.

**MULTIPLE USES:** *Keep a gauge swatch to test blocking and cleaning methods.*

## CALCULATING YARN AMOUNTS

Each of the patterns in this book has yarn requirements provided. These are approximate and based on using the same yarn and hook size. If you choose to use thinner or thicker weight yarn for your afghan, or a different-sized hook, the yarn requirements needed may be different. The best way to work out how much yarn you will need is to make a few blocks in the yarn and color combination you intend to use, then unravel it. It seems a shame to unravel something you've just made, but it's worth it in the long run. Measure the amount of yarn used for each color in the blocks and, taking the average yardage, multiply by the number of blocks you intend to make. Don't forget to add extra yarn for joining the blocks and working the edgings.

Here, the same block is worked in different-weight yarn and appropriate hook sizes.

Yarn: Fingering (4-ply)
Hook: E size (4 mm)

Yarn: Worsted
Hook: H size (5 mm)

# Working with Colors

Colors are the most important element of your project and you need to be happy with your selection from the start. But how do you pick the right palette? What is the secret of a successful color combination?

After the initial excitement surrounding yarn choices, fiber contents, and textures, you now have to choose colors. We have all stood in the yarn store, arms overflowing with scrumptious yarns in myriad colors, mind buzzing with possibilities.

There is no golden rule or big secret to picking a perfect palette for your project. There are no "wrong" colors. Color triggers an emotional response, and color choice will be different for each person. Combinations that we are drawn to will be unique. Bold, bright colors can be invigorating, while cool, light colors can be calming.

## Color combinations

Before setting foot in the yarn store with the intention to buy, spend some time working out the color combinations you are drawn to—see opposite for some inspiration. Once you have a collection of yarns to work with, try adding new colors and taking colors away. Fiddle about for as long as necessary to get a selection you are happy with.

Another thing to consider is that while a bundle of yarn skeins will look good together, once crocheted they can look surprisingly different from how you imagined. The use of color can change the look of a crochet block, depending on where you place each color. The best course of action is to make test swatches of different combinations before you buy enough yarn to make an afghan.

## Gathering inspiration

You can find inspiration anywhere and everywhere. Color is used in everything: clothing, logos, packaging, toys, flowers, fabric, birds, magazines, websites, and, of course, art. A trip to your local museum or gallery can trigger your creative imagination and open your eyes to new color combinations. Another good trick is collect paint cards, snip out the colors you are drawn to, and mix and match.

Trust your gut feeling when picking colors. If you've chosen greens and blues but the yarn store doesn't have the range you were hoping for, add a sploosh of yellow or hot pink. Be brave and experiment!

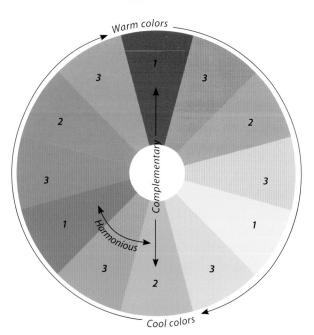

## COLOR WHEEL

You can use an artist's color wheel to help you choose colors that go together.

The color wheel is made of three primary colors (1): red, blue, and yellow. These are mixed in pairs to create the secondary colors (2): purple, green, and orange. These in turn are mixed with their neighbors to create tertiary colors (3).

Opposite colors on the wheel (such as green and red) are "complementary" colors.

Adjacent colors on the wheel are harmonious—for example, blue, turquoise, and green.

**COLORS THAT POP:** *Sometimes, adding a color that you think won't go works surprisingly well. A clashing color really adds some vibrancy to your work.*

## Cool collection

Cool colors take up one half of the color wheel. A combination of these cool shades will be calming and refreshing. Try adding a touch or cream, black, gray, or white to brighten up the palette. Or, for a really eye-popping palette, add an accent of bright orange.

## Warm glow

Warm colors take up the other half of the color wheel. Combinations of warm, earthy, fall colors are perfect for a cozy fireside afghan. Add a few cool colors or cream to lighten the palette.

## Pretty pastels

Pale, pastel colors are suitable for baby items or spring and summer throws. Combinations of pastel colors look fresh and airy. Try adding a touch of a bright color to a pastel palette for contrast.

## Fun with brights

Bright, vivid, and fluorescent colors are eye catching and fun to use in crochet projects. Using a neutral color like black or white to edge granny squares made in bright colors helps to unite the colors.

## Making a statement

Although black and white are not true colors, when used together they are bold and striking. Add gray and a bold statement color, such as red or electric blue, for a stunning afghan.

## Personal palette

Begin with your favorite color (here, green). Add one or two shades of that color. Then have a look at the color wheel and choose a complementary color (pink). Think about adding a splash of white or black for extra zing. Then add a color two wedges away in either direction from your favorite color on the color wheel.

# Design Your Own Project

All of the blocks in this book can be mixed and matched to create a huge array of possible combinations. You could crochet a project using one block design in different colors, or using all of the squares in the book. The choices are endless, so whether you are making a pillow cover or a bedspread, the following guidelines will help you design your own unique item.

First, decide what you are making and who it is for. This will affect your choice of yarns and colors. For instance, if you are making a baby throw for a girl, perhaps you will choose pink as your main color, and a machine-washable yarn. Or, if you're making a throw for yourself, pick colors and yarns that you love.

## Choosing blocks
Choose blocks that are appropriate for your skill level and that you are comfortable making. Start by choosing just one or a few of your favorite blocks. You can mix and match squares of different sizes.

## Choosing yarns
Pick yarns that are suitable for the finished item. For instance, a baby blanket may be worked in light worsted or sport-weight yarn. Or a pillow cover could work in smooth, silky yarn. Think about the feel and drape of the finished item and whether the yarn needs to be machine-washable.

## Choosing colors
If you're making a throw for your favorite armchair, choose colors that will match the decor of the room if you want the throw to blend in, or go for contrasting colors if you'd like the throw to be a feature. If you're making a baby blanket, decide whether you'd like soft, pastel colors or bright, cheery colors. You can also make a striking throw by using up scraps in a variety of colors, and edging each block in a neutral color such as cream, white, or black.

## Planning and drawing your design
Use graph paper or a program on your computer to design your layout. Color the squares in the palette you've chosen to see if it works well. Leave space to add notes on yarn requirements.

## Joining method
Decide which joining method you'd like to use (see page 26). Do you want the joins to be visible and part of the design, or would you rather they were hidden?

## Edging
Pick an edging than complements your layout (see page 28). Decide on the color or colors you'd like the edging to be in. A fringe can add softness while a simple border of single crochet can neaten a busy design.

## Work out yarn quantities
Make test squares and then unravel them. Measure how much of each color you have used for the squares and then multiply by the number of blocks you'll be making. Add extra yarn for joining and edging. If you're not sure you'll have enough yarn, it's preferable to buy an extra skein just in case!

54 in. (137 cm)

36 in. (91 cm)

A: 594 yds/543 m
B: 360 yds/329 m
C: 738 yds/675 m
D: 360 yds/329 m
E: 576 yds/527 m

Plan your layout design. Here, Swirly squares (page 136) in four color combinations have been mixed with Eye-popping Popcorn (page 72) in two color combinations.

## Test swatch

Once you have settled on your design, make a test swatch of four or more squares. This is a great way to double check that your yarn, color, and block choices work well together and it's also a great way to trial blocking, joining, and washing methods. Block each square and join them with your chosen method, then work the edging you've picked around the swatch. This mini-project will give you a tangible idea of how the actual finished project will look and feel.

## The importance of blocking

When you've made all of the blocks required, take the time to block them. It really does help to set the stitches and make neat edges for joining and edging. See page 26 for more about blocking.

A test swatch helps visualize the completed project. A Popcorn Fringe (see page 30) has been added here to test if the edging fits the design.

### YARN QUANTITIES

Each block design in this book has estimated yarn quantities for making afghans in three sizes: baby blanket, lap throw, and bedspread. So, for instance, a baby blanket made of Daisy Chain blocks (see page 37) requires 36 squares joined in six rows of six squares, and will measure approximately 36 in. (91 cm) square without an edging. The yarn quantities can be found with the instructions for each block; all you need to add to these quantities is the yarn for joining and edging.

BABY BLANKET: 36 in. (91 cm) square. Make 36 squares and join in 6 rows of 6 squares.
LAP THROW: 54 x 42 in. (137 x 107 cm). Make 63 squares and join in 9 rows of 7 squares.
BEDSPREAD: 85 x 66 in. (216 x 168 cm). Make 154 squares and join in 14 rows of 11 squares.

# Blocking and Joining

To finish off your squares neatly, you'll need to block them before using one of the joining methods. You can choose to sew or crochet your squares together, and opt for either a visible join at the front of your work or keeping it out of sight at the back. A single-crochet join in a contrasting color to your blocks can add texture and interest. A woven seam can be used if you don't want the join to be seen.

## Blocking

Blocking is crucial to set the stitches and even out the squares ready for joining. Choose a method based on the care label of your yarn or, if none is provided, take into account the fiber content. When in doubt, use the wet method.

Use an ironing board, pillow, or old quilt. Or, you may find it useful to make a blocking board by securing one or two layers of quilter's batting, covered with a sheet of cotton fabric, over a piece of flat board.

### Wet method—acrylic and wool/acrylic blends

Using rustproof pins, pin your squares to the correct measurements on a flat surface and dampen using a spray bottle of cold water. Pat the fabric to help the moisture penetrate more easily. Ease stitches into position, keeping rows and stitches straight. Allow to dry before removing pins.

### Steam method—wools and cottons

With wrong sides facing up, pin pieces to the correct measurements using rustproof and glass-headed pins. For blocks with raised stitches, pin them with right sides facing up to avoid squashing the stitches. Steam lightly, holding the iron 1 in. (2.5 cm) above your work. Allow the steam to penetrate the block for several seconds. It is safer to avoid pressing, but if you choose to do so, cover with a clean towel or cloth first and press lightly to avoid flattening the stitches. Allow to dry before removing pins.

## Joining

Squares can be joined together by sewing or by crochet. Place markers and pin seams together to help match blocks up and give a neat finish. Use the same yarn that you used for the squares, or a finer yarn, preferably with the same fiber content.

### Overcast seam

Pieces of crochet can be joined by overcasting the seam. The overcasting stitches can be worked through just the back of the crochet loops or the whole loops. Place the pieces to be joined side by side on a flat surface with right sides up and edges together. Thread a large, blunt-ended sewing needle with yarn.

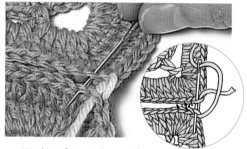

1 Working from right to left, overcast the seam by inserting the needle into the back loop of corresponding stitches. For extra strength, you can work two stitches into the end loops.

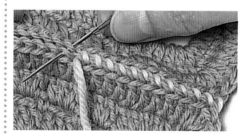

2 Continue overcasting the seam, making sure you join only the back loops of the edges together, until you reach the end of the seam. Secure the yarn at the beginning and end of the stitching.

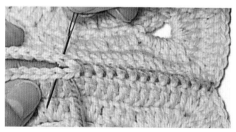

Alternatively, overcast the two pieces together by inserting the needle through the whole loops of corresponding stitches. This gives a less neat join than sewing through just the back of the loops.

## Backstitch seam

A backstitch seam creates a strong but non-elastic seam and is suitable where firmness is required and for lightweight yarns. With right sides facing, pin together the pieces to be joined. Insert the pins at right angles to the edge evenly across the fabric. Thread a large, blunt-ended sewing needle with yarn.

1 Secure the end of the seam and yarn by taking the needle twice around the outer edges of the fabric, from back to front. Take the yarn around the outside edge once more, but this time insert the needle through the work from back to front no more than ¹/₂ in. (1.3 cm) from where the yarn last emerged. Insert the needle from front to back where the first stitch began, then bring the needle back through to the front, the same distance along the edge as before.

2 Work in backstitch from right to left along the whole seam, staying close to the edge and going through both pieces of fabric. Secure the end with a couple of overlapping stitches.

## Mattress stitch/woven stitch

Place the pieces to be joined side by side on a flat surface, wrong sides up and edges together. Thread a large, blunt-ended sewing needle with yarn. Starting at the bottom and working from right to left, place the needle under the loop of the first stitch on both pieces and draw the yarn through. Move up one stitch and repeat this process, going from left to right. Continue to zigzag loosely from edge to edge. Pull the yarn tight every inch or so, allowing the edges to join together. A woven seam gives a flatter finish than a backstitch seam and works better for baby garments and fine work.

## Slip stitch crochet seam

A slip stitch crochet seam can be worked with right sides together, and will form a ridge at the back of the work. Or, work with wrong sides together for a ridge on the right side of the work. This can be effective worked in a different color from the squares.

Hold pieces with right sides facing. You can work through both loops, which creates a thick seam, or through one loop for a less bulky seam. Insert the hook under the back loop only of the nearest edge and the front loop only of the farther edge.

## Single crochet seam

Again, this is a method that can be used at the front or back of the work. Work as for the slip stitch seam, but in single crochet.

# Edgings

A crochet edging doesn't just finish off your project with style; it also helps your project hold its shape and keeps the edges from stretching.

Use a hook a size or two smaller than the one you used for the main project. Always start by working a round of single crochet around the project, working three stitches in each corner stitch. This gives you a base to work from if you are making a grown-on or sewn-on edging.

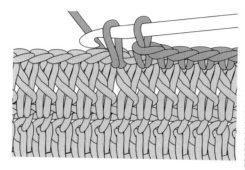

### Working across the top or bottom edge

When working across the top of a row, work 1 sc into each stitch as you would if working another row. When working across the bottom edge of chain stitches, work 1 sc in remaining loop of each foundation chain.

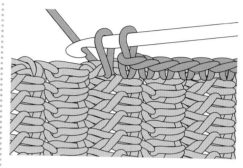

### Working along sides of row ends

When working on a side edge of a block worked in rows, insert the hook under two threads of the first (or last) stitch of each row. Place the stitches an even distance apart along the edge. Try a short length to test the number of stitches required for a flat result. As a guide:

**ROWS OF SC:** 1 sc in side edge of each row.
**ROWS OF HDC:** 3 sc in side edge of every two rows.
**ROWS OF DC:** 2 sc in side edge of every row.
**ROWS OF TR:** 3 sc in side edge of each row.

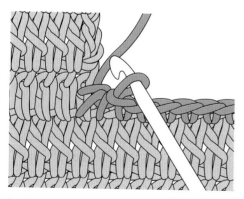

Inward corner

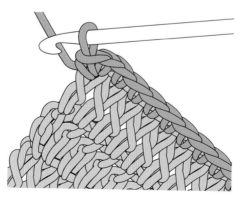

Outer corner

### Working around corners

You'll need to add a couple of stitches at each corner to allow the edging to turn without distorting your work. As a guide, corners are normally turned by working 3 sc (or sc, hdc, sc) into the corner. If you find the edging is too wavy or too taut after the first round has been completed, it will probably get worse once the rest of the edging has been worked. Take time at this point to pull out the first row or round and redo it using fewer stitches.

## Sewn-on edgings

Sewn-on edgings are usually worked sideways by working a few stitches on each row for the length required. Make the edging longer than it appears to need to be. If possible, sew the edging in place as you make it, adding any extra length as you go.

When calculating the amount you need, add about an extra 2–4 in. (5–10 cm) for every 39½ in. (100 cm) of edging. Allow extra to turn corners. Try out the edging on your gauge swatch to help you work out the correct number of stitches you will need for the edging to sit correctly around corners.

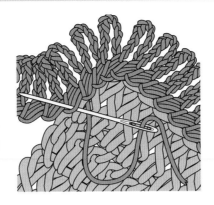

## Attaching sewn-on edgings

Don't break your yarn in case you need to make adjustments to its length. Hold the working loop of your edging with a slip marker to keep it from unraveling. Place the edge of the afghan and the edge of the edging to be attached so that their right sides are together. Use quilter's pins or safety pins to hold in place and sew on the edging using overcast stitch. Make any adjustments to the length of the edging, then end the yarn using the tail to join together the two ends of the border.

## Jagged Edging

- **SKILL LEVEL:** *Beginner*
**FOUNDATION ROW:** Ch 8.
**ROW 1:** 4 dc in 8th ch from hook, ch 4, turn. (4 sts.)
**ROW 2:** Sc in next 4 sts, ch 2, skip 2 ch, sc in next ch, turn. (5 sts, 1 ch sp.)

**ROW 3:** Ch 5, 4 dc in ch-2 sp, ch 4, turn. (4 sts, 1 ch sp.)
Repeat Rows 2 and 3 for desired length.

## Loopy Fringe

- **SKILL LEVEL:** *Beginner*
**FOUNDATION ROW:** Ch 4.
**ROW 1:** Sc in 2nd ch from hook and in next 2 ch, ch 1, turn. (3 sts.)
**ROW 2:** Sc in next 3 sts, ch 7, turn. (3 sts, 1 ch sp.)

**ROW 3:** Sc in next 3 sts, ch 1, turn. (3 sts.)
Repeat Rows 2 and 3 for desired length.

## Blooming Border

- **SKILL LEVEL:** *Intermediate*
**SPECIAL STITCHES:**
- Cluster—Cl: Made of 2 tr.
- Slip Cluster—Sl Cl: Make 1 unfinished tr (2 loops on hook), remove hook and insert, from back to front, into top of 6th cluster of last motif made, pull through 1 loop, remove hook and pick up all 3 loops on hook, finish as for Cl.
**1ST MOTIF:** Ch 12, sl st in 7th ch from

hook to form a ring, ch 1, turn, sc into ring, [ch 3, Cl, ch 3, sc into ring] 6 times.
**2ND MOTIF:** Ch 17, sl st into 7th ch from hook to form a ring, ch 1, turn, sc into ring, (ch 3, Sl Cl, ch 3, sc into ring), [ch 3, Cl, ch 3, sc into ring] 5 times.
Repeat instructions for 2nd Motif until edging is desired length, ch 5.

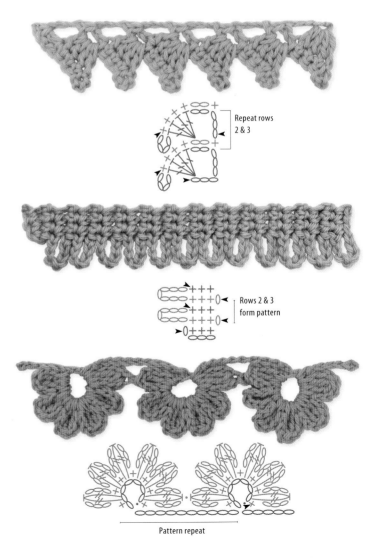

Repeat rows 2 & 3

Rows 2 & 3 form pattern

Pattern repeat

## Picot Flower Edging

- **SKILL LEVEL:** *Beginner*
**SPECIAL STITCH:**
- Picot Flower: Ch 5, sl st into 6th ch from hook, [ch 5, sl st into same ch as last picot] twice.
**ROW 1:** Using Color A, ch 1, * make Picot Flower, ch 9; rep from * for desired length.
Attach edging.

**ROW 2:** Join Color B with sl st into 2nd picot of Picot Flower, *ch 6, make Picot Flower, ch 5, sl st into 2nd picot of next Picot Flower; rep from * around, join into first sl st made. End Color B.

Pattern repeat

## Working grown-on edgings

Always begin with a round of single crochet. Calculate how many stitches the edging pattern needs, including corners. If you need to add or subtract a few stitches, add another round of single crochet, adjusting the number of stitches evenly. Using split markers to mark where pattern repeats will lie will help you to visualize it.

## Popcorn Fringe

- **SKILL LEVEL:** *Beginner*
**SPECIAL STITCH:**
- Popcorn—PC: Made of 5 dc.
Multiple of 5 + 4 + 1 turning ch.
**ROUND 1:** Using Color A, work a round of sc, working 3 sc in each corner. End Color A.
**ROUND 2:** Using Color B, work a round of sc, working 3 sc in each corner. After working this round, place markers or scraps of yarn to mark each repeat. Try to place a PC in each corner stitch. You may need to increase or decrease the number of stitches on this round before working Round 3. End Color B.

**ROUND 3:** Join Color C, ch 1, *[sc in next 4 sts, make PC in next st; rep from * until 4 sts from corner, sc in next 4 sts, PC in corner st] 4 times, join to first sc made. End Color C.
**ROUND 4:** Join Color D, ch 2 (counts as 1 hdc), sc in next 2 sts, * hdc in next st, (dc, ch 1, dc) in PC, hdc in next st, sc in next 2 sts; rep from * around, join to top of beginning ch. End Color D.
Make fringe using three strands of Color B and fasten through each ch sp.

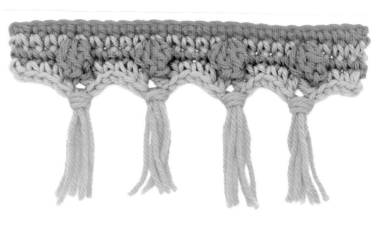

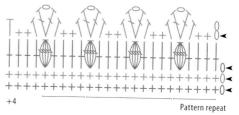

+4

Pattern repeat

## Simple Ridged Band

• **SKILL LEVEL:** *Beginner*

Any number of stitches.

**ROUND 1:** Using Color A, work a round of sc, working 3 sc in each corner, join to first sc made. End Color A.

**ROUND 2:** Join Color B tbl, ch 1 and sc tbl in same place, sc tbl in each st around, working 3 sc tbl in corner stitches, join to first sc made. End Color B.

**ROUND 3:** Join Color C tbl and repeat Round 2. End Color C.

**ROUND 4:** Join Color D tbl and repeat Round 2. End Color D.

Any number of stitches

## Shell Edging

• **SKILL LEVEL:** *Beginner*

**SPECIAL STITCH:**

• Shell: Made of 3 dc, ch 1, 3 dc in same place.

Multiple of 6.

**ROUND 1:** Work a round of sc, working 3 sc in each corner. After working this round, place markers or scraps of yarn to mark out each multiple of six. Try to place a Shell in each corner stitch. You may need to increase or decrease the number of stitches on this round before working Round 2.

**ROUND 2:** Join Color B in 3rd st to left of any corner, * ch 1 and sc into same st, skip 2 sts, make Shell in next st, skip 2 sts; rep from * around, join into first sc made. End Color B.

**ROUND 3:** Join Color C, ch 1 and sc into same st, * sc in next 3 dc, ch 3, sc in next 3 dc, sc in next sc; rep from * around, sc in last st, join to first sc made. End Color C.

Multiple of 6

## Flower Border

• **SKILL LEVEL:** *Beginner*

Multiple of 8 + 1 turning ch.

Make Flowers separately.

**FLOWER:**

**FOUNDATION RING:** Using Color A, make a Magic Ring.

**ROUND 1:** Ch 1, [sc into ring, ch 2] 5 times, join to first sc made. End Color A.

**ROUND 2:** Join Color B, C or D in ch sp, [(ch 2, 1 dc, ch 1, 1 dc, ch 2, sl st) into same ch sp, sl st into next ch sp] 5 times. End Color. (5 petals made.)

**EDGING:**

**ROUND 1:** Using Color A, work a round of sc, working 3 sc in each corner, join to first sc made. End Color A.

**ROUND 2:** Join Color E, ch 1 and sc in same place, sc in next 2 sts, * (ch 2, sl st into ch-1 sp of Flower petal, ch 2, sl st into top of same sc), sc in next 5 sts, (ch 2, sl st into next petal of same Flower, ch 2, sl st into last sc made), sc in next 3 sts; rep from * around, join to first sc made. End Color E.

Flowers taken from appliqué block chain stitch added

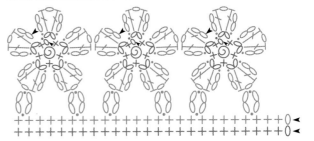

Appliqué, beads, and surface crochet

Buttons, appliqué motifs, and ribbons

# Embellishments

You can embellish and personalize your crochet blocks with appliqué, cross stitch, embroidery, buttons, ribbons, and beads. Make a few blocks in single crochet, dig out your sewing box, and let your imagination run free!

For embroidery work it's best to use a blunt wool needle to avoid damaging your crochet block by splitting the threads. A same-weight yarn is good for cross stitch, but for embroidery you can create attractive effects by experimenting with different yarns of different weights and fibers. Cross stitch and embroidery are best worked on a solid stitch pattern such as single crochet, rather than on bigger stitches.

## Cross stitch

Working cross stitch on a crochet block can be tricky at first. Finding where the holes are is harder than with cross stitch fabric; try holding up the square to the light to see where they are.

## Embroidery

Use simple embroidery stitches such as backstitch, running stitch, and lazy daisy to create your own designs. Try embroidering a name or phrase onto a block as a personal touch.

## Surface crochet

Working surface crochet onto a block is another way of embroidering and embellishing your work. Work simple chain stitches onto the block to create swirly lines or letters.

## Appliqué motifs

Sewing crochet motifs to blocks is another great way to embellish your work. Motifs worked in a yarn with different fiber content can add interest.

## Buttons

Try attaching simple, shaped, or vintage buttons to the corners or in the center of a flower granny square. Just one button placed neatly in the center or many buttons dotted all around both look great.

## Beads

Sew beads or sequins to the finished block to add a splash of sparkle. Use sewing thread and attach securely.

## Ribbons

Weave ribbons through larger stitches and secure at the back of the work to add some shimmer.

Ribbons and surface crochet

Buttons and appliqué motifs

Cross stitch and appliqué motifs

Embroidery

# Caring For Your Project

Your project is complete! Before you snuggle up in it, or give it away as a gift, it's a good idea to sew a care label onto it for future reference.

You can purchase labels at craft stores or else use a scrap of plain material. Check the yarn label for instructions then, using a permanent ink pen, write the care instructions on the label and sew it onto your project. Don't be tempted to use an iron-on label, as this could ruin all your hard work. It's especially important to include a care label if you're giving the project to someone as a gift to avoid any laundry disasters in the future.

to dry on a flat surface, reshape, and allow to dry thoroughly before moving it. Never hang dry when wet or your project will stretch. You can air your project on the washing line when it is almost dry.

## Storage

If you want to store your project for any length of time, make sure that it is clean and dry. A woolen blanket can sweat in plastic, so acid-free tissue paper is preferable to a plastic bag or box. Place sheets of paper between the folds and then wrap the project completely in the paper. Not only does the paper absorb any sweating, but this also protects it from dust. Store in a dry area, adding a sachet of lavender or cedar wood chippings to keep it smelling fresh and to scare off any unwanted pests. Alternatively, you can use a cotton pillowcase to keep your project free from dust.

## Machine washing

Machine wash on a "gentle," "synthetic," "wool," "handwash," or "delicates" setting using cool water and detergent that doesn't contain bleaching agents. Add some fabric softener to the final rinse to help keep your afghan feeling soft and supple.

Tumble dry on a "low" or "perm press" setting, and remember to check the yarn label, as not all yarns can be tumble dried.

## Hand washing

Hand washing is always the safest option with natural fibers, unless the yarn specifically states "dry clean only."

Wash gently, with as little agitation as possible, in warm water using detergent without bleaching agents. Ensure that the project doesn't stretch out of shape during washing and rinsing. Gently squeeze out excess water and roll inside a towel. Spread the project

## INTERNATIONAL CARE SYMBOLS  These symbols may be found on ball bands.

Do not wash by hand or machine

Hand-washable in warm water at stated temperature

Machine-washable in warm water at stated temperature

Machine-washable in warm water at stated temperature, short spin

Machine-washable in warm water at stated temperature, cool rinse, and short spin

Bleaching not permitted

Bleaching permitted (with chlorine)

Do not press

Press with a cool iron

Press with a warm iron

Press with a hot iron

Do not dry clean

May be dry cleaned with all solutions

May be dry cleaned with perchlorethylene, fluorocarbon, or petroleum-based solvents

May be dry cleaned with fluorocarbon or petroleum-based solvents only

## IGNORING THE CARE INSTRUCTIONS

Some yarns specify that they are "hand wash only." If you decide to machine wash a hand-wash-only yarn, do so with extreme care! Washing your project in the machine can be fine, providing you use a suitably delicate setting. You need a cool water wash with as little agitation as possible to avoid felting, pilling, stretching, shrinking, and other horrors. The best idea is to make a few test swatches and experiment before washing the whole thing.

# CHAPTER 2

# Block and Stitch Designs

# Daisy

A:  8 yds/7.3 m
B:  11 yds/10 m
C:  12 yds/11 m
D:  8 yds/7.3 m

• **SKILL LEVEL:** *Intermediate*

## Method

**FOUNDATION RING:** Using Color A, ch 5 and join with slip st to form a ring.

**ROUND 1:** Ch 1, * sc into ring, ch 2; rep from * 7 more times, join with slip st into first sc made. End Color A. (8 sc, 8 sps.)

**ROUND 2:** Join Color B in ch-2 sp, * in ch-2 sp work ([ch 2, dc] twice, ch 2, slip st), ch 1 **, slip st into next ch-2 sp; rep from * 6 more times, then from * to ** once more, join with slip st into base of beginning ch. End Color B. (8 petals.)

**ROUND 3:** Join Color C in ch-1 sp between two petals, ch 1 and sc in same space, * ch 3, sc in next ch-1 sp between two petals; rep from * 6 more times, ch 3, join with slip st into first sc made. (8 sc, 8 ch sps.)

**ROUND 4:** Slip st into ch-3 sp, ch 3 (counts as 1 dc), 2 dc in same ch-3 sp, * ch 1, (2 dc, ch 2, 2 dc) in next ch-3 sp, ch 1 **, 3 dc in next ch sp; rep from * twice more, then from * to ** once more, join with slip st into top of beginning ch. (28 sts, 12 ch sps.)

**ROUND 5:** Slip st in next 2 sts and into ch-1 sp, 3 ch (counts as 1 dc), 2 dc in same ch sp,

* ch 1, (2 dc, ch 2, 2 dc) in corner ch-2 space **, (ch 1, 3 dc in next ch-1 sp) twice more; rep from * 2 more times, then from * to ** once more, ch 1, 3 dc in next ch-1 sp, ch 1, join with slip st into top of beginning ch. End Color C. (40 sts, 16 ch sps.)

**ROUND 6:** Join Color D in corner ch-2 sp, ch 3 (counts as 1 dc), dc in same ch-2 sp, * ch 1, [3 dc in next ch-1 sp, ch 1] 3 times **, (2 dc, ch 2, 2 dc) in corner ch-2 sp; rep from * twice more, then from * to ** once more, (2 dc, ch 2) in same ch-2 space as beginning of round, join with slip st into top of beginning ch. End Color D. (52 sts, 20 ch sps.)

**ROUND 7:** Join Color B in corner ch-2 sp, ch 1, * (sc, hdc, sc) in corner ch-2 sp **, sc in each st and ch to next corner ch-2 sp; rep from * 3 more times, join with slip st into first sc made. End Color B. (80 sts.)

**ROUND 8:** Join Color A in corner hdc, ch 1, * (sc, hdc, sc) in corner hdc **, sc in each st to next corner hdc; rep from * 3 more times, join with slip st into first sc made. End Color A. (88 sts.)

Daisy

Daisy 2

## COLOR VARIATION

## Daisy 2

Follow the written instructions or the chart, using colors as follows:

A:  8 yds/7.3 m
B:  11 yds/10 m
C:  12 yds/11 m
D:  8 yds/7.3 m

Daisy Chain

Daisy

Daisy Chain

## STITCH VARIATION

## Daisy Chain

- **SKILL LEVEL:** Intermediate

- A: 17 yds/15.5 m
- B: 5 yds/4.6 m
- C: 13 yds/11.9 m

## Method

**FOUNDATION RING:** Using Color A, ch 5 and join with slip st to form a ring.

**ROUND 1:** Ch 1, * sc into ring, ch 2; rep from * 7 more times, join with slip st into first sc made. End Color A. (8 sts, 8 ch sps.)

**ROUND 2:** Join Color B in ch-2 sp, * in ch sp work ([ch 2, dc] twice, ch 2, slip st), ch 1 **, slip st into next ch-2 sp; rep from * 6 more times, then from * to ** once more, join with slip st into base of beginning ch. End Color B. (8 petals.)

**ROUND 3:** Join Color C in ch-1 sp between two petals, ch 1 and slip st in same space, * ch 3, slip st in next ch-1 sp between two petals; rep from * 6 more times, ch 3, join with slip st into first sc made. (8 ch sps, 8 sts.)

**ROUND 4:** Slip st into ch-3 sp, * ch 4, slip st in same space, [ch 3 **, slip st in next ch-3 sp] twice; rep from * twice more, then from * to ** once more, slip st into base of beginning ch. (12 slip sts, 12 ch sps.)

**ROUND 5:** Slip st into ch-4 sp, * ch 4, slip st in same space, [ch 3 **, slip st in next ch-3 sp] 3 times; rep from * twice more, then from * to ** once more, slip st into base of beginning ch. (16 slip sts, 16 ch sps.)

**ROUND 6:** Slip st into ch-4 sp, * ch 4, slip st in same space, [ch 3 **, slip st in next ch-3 sp] 4 times; rep from * twice more, then from * to ** once more, slip st into base of beginning ch. (20 slip sts, 20 ch sps.)

**ROUND 7:** Slip st into ch-4 sp, * ch 4, slip st in same space, [ch 3 **, slip st in next ch-3 sp] 5 times; rep from * twice more, then from * to ** once more, slip st into base of beginning ch. End Color C. (24 slip sts, 24 ch sps.)

**ROUND 8:** Join Color A in corner ch-4 sp, ch 1, *(sc, hdc, sc) in ch-4 sp, [ch 2, sc in next ch-3 sp] 5 times, ch 2: rep from * 3 more times, join with slip st into first sc made. (32 sts, 24 ch sps.)

**ROUND 9:** Slip st into corner hdc, ch 3 (counts as 1 dc), tr, dc in same space, * [ch 1, 3 dc in next ch-2 sp] 6 times, ch 1 **, (dc, tr, dc) in corner hdc; rep from * twice more, then from * to ** once more, join with slip st into top of beginning ch. End Color A. (84 sts, 28 ch sps.)

## Yarn requirement for throws

**NOTE:** *All yarn requirements are estimated using an H-size (5 mm) crochet hook and worsted/10-ply yarn. Measurements and yarn requirements do not include joining and edging.*

### Daisy

| | BABY | LAP | BED |
|---|---|---|---|
| A | 288 yds/263 m | 504 yds/461 m | 1232 yds/1127 m |
| B | 396 yds/362 m | 693 yds/634 m | 1694 yds/1549 m |
| C | 432 yds/395 m | 756 yds/691 m | 1848 yds/1690 m |
| D | 288 yds/263 m | 504 yds/461 m | 1232 yds/1127 m |

### Daisy 2

| | BABY | LAP | BED |
|---|---|---|---|
| A | 288 yds/263 m | 504 yds/461 m | 1232 yds/1127 m |
| B | 396 yds/362 m | 693 yds/634 m | 1694 yds/1549 m |
| C | 432 yds/395 m | 756 yds/691 m | 1848 yds/1690 m |
| D | 288 yds/263 m | 504 yds/461 m | 1232 yds/1127 m |

### Daisy Chain

| | BABY | LAP | BED |
|---|---|---|---|
| A | 612 yds/560 m | 1071 yds/979 m | 2618 yds/2394 m |
| B | 180 yds/165 m | 315 yds/288 m | 770 yds/704 m |
| C | 468 yds/428 m | 819 yds/749 m | 2002 yds/1831 m |

# Spiked Lines

A: 23 yds/21 m
B: 10 yds/9.1 m
C: 10 yds/9.1 m

- **SKILL LEVEL:** *Beginner*

## Method

**FOUNDATION ROW:** Using Color A, ch 20. (19 sts + 1 turning ch.)

**ROW 1:** Begin with 2nd ch from hook and sc into each ch across, turn. (19 sts.)

**ROW 2:** Ch 1, sc in each st across, turn. (19 sts.)

**ROW 3:** Rep Row 2. End Color A. (19 sts.)

**ROW 4 (RS):** Join Color B, ch 1, sc in next 2 sts, * (sc into st 2 rows below) 3 times **, sc into next 3 sts; rep from * once more, then from * to ** once more, sc in next 2 sts, turn. (19 sts.)

**ROW 5:** Rep Row 2. (19 sts.)

**ROW 6:** Rep Row 2. End Color B. (19 sts.)

**ROWS 7–9:** Join Color A and rep Rows 4–6. End Color A. (19 sts.)

**ROWS 10–12:** Join Color C and rep Rows 4–6. End Color C. (19 sts.)

**ROWS 13–15:** Join Color A and rep Rows 4–6. End Color A. (19 sts.)

**ROWS 16–18:** Join Color B and rep Rows 4–6. End Color B. (19 sts.)

**ROWS 19–21:** Join Color A and rep Rows 4–6. End Color A. (19 sts.)

**ROWS 22–24:** Join Color C and rep Rows 4–6. End Color C. (19 sts.)

**ROW 25:** Join Color A and rep Row 4. End Color A. (19 sts.)

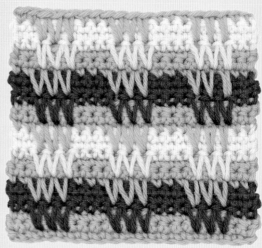

Spiked Lines

**COLOR VARIATION**

## Spiked Lines 2

Follow the written instructions or the chart, using colors as follows:

A: 23 yds/21 m
B: 10 yds/9.1 m
C: 10 yds/9.1 m

Spiked Lines 2

V-Spiked Lines

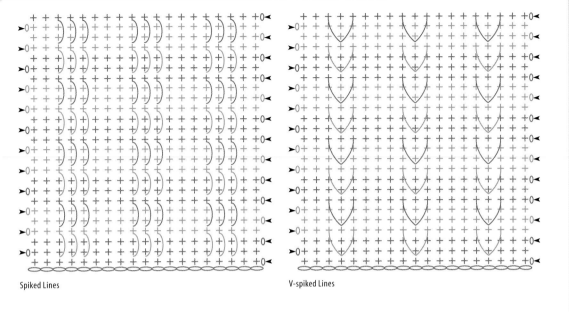

Spiked Lines

V-spiked Lines

## Yarn requirement for throws

**NOTE:** *All yarn requirements are estimated using an H-size (5 mm) crochet hook and worsted/10-ply yarn. Measurements and yarn requirements do not include joining and edging.*

### Spiked Lines

|   | BABY | LAP | BED |
|---|------|-----|-----|
| **A** | 828 yds/757 m | 1449 yds/1325 m | 3542 yds/3239 m |
| **B** | 360 yds/329 m | 630 yds/576 m | 1540 yds/1408 m |
| **C** | 360 yds/329 m | 630 yds/576 m | 1540 yds/1408 m |

### Spiked Lines 2

|   | BABY | LAP | BED |
|---|------|-----|-----|
| **A** | 828 yds/757 m | 1449 yds/1325 m | 3542 yds/3239 m |
| **B** | 360 yds/329 m | 630 yds/576 m | 1540 yds/1408 m |
| **C** | 360 yds/329 m | 630 yds/576 m | 1540 yds/1408 m |

### V-spiked Lines

|   | BABY | LAP | BED |
|---|------|-----|-----|
| **A** | 828 yds/757 m | 1449 yds/1325 m | 3542 yds/3239 m |
| **B** | 360 yds/329 m | 630 yds/576 m | 1540 yds/1408 m |
| **C** | 360 yds/329 m | 630 yds/576 m | 1540 yds/1408 m |

## STITCH VARIATION

## V-spiked Lines

- A: 23 yds/21 m
- B: 10 yds/9.1 m
- C: 10 yds/9.1 m

• **SKILL LEVEL:** *Beginner*

## Method

**SPECIAL STITCH:** Spiked V-stitch—SV: Skip 1 sc, sc into next st 2 rows below, sc into next st on current row, sc into same st 2 rows below.

**FOUNDATION RING:** Using Color A, ch 20, turn. (19 sts + 1 turning ch.)

**ROW 1:** Begin with 2nd ch from hook, 1 sc into each ch across, turn. (19 sts.)

**ROW 2:** Ch 1, sc in each st across, turn. (19 sts.)

**ROW 3:** Rep Row 2. End Color A. (19 sts.)

**ROW 4 (RS):** Join Color B, ch 1, sc in next 2 sts, * SV over next 3 sts **, sc into next 3 sts; rep from * once more, then from * to ** once more, sc in next 2 sts, turn.

**ROW 5:** Rep Row 2.

**ROW 6:** Rep Row 2. End Color B.

**ROWS 7–9:** Join Color A and rep Rows 4–6. End Color A. (19 sts.)

**ROWS 10–12:** Join Color C and rep Rows 4–6. End Color C.

**ROWS 13–15:** Join Color A and rep Rows 4–6. End Color A.

**ROWS 16–18:** Join Color B and rep Rows 4–6. End Color B.

**ROWS 19–21:** Join Color A and rep Rows 4–6. End Color A.

**ROWS 22–24:** Join Color C and rep Rows 4–6. End Color C.

**ROW 25:** Join Color A and rep Row 4. End Color A.

# My Heart

● A:  31 yds/28.3 m
● B:  9 yds/8.2 m
● C:  8 yds/7.3 m

• **SKILL LEVEL:** *Intermediate*

## Method

**FOUNDATION ROW:** Using Color A, ch 22. (21 sts + 1 turning ch.)

**ROW 1:** Begin with 2nd ch from hook, 1 sc in each ch across, turn. (21 sts.)

**ROW 2:** Ch 1, sc in each st across, turn. (21 sts.)

Rep Row 2 for 23 more rows. End Color A.

**WORKING THE PATTERN:** Starting at the bottom right-hand corner of the chart, work the 25-row pattern in sc. When following the chart, read odd-numbered rows (right-side rows) from right to left and even-numbered rows (wrong-side rows) from left to right.

Also, remember to insert hook under the strand of yarn that you carried across on the last row.

**OPTIONAL SURFACE CROCHET:** With two strands of Color C, work slip st around heart.

My Heart

My Heart 2

**COLOR VARIATION**

## My Heart 2

● A:  31 yds/28.3 m
● B:  9 yds/8.2 m

Follow the written instructions (omitting the optional surface-crochet stitches) and the chart, using colors as follows:

Cross My Heart

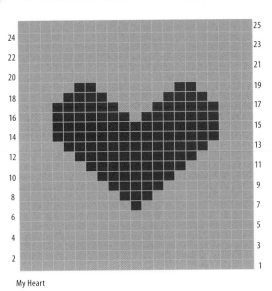

My Heart

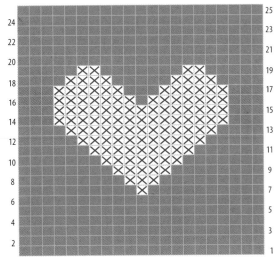

Cross My Heart

## Yarn requirement for throws

**NOTE:** *All yarn requirements are estimated using an H-size (5 mm) crochet hook and worsted/10-ply yarn. Measurements and yarn requirements do not include joining and edging.*

| My Heart | | | |
|---|---|---|---|
| | **BABY** | **LAP** | **BED** |
| **A** | 1116 yds/1020 m | 1953 yds/1786 m | 4774 yds/4365 m |
| **B** | 324 yds/296 m | 567 yds/518 m | 1386 yds/1267 m |
| **C** | 288 yds/263 m | 504 yds/461 m | 1232 yds/1127 m |

| My Heart 2 | | | |
|---|---|---|---|
| | **BABY** | **LAP** | **BED** |
| **A** | 1116 yds/1020 m | 1953 yds/1786 m | 4774 yds/4365 m |
| **B** | 324 yds/296 m | 567 yds/518 m | 1386 yds/1267 m |

| Cross My Heart | | | |
|---|---|---|---|
| | **BABY** | **LAP** | **BED** |
| **A** | 1404 yds/1284 m | 2457 yds/2247 m | 6006 yds/5492 m |
| **B** | 324 yds/296 m | 567 yds/518 m | 1386 yds/1267 m |
| **C** | 144 yds/132 m | 252 yds/230 m | 616 yds/563 m |

**STITCH VARIATION**

## Cross My Heart

A: 39 yds/35.7 m
B: 9 yds/8.2 m
C: 4 yds/3.7 m

• **SKILL LEVEL:** *Beginner*

## Method

**FOUNDATION ROW:** Using Color A, ch 22. (21sts + 1 turning ch.)

**ROW 1:** Begin with 2nd ch from hook, 1 sc in each ch across, turn. (21 sts.)

**ROW 2:** Ch 1, 1 sc in each st across, turn. (21 sts.)

Rep Row 2 for 23 more rows. End Color A.

**CROSS-STITCH HEART:** Starting at the bottom left-hand corner of the chart, work cross stitch using one strand of Color B.

**OPTIONAL SURFACE CROCHET:** With one strand of Color C, work slip st around the heart.

# Carnival

• **SKILL LEVEL:** *Intermediate*

- A: 3 yds/2.7 m
- B: 5 yds/4.6 m
- C: 5 yds/4.6 m
- D: 11 yds/10 m
- E: 5 yds/4.6 m
- F: 7 yds/6.4 m

## Method

**SPECIAL STITCHES:**
- Beg 3-st Cluster—Beg Cl: Made of 2ch, 2 dc.
- 3-st Cluster—3st Cl: Made of 3 dc.
- 4-st Cluster—4st Cl: Made of 4 dc.

**FOUNDATION RING:** Using Color A, make a Magic Ring.

**ROUND 1:** Beg Cl, * ch 3, 3-st Cl; rep from * twice more, ch 3, join with slip st into top of Beg Cl. End Color A. (4 Clusters, 4 ch sps.)

**ROUND 2:** Join Color B in ch-3 sp, 3ch (counts as 1 dc), (2 dc, tr, 3 dc) in same ch-3 sp, * (3 dc, tr, 3 dc) in next ch-3 sp; rep from * twice more, join with slip st into top of beginning ch. End Color B. (28 sts.)

**ROUND 3:** Join Color C, ch 4 (counts as 1 tr), * dc in next st, hdc in next st, 3 sc in next st, hdc in next st, dc in next st **, tr in next 2 sts; rep from * twice more, then from * to ** once more, tr in next st, join with slip st into top of beginning ch. End Color C. (36 sts.)

**ROUND 4:** Join Color D, ch 3 (counts as 1 tr), * dc in next st, hdc in next st, sc in next 3 sts, hdc in next st, dc in next st **, tr in next st,

ch 3, tr in next st; rep from * twice more, then from * to ** once more, tr in next st, ch 3, join with slip st into top of beginning ch. End Color D. (36 sts, 4 ch sps.)

**ROUND 5:** Join Color E, ch 1 and sc in same sp, * sc in each st to corner ch-3 sp, ch 2, 4-st Cl in ch-3 sp, ch 2; rep from * 3 more times, join with slip st into first sc made. (36 sts, 4 Clusters, 8 ch sps.)

**ROUND 6:** Join Color F, ch 4 (counts as 1 dc, ch 1), * (skip 1 st, dc in next st, ch 1) 4 times, dc in ch-2 sp, ch 1, (dc, tr, dc) in 4-st Cl, ch 1, dc in ch-2 sp, ch 1 **, dc in next st, ch 1; rep from * 3 more times, then from * to ** once more, join with slip st into 3rd ch of beginning ch. End Color F. (40 sts, 32 ch sps.)

**ROUND 7:** Join Color D, ch 1 and sc in same sp, * sc in each st and ch-sp to corner tr, (sc, hdc, sc) in tr; rep from * 3 more times, sc to end of round, join with slip st into first sc made. End Color D. (80 sts.)

Carnival

Carnival 2

**COLOR VARIATION**

## Carnival 2

Follow the written instructions or the chart, using colors as follows:

- A: 8 yds/7.3 m
- B: 5 yds/4.6 m
- C: 5 yds/4.6 m
- D: 5 yds/4.6 m
- E: 7 yds/6.4 m
- F: 6 yds/5.5 m

**FOUNDATION RING AND ROUND 1:** Color A
**ROUND 2:** Color B
**ROUND 3:** Color C
**ROUND 4:** Color D
**ROUND 5:** Color A
**ROUND 6:** Color E
**ROUND 7:** Color F

Parade

Carnival

Parade

## STITCH VARIATION

## Parade

- **SKILL LEVEL:** *Intermediate*

## Method

**SPECIAL STITCHES:**
- Beg 3-st Cluster—Beg Cl: Made of 2ch, 2 dc.
- 3-st Cluster—3-st Cl: Made of 3 dc.
- 4-st Cluster—4-st Cl: Made of 4 dc.

**FOUNDATION RING:** Using Color A, make a Magic Ring.

**ROUND 1:** Beg Cl, * ch 3, 3-st Cl; rep from * twice more, ch 3, join with slip st into top of Beg Cl. End Color A. (4 Clusters, 4 ch sps.)

**ROUND 2:** Join Color B in ch-3 sp, ch 3 (counts as 1 dc), (2 dc, tr, 3 dc) in same ch-3 sp, * (3 dc, tr, 3 dc) in next ch-3 sp; rep from * twice more, join with slip st into top of beginning ch. End Color B. (28 sts.)

**ROUND 3:** Join Color C by working back post slip st around dc of Round 2, ch 4 (counts as 1 tr), * bpdc around next st, bphdc around next, 3 bpsc around next st, bphdc around next st, bpdc around next st **, bptr around next 2 sts; rep from * twice more, then from * to ** once more, bptr around next st, join with slip st into top of beginning ch. End Color C. (36 sts.)

**ROUND 4:** Join Color D, ch 3 (counts as 1 dc), * dc in next st, hdc in next st, sc in next 3 sts, hdc in next st, dc in next 2 sts **, ch 3, dc in next st; rep from * twice more, then

from * to ** once more, ch 3, join with slip st into top of beginning ch. End Color D. (36 sts, 4 ch sps.)

**ROUND 5:** Join Color E, ch 1 and sc in same sp, * sc in each st to corner ch sp, ch 2, 4-st Cl in ch-3 sp, ch 2; rep from * 3 more times, join with slip st into first sc made. (36 sts, 4 Clusters, 8 ch sps.)

**ROUND 6:** Join Color F, ch 4 (counts as 1 dc, ch 1), * (skip 1 st, dc in next st, ch 1) 4 times, dc in ch-2 sp, ch 1, (dc, tr, dc) in 4-st Cl, ch 1, dc in ch-2 sp, ch 1 **, dc in next st, ch 1; rep from * 3 more times, then from * to ** once more, join with slip st into 3rd ch of beginning ch. End Color F. (40 sts, 32 ch sps.)

**ROUND 7:** Join Color D, ch 1 and sc in same sp, (sc into sc of Round 5, sc in next st of Round 6) 4 times, sc into ch sp of Round 5, sc into next st of Round 6, * sc in ch sp, sc in next st, (sc, hdc, sc) in tr, sc in next st, sc in ch sp**, (sc in next st of Round 6, sc into sc of Round 5) 5 times, sc in next st, sc into ch sp of Round 5, sc into next st of Round 6; rep from * twice more, then from * to ** once more, sc in next st of Round 6, sc into sc of Round 5, join with slip st into first sc made. End Color D. (80 sts.)

● A: 3 yds/2.7 m
● B: 5 yds/4.6 m
● C: 5 yds/4.6 m
● D: 11 yds/10 m
● E: 5 yds/4.6 m
● F: 7 yds/6.4 m

## Yarn requirement for throws

**NOTE:** *All yarn requirements are estimated using an H-size (5 mm) crochet hook and worsted/10-ply yarn. Measurements and yarn requirements do not include joining and edging.*

| Carnival | BABY | LAP | BED |
|---|---|---|---|
| A | 108 yds/99 m | 189 yds/173 m | 462 yds/422 m |
| B | 180 yds/165 m | 315 yds/288 m | 770 yds/704 m |
| C | 180 yds/165 m | 315 yds/288 m | 770 yds/704 m |
| D | 396 yds/362 m | 693 yds/634 m | 1694 yds/1549 m |
| E | 180 yds/165 m | 315 yds/288 m | 770 yds/704 m |
| F | 252 yds/230 m | 441 yds/403 m | 1078 yds/986 m |

| Carnival 2 | BABY | LAP | BED |
|---|---|---|---|
| A | 288 yds/263 m | 504 yds/461 m | 1232 yds/1127 m |
| B | 180 yds/165 m | 315 yds/288 m | 770 yds/704 m |
| C | 180 yds/165 m | 315 yds/288 m | 770 yds/704 m |
| D | 180 yds/165 m | 315 yds/288 m | 770 yds/704 m |
| E | 252 yds/230 m | 441 yds/403 m | 1078 yds/986 m |
| F | 216 yds/198 m | 378 yds/346 m | 924 yds/845 m |

| Parade | BABY | LAP | BED |
|---|---|---|---|
| A | 108 yds/99 m | 189 yds/173 m | 462 yds/422 m |
| B | 180 yds/165 m | 315 yds/288 m | 770 yds/704 m |
| C | 180 yds/165 m | 315 yds/288 m | 770 yds/704 m |
| D | 396 yds/362 m | 693 yds/634 m | 1694 yds/1549 m |
| E | 180 yds/165 m | 315 yds/288 m | 770 yds/704 m |
| F | 252 yds/230 m | 441 yds/403 m | 1078 yds/986 m |

# Flame Flower

A: 12 yds/11 m
B: 14 yds/12.8 m
C: 33 yds/30.1 m

• **SKILL LEVEL:** *Advanced*

## Method

**FOUNDATION RING:** Using Color A, ch 4, join to form a ring.

**ROUND 1:** Ch 4 (counts as 1 dc, ch 1), * dc into ring, ch 1; rep from * 6 more times, join with slip st into 3rd ch of beginning ch. (8 sts, 8 ch sps.)

**ROUND 2:** Ch 1 and sc in same sp, * slip st into next ch-1 sp, ch 9, slip st into same ch-1 sp **, sc in dc; rep from * 6 more times, then from * to ** once more, join with slip st into first sc made. (8 sts, 8 ch sps.)

**ROUND 3:** Ch 1, * (5 sc, ch 2, 5 sc) into ch-9 sp **, slip st into sc; rep from * 6 more times, then from * to ** once more, join with slip st into first slip st made. End Color A. (80 sts, 8 ch sp, 16 slip sts.)

**ROUND 4:** Join Color B, ch 1, * sc in first sc of petal, hdc in next 2 sts, dc in next 2 sc, (2 dc, ch 2, 2 dc) in ch-2 sp, dc in next 2 sts, hdc in next 2 sts, sc in next st **, fpsc around dc of Round 1; rep from * six more times, then from * to ** once more, join with slip st into first sc of petal. End Color B. (120 sts, 8 ch sps.)

**ROUND 5:** Join Color C by working * back post slip st around dc of Round 1, ch 3, skip 1 dc; rep from * 3 more times, join with slip st into first slip st made. (4 bp slip sts, 4 ch sps.)

**ROUND 6:** Slip st into ch-3 sp, ch 3 (counts as 1 dc), 2 dc, ch 2, 3 dc in same ch sp, ch 1, * (3 dc, ch 2, 3 dc) in next ch-3 sp, ch 1; rep from * twice more, join with a slip st into top of beginning ch. (24 sts, 8 ch sps.)

**ROUND 7:** Slip across into ch-2 sp, ch 3 (counts as 1 dc), 2 dc, ch 2, 3 dc in same ch-2 sp, ch 1, * 3 dc in ch-1 sp, ch 1 **, (3 dc, ch 2, 3 dc) in next ch-2 sp, ch 1; rep from * twice more, then from * to ** once more, join with slip st into top of beginning ch. (36 sts, 12 ch sps.)

**ROUND 8:** Slip st across into ch-2 sp, ch 3 (counts as 1 dc), 2 dc, ch 2, 3 dc in same ch sp, ch 1, * [3 dc in ch-1 sp] twice **, (3 dc, ch 2, 3 dc) in next ch-2 sp, ch 1; rep from * twice more, then from * to ** once more, join with slip st into top of beginning ch. (48 sts, 16 ch sps.)

**ROUND 9:** Slip st across into ch-2 sp, ch 3 (counts as 1 dc), 2 dc, ch 2, 3 dc in same ch sp, ch 1, * [3 dc in ch-1 sp, ch 1] 3 times **, (3 dc, ch 2, 3 dc) in next ch-2 sp, ch 1; rep from * twice more, then from * to ** once more, join with slip st into top of beginning ch. (60 sts, 20 ch sps.)

**ROUND 10:** Ch 1 and sc in same sp, sc in next 2 sts, * (sc, hdc, sc) in ch-2 sp, sc in next 5 sts and ch sp, sc through ch-2 sp of Round 4 petal and into next st, sc in next 7 sts and ch sps, sc through ch-2 sp of Round 4 petal and into next st **, sc in 5 sts and ch sp to corner ch-2 sp; rep from * twice more, then from * to ** once more, sc to end, join with slip st into first sc made. End Color C. (88 sts.)

Flame Flower

Flame Flower 2

---

**COLOR VARIATION**

## Flame Flower 2

Follow the written instructions or the chart, using colors as follows:

A: 12 yds/11 m
B: 14 yds/12.8 m
C: 33 yds/30.2 m

Fire Star

Flame Flower

Fire Star

## STITCH VARIATION

## Fire Star

- **SKILL LEVEL:** *Advanced*

⬤ A: 12 yds/11 m
⬤ B: 33 yds/30 m

## Method

**SPECIAL STITCH:** Picot: 3ch, slip st into first ch.

**FOUNDATION RING:** Using Color A, ch 4, join to form a ring.

**ROUND 1:** Ch 4 (counts as 1 dc, ch 1), * dc into ring, ch 1; rep from * 6 more times, join with slip st into top of beginning ch. (8 sts, 8 ch sps.)

**ROUND 2:** Ch 1 and sc in same sp, * slip st into next ch sp, ch 9, slip st into same ch sp **, sc in dc; rep from * 6 more times, then from * to ** once more, join with slip st into first sc made. (8 sts, 8 ch sps.)

**ROUND 3:** Ch 1, * (5 sc, Picot, 5 sc) into ch-9 sp **, slip st into sc; rep from * 6 more times, then from * to ** once more, join with slip st into first slip st made. End Color A. (80 sts, 8 picots, 16 slip sts.)

**ROUND 4:** Join Color B by working * bp slip st around dc of Round 1, ch 3, skip 1 dc; rep from * 3 more times, join with slip st to first slip st made. (4 bp slip sts, 4 ch sps.)

**ROUND 5:** Slip st into ch sp, ch 3 (counts as 1 dc), 2 dc, ch 2, 3 dc in same ch sp, ch 1, * (3 dc, ch 2, 3 dc) in next ch-3 sp, ch 1; rep from * twice more, join with slip st into top of beginning ch. (24 sts, 8 ch sps.)

**ROUND 6:** Slip st across into ch-2 sp, ch 3 (counts as 1 dc), 2 dc, ch 2, 3 dc in same ch sp, ch 1, * 3 dc in ch-1 sp, ch 1 **, (3 dc, ch 2, 3 dc) in next ch-2 sp, ch 1; rep from * twice more, then from * to ** once more, join with slip st into top of beginning ch. (36 sts, 12 ch sps.)

**ROUND 7:** Slip st across into ch-2 sp, ch 3 (counts as 1 dc), 2 dc, ch 2, 3 dc in same ch sp, ch 1, * [3 dc in ch-1 sp, ch 1] twice **, (3 dc, ch 2, 3 dc) in next ch-2 sp, ch 1; rep from * twice more, then from * to ** once more, join with slip st into top of beginning ch. (48 sts, 16 ch sps.)

**ROUND 8:** Slip st across into ch-2 sp, ch 3 (counts as 1 dc), 2 dc, ch 2, 3 dc in same ch sp, * ch 1, 1 dc in next ch sp, 1 dc through Picot of Round 3 petal and into ch sp, 1 dc in same ch sp, ch 1, 3 dc in next ch sp, ch 1, 1 dc in next ch sp, 1 dc through Picot of Round 3 petal and into ch sp, 1 dc in same ch sp, ch 1 **, (3 dc, ch 2, 3 dc) in corner ch-2 sp; rep from * twice more, then from * to ** once more, join with slip st into top of beginning ch. (60 sts, 20 ch sps.)

**ROUND 9:** Ch 1, sc in same sp, sc in next 2 sts, * (sc, hdc, sc) in corner ch-2 sp **, sc in each st and ch-1 sp to next corner ch-2 sp; rep from * twice more, then from * to ** once more, sc in each st and ch sp to end of round, join with slip st into first sc made. End Color B. (88 sts.)

## Yarn requirement for throws

**NOTE:** *All yarn requirements are estimated using an H-size (5 mm) crochet hook and worsted/10-ply yarn. Measurements and yarn requirements do not include joining and edging.*

### Flame Flower

| | BABY | LAP | BED |
|---|---|---|---|
| A | 432 yds/395 m | 756 yds/691 m | 1848 yds/1690 m |
| B | 504 yds/461 m | 882 yds/807 m | 2156 yds/1971 m |
| C | 1188 yds/1086 m | 2079 yds/1901 m | 5082 yds/4647 m |

### Flame Flower 2

| | BABY | LAP | BED |
|---|---|---|---|
| A | 432 yds/395 m | 756 yds/691 m | 1848 yds/1690 m |
| B | 504 yds/461 m | 882 yds/807 m | 2156 yds/1971 m |
| C | 1188 yds/1086 m | 2079 yds/1901 m | 5082 yds/4647 m |

### Fire Star

| | BABY | LAP | BED |
|---|---|---|---|
| A | 432 yds/395 m | 756 yds/691 m | 1848 yds/1690 m |
| B | 1188 yds/1086 m | 2079 yds/1901 m | 5082 yds/4647 m |

# Darts

• **SKILL LEVEL:** *Intermediate*

## Method

**FOUNDATION ROW:** Using Color A, 19 ch. (18 sts + 1 turning ch.)

**ROW 1:** Begin with 2nd ch from hook, 1 sc in each ch across, turn. (21 sts.)

**ROW 2:** Ch 1, 1 sc in each st across turn. (21 sts.)

Rep Row 2 for 22 more rows. End both colors.

**WORKING THE PATTERN:** Starting at the bottom right-hand corner of the chart, work the 24-row pattern in sc.

● A: 10 yds/9.1 m
  B: 20 yds/18.2 m
● C: 5 yds/4.6 m
◐ D: 5 yds/4.6 m

When following the chart, read odd-numbered (right-side) rows from right to left and even-numbered (wrong-side) rows from left to right. Work rows using one strand of working color and one strand of second color. Carry the unused strand along the top of the previous row. Work each stitch over the carried yarn, locking it in place, and under the carried yarn on the previous row. Switch colors as needed.

## COLOR VARIATION

## Darts 2

Follow the written instructions and the chart, using colors as follows:

● A: 10 yds/9.1 m
◍ B: 20 yds/18.2 m
◯ C: 5 yds/4.6 m
◐ D: 5 yds/4.6 m

Darts

Darts 2

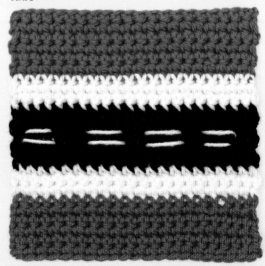

Lines

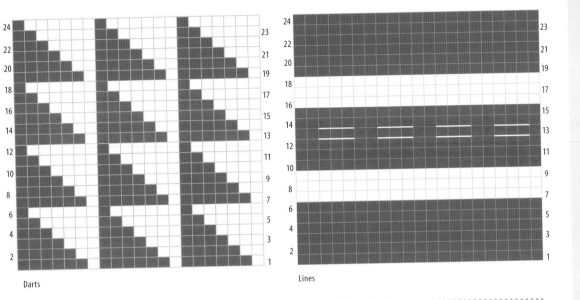

Darts

Lines

## Yarn requirement for throws

**NOTE:** *All yarn requirements are estimated using an H-size (5 mm) crochet hook and worsted/10-ply yarn. Measurements and yarn requirements do not include joining and edging.*

**Darts**

|   | BABY | LAP | BED |
|---|------|-----|-----|
| **A** | 360 yds/329 m | 630 yds/576 m | 1540 yds/1408 m |
| **B** | 720 yds/658 m | 1260 yds/1152 m | 3080 yds/2816 m |
| **C** | 180 yds/165 m | 315 yds/288 m | 770 yds/704 m |
| **D** | 180 yds/165 m | 315 yds/288 m | 770 yds/704 m |

**Darts 2**

|   | BABY | LAP | BED |
|---|------|-----|-----|
| **A** | 360 yds/329 m | 630 yds/576 m | 1540 yds/1408 m |
| **B** | 720 yds/658 m | 1260 yds/1152 m | 3080 yds/2816 m |
| **C** | 180 yds/165 m | 315 yds/288 m | 770 yds/704 m |
| **D** | 180 yds/165 m | 315 yds/288 m | 770 yds/704 m |

**Lines**

|   | BABY | LAP | BED |
|---|------|-----|-----|
| **A** | 216 yds/198 m | 378 yds/346 m | 924 yds/845 m |
| **B** | 216 yds/198 m | 378 yds/346 m | 924 yds/845 m |
| **C** | 216 yds/198 m | 378 yds/346 m | 924 yds/845 m |
| **D** | 216 yds/198 m | 378 yds/346 m | 924 yds/845 m |

## STITCH VARIATION

## Lines

- **SKILL LEVEL:** *Beginner*

● A: 6 yds/5.5 m
○ B: 6 yds/5.5 m
● C: 6 yds/5.5 m
● D: 6 yds/5.5 m

## Method

**FOUNDATION ROW:** Using Color A, ch 22. (21 sts + 1 turning ch.)

**ROW 1:** Begin with 2nd ch from hook, 1 sc in each ch across, turn. (21 sts.)

**ROW 2:** Ch 1, 1 sc in each st across, turn. (21 sts.)

Rep Row 2 for 22 more rows. End D.

**WORKING THE PATTERN:** Starting at the bottom right-hand corner of the chart, work the 24-row pattern in sc. When following the chart, read odd-numbered (right-side) rows from right to left and even-numbered (wrong-side) rows from left to right.

**EMBROIDERY:** Using Color B, follow the chart, working in running stitch.

# Popcorn

• **SKILL LEVEL:** *Intermediate*

## Method

**SPECIAL STITCHES:**

• Beginning Popcorn—Beg PC: Made of ch 3, 3 dc, ch 1.

• Popcorn—PC: Made of 4 dc, ch 1.

**FOUNDATION RING:** Using Color A, ch 5 and join with slip st to form a ring.

**ROUND 1:** Beg PC into ring, ch 4, * PC into ring, ch 4: rep from * twice more, join with slip st into ch at top of Beg PC. End Color A. (4 PC, 4 ch sps.)

**ROUND 2:** Join Color B in any ch-4 sp, Beg PC, ch 4, PC in same ch-4 sp, * ch 2, (PC, ch 4, PC) in next ch-4 sp; rep from * twice more, ch 2, join with slip st into ch at top of Beg PC. End Color B. (8 PC, 8 ch sps.)

**ROUND 3:** Join Color C in any ch-4 sp, Beg PC, ch 4, PC in same ch-4 sp, * ch 2, PC in ch-2 sp, ch 2 **, (PC, ch 4, PC) in next ch-4 sp; rep from * twice more, then from * to ** once more, join with slip st into ch at top of Beg PC. End Color C. (12 PC, 12 ch sps.)

- A: 4 yds/3.7 m
- B: 6 yds/5.5 m
- C: 8 yds/7.3 m
- D: 10 yds/9.1 m
- E: 9 yds/8.2 m

**ROUND 4:** Join Color D in any ch-4 sp, Beg PC, ch 4, PC in same ch-4 sp, * (ch 2, PC in next ch-2 sp) twice, ch 2 **, (PC, ch 4, PC) in next ch-4 sp; rep from * twice more, then from * to ** once more, join with slip st into ch at top of Beg PC. End Color D. (16 PC, 16 ch sps.)

**ROUND 5:** Join Color E in any ch-4 sp, ch 3 (counts as 1 dc), 2 dc, ch 2, 3 dc into same ch-4 sp, * [ch 1, 3 dc] into each ch-2 sp along side of square, ch 1, ** (3 dc, ch 2, 3 dc) into next corner ch-4 sp; rep from * twice more, then from * to ** once more, join with slip st into top of beginning ch. End Color E. (60 sts, 20 ch sps.)

Popcorn

Popcorn 2

**COLOR VARIATION**

## Popcorn 2

Follow the written instructions or the chart, using colors as follows:

- A: 4 yds/3.7 m
- B: 6 yds/5.5 m
- C: 8 yds/7.3 m
- D: 10 yds/9.1 m
- E: 9 yds/8.2 m

Popcorn kernel

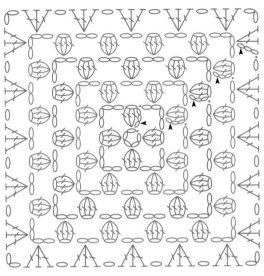

Popcorn Granny Square

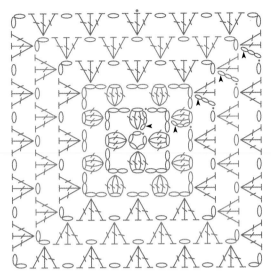

Popcorn Kernel

## Yarn requirement for throws

**NOTE:** *All yarn requirements are estimated using an H-size (5 mm) crochet hook and worsted/10-ply yarn. Measurements and yarn requirements do not include joining and edging.*

### Popcorn

| | BABY | LAP | BED |
|---|---|---|---|
| A | 144 yds/132 m | 252 yds/230 m | 616 yds/563 m |
| B | 216 yds/198 m | 378 yds/346 m | 924 yds/845 m |
| C | 288 yds/263 m | 504 yds/461 m | 1232 yds/1127 m |
| D | 360 yds/329 m | 630 yds/576 m | 1540 yds/1408 m |
| E | 324 yds/296 m | 567 yds/518 m | 1386 yds/1267 m |

### Popcorn 2

| | BABY | LAP | BED |
|---|---|---|---|
| A | 144 yds/132 m | 252 yds/230 m | 616 yds/563 m |
| B | 216 yds/198 m | 378 yds/346 m | 924 yds/845 m |
| C | 288 yds/263 m | 504 yds/461 m | 1232 yds/1127 m |
| D | 360 yds/329 m | 630 yds/576 m | 1540 yds/1408 m |
| E | 324 yds/296 m | 567 yds/518 m | 1386 yds/1267 m |

### Popcorn Kernel

| | BABY | LAP | BED |
|---|---|---|---|
| A | 144 yds/132 m | 252 yds/230 m | 616 yds/563 m |
| B | 216 yds/198 m | 378 yds/346 m | 924 yds/845 m |
| C | 216 yds/198 m | 378 yds/346 m | 924 yds/845 m |
| D | 288 yds/263 m | 504 yds/461 m | 1232 yds/1127 m |
| E | 324 yds/296 m | 567 yds/518 m | 1386 yds/1267 m |

## STITCH VARIATION

## Popcorn Kernel

• **SKILL LEVEL:** *Intermediate*

## Method

**SPECIAL STITCHES:**
• Beginning Popcorn—Beg PC: Made of ch 3, 3 dc, ch 1.
• Popcorn—PC: Made of 4 dc, ch 1.

**FOUNDATION RING:** Using Color A, ch 5 and join with slip st to form a ring.

**ROUND 1:** Beg PC into ring, ch 4, * PC into ring, ch 4: rep from * twice more, join with slip st into ch at top of Beg PC. End Color A. (4 PC, 4 ch sps.)

**ROUND 2:** Join Color B in any ch 4 sp, Beg PC, ch 4, PC in same ch-4 sp, * ch 2, (PC, ch 4, PC) in next ch-4 sp; rep from * twice more, ch 2, join with slip st into ch at top of Beg PC. End Color B. (8 PC, 8 ch sps.)

**ROUND 3:** Join Color C in any ch-4 sp, ch 3 (counts as 1 dc), 2 dc, ch 2, 3 dc into same ch sp, * ch 1, 3 dc into ch-2 sp, ch 1 ** (3 dc, ch 2, 3 dc) into next corner ch-4 sp; rep from * twice more, then from * to ** once more, join with slip st into top of beginning ch. End Color C. (36 sts, 12 ch sps.)

**ROUND 4:** Join Color D in any ch-2 sp, ch 3 (counts as 1 dc), 2 dc, ch 2, 3 dc into same ch sp, * [ch 1, 3 dc] into each ch sp along side of square, ch 1, ** (3 dc, ch 2, 3 dc) into next corner ch-2 sp; rep from * twice more, then from * to ** once more, join with slip st into top of beginning ch. End Color D. (48 sts, 16 ch sps.)

**ROUND 5:** Join Color E in any ch-2 sp, ch 3 (counts as 1 dc), 2 dc, ch 2, 3 dc into same ch sp, * [ch 1, 3 dc] into each ch sp along side of square, ch 1, ** (3 dc, ch 2, 3 dc) into next corner ch-2 sp: rep from * twice more, then from * to ** once more, join with slip st into top of beginning ch. End Color E. (60 sts, 20 ch sps.)

● A: 4 yds/3.7 m
● B: 6 yds/5.5 m
● C: 6 yds/5.5 m
● D: 8 yds/7.3 m
● E: 9 yds/8.2 m

# Tutti Frutti

- A: 10 yds/9.1 m
- B: 10 yds/9.1 m
- C: 10 yds/9.1 m

• **SKILL LEVEL:** *Beginner*

## Method

**FOUNDATION ROW:** Using Color A, ch 20. (19 sts + 1 turning ch.)

**ROW 1:** Begin with 2nd ch from hook and sc in each ch across, turn. (19 sts.)

**ROW 2:** Ch 3 (counts as 1 dc), dc in each st across, turn. End Color A. (19 sts.)

**ROW 3:** Join Color B, ch 1 and sc in same st, sc in each st across, turn. (19 sts.)

**ROW 4:** Ch 4 (counts as 1 tr), tr in each st across, turn. End Color B. (19 sts.)

**ROW 5:** Join Color C and repeat Row 3.

**ROW 6:** Repeat Row 2. End Color C.

**ROW 7:** Join Color A and repeat Row 3.

**ROW 8:** Repeat Row 2. End Color A.

**ROW 9:** Join Color B and repeat Row 3.

**ROW 10:** Repeat Row 4. End Color B.

**ROW 11:** Join Color C and repeat Row 3.

**ROW 12:** Repeat Row 2. End Color C.

## COLOR VARIATION

### Tutti Frutti 2

Follow the written instructions or the chart, using colors as follows:

- A: 10 yds/9.1 m
- B: 10 yds/9.1 m
- C: 10 yds/9.1 m

Tutti Frutti

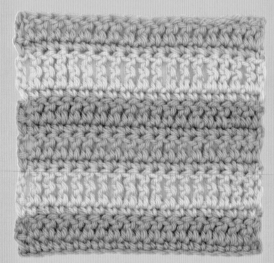

Tutti Frutti 2

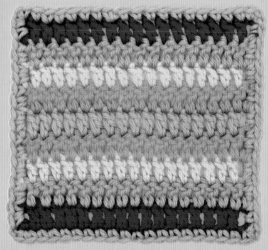

Fruit Salad

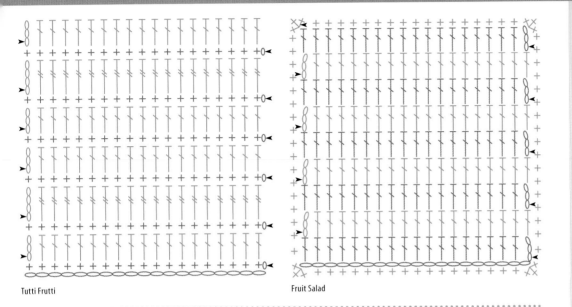

Tutti Frutti

Fruit Salad

## Yarn requirement for throws

**NOTE:** *All yarn requirements are estimated using an H-size (5 mm) crochet hook and worsted/10-ply yarn. Measurements and yarn requirements do not include joining and edging.*

### Tutti Frutti

|   | BABY | LAP | BED |
|---|------|-----|-----|
| A | 360 yds/329 m | 630 yds/576 m | 1540 yds/1408 m |
| B | 360 yds/329 m | 630 yds/576 m | 1540 yds/1408 m |
| C | 360 yds/329 m | 630 yds/576 m | 1540 yds/1408 m |

### Tutti Frutti 2

|   | BABY | LAP | BED |
|---|------|-----|-----|
| A | 360 yds/329 m | 630 yds/576 m | 1540 yds/1408 m |
| B | 360 yds/329 m | 630 yds/576 m | 1540 yds/1408 m |
| C | 360 yds/329 m | 630 yds/576 m | 1540 yds/1408 m |

### Fruit Salad

|   | BABY | LAP | BED |
|---|------|-----|-----|
| A | 216 yds/198 m | 378 yds/346 m | 924 yds/845 m |
| B | 216 yds/198 m | 378 yds/346 m | 924 yds/845 m |
| C | 216 yds/198 m | 378 yds/346 m | 924 yds/845 m |
| D | 216 yds/198 m | 378 yds/346 m | 924 yds/845 m |
| E | 324 yds/296 m | 567 yds/518 m | 1386 yds/1267 m |

**STITCH VARIATION**

## Fruit Salad

• **SKILL LEVEL:** *Beginner*

- ● A: 6 yds/5.5 m
- ● B: 6 yds/5.5 m
- ● C: 6 yds/5.5 m
- ● D: 6 yds/5.5 m
- ● E: 9 yds/8.2 m

## Method

**FOUNDATION ROW:** Using Color A, ch 22. (19 sts + 3 turning chs.)

**ROW 1:** Begin in 5th ch from hook and dc in each ch across, turn. End Color A. (19 sts.)

**ROW 2:** Join Color B, ch 3 (counts as 1 dc), dc in each st across, turn. End Color B. (19 sts.)

**ROW 3:** Join Color C and repeat Row 2. End Color C. (19 sts.)

**ROW 4:** Join Color D and repeat Row 2. End Color D. (19 sts.)

**ROW 5:** Join Color E and repeat Row 2. End Color E. (19 sts.)

**ROW 6:** Join Color D and repeat Row 2. End Color D. (19 sts.)

**ROW 7:** Join Color C and repeat Row 2. End Color C. (19 sts.)

**ROW 8:** Join Color B and repeat Row 2. End Color B. (19 sts.)

**ROW 9:** Join Color A and repeat Row 2. End Color A. (19 sts.)

**ROUND 10:** Join Color E, ch 1 and 3 sc in same corner st, sc around each column and in base of each st along side, 3 sc in first foundation ch, sc in each foundation ch to last ch, 3 sc in last ch, sc around each column and in base of each st along side, 3 sc in corner st, sc in each st to end of round, join with slip st into first sc made. End Color E. (80 sts.)

# Flower in Web

- **A:** 10 yds/9.1 m
- **B:** 4 yds/3.7 m
- **C:** 11 yds/10 m
- **D:** 10 yds/9.1 m

• **SKILL LEVEL:** *Beginner*

## Method

**FOUNDATION RING:** Using Color A, make a Magic Ring.

**ROUND 1:** Ch 3 (counts as 1 dc), 2 dc into ring, ch 3, * 3 dc into ring, ch 3; rep from * twice more, join with slip st into top of beginning ch. End Color A. (12 sts, 4 ch sps.)

**ROUND 2:** Join Color B, slip st into next dc, skip 1 dc, * ([2dc, 2ch] twice, 2 dc) in ch-3 sp **, skip 1 dc, slip st in next dc, skip 1 dc; rep from * twice more, then from * to ** once more, join with slip st into first slip st made. End Color B. (24 sts, 8 ch sps, 4 slip sts.)

**ROUND 3:** Join Color C, ch 5 (counts as 1 dc, ch 2), * sc in ch-2 sp, ch 2, sc in ch-2 sp, ch 2 **, dc in slip st, ch 2; rep from * twice more, then from * to ** once more, join with slip st into 3rd ch of beginning ch. (12 sts, 12 ch sps.)

**ROUND 4:** Ch 7 (counts as 1 dc, ch 4), * sc in next sc, 3 sc in ch-2 sp, sc in next sc, ch 4 **, dc in dc, ch 4; rep from * twice more, then from * to ** once more, join with slip st into

3rd ch of beginning ch. End Color C. (24 sts, 8 ch sps.)

**ROUND 5:** Join Color D, ch 3 (counts as 1 dc), tr, dc in same st, * 5 dc in ch-4 sp, dc in next 5 sts, 5 dc in ch-4 sp **, dc, tr, dc in corner dc; rep from * twice more, then from * to ** once more, join with slip st into top of beginning ch. End Color D. (72 sts.)

**ROUND 6:** Join Color C, ch 1 and sc in same space, * (sc, hdc, sc) in tr **, sc in each dc to tr; rep from * twice more, then from * to ** once more, sc in each st to end of round, join with slip st into first sc made. (80 sts.)

**ROUND 7:** Join Color A, ch 1 and sc in same space, sc in next st, * (sc, hdc, sc) in hdc **, sc in each sc to hdc; rep from * twice more, then from * to ** once more, sc in each st to end of round, join with slip st into first sc made. End Color A. (84 sts.)

Flower in Web

Flower in Web 2

---

## COLOR VARIATION

### Flower in Web 2

Follow the written instructions or the chart, using colors as follows:

- **A:** 10 yds/9.1 m
- **B:** 4 yds/3.7 m
- **C:** 5 yds/4.6 m
- **D:** 10 yds/9.1 m
- **E:** 6 yds/5.5 m

**FOUNDATION RING:** Color A
**ROUND 1:** Color A
**ROUND 2:** Color B
**ROUNDS 3 AND 4:** Color C
**ROUND 5:** Color D
**ROUND 6:** Color E
**ROUND 7:** Color A

Webbed Flower

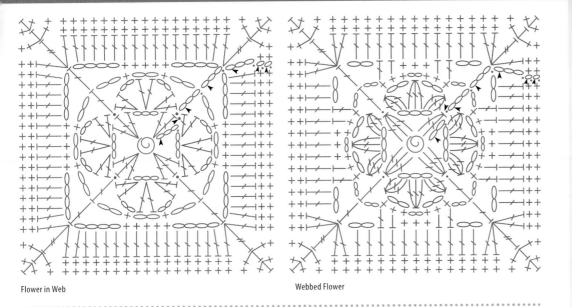

Flower in Web

Webbed Flower

## STITCH VARIATION

## Webbed Flower

- **SKILL LEVEL:** *Beginner*

## Method

**SPECIAL STITCHES:**
- Beginning Cluster—Beg Cl: Made of 2ch, 2dc.
- Cluster—Cl: Made of 3dc.

**FOUNDATION RING:** Using Color A, make a Magic Ring.

**ROUND 1:** Work Beg Cl into ring, * ch 3, Cl; rep from * twice more, ch 3, join with slip st into top of Beg Cl. End Color A. (4 CL, 4 ch sps.)

**ROUND 2:** Join Color B, slip st into top of first Cl, * ([Cl, ch 2] twice, Cl) into ch-3 sp **, slip st into top of next Cl; rep from * twice more, then from * to ** once more, join with slip st into first slip st made. End Color B. (12 CL, 8 ch sps, 4 slip sts.)

**ROUND 3:** Join Color C, ch 5 (counts as 1 dc, ch 2), * (3 sc in ch-2 sp, ch 2) twice **, dc in slip st, ch 2; rep from * twice more, then from * to ** once more, join with slip st into 3rd ch of beginning ch. (28 sts, 12 ch sps.)

**ROUND 4:** Ch 5 (counts as 1 dc, ch 2), * dc in next st, hdc in next st, sc in next st, sc in ch-2 sp, sc in next st, hdc in next st, dc in next st, ch 2 **, dc in dc, ch 2: rep from * twice more, then from * to ** once more, join with slip st into 3rd ch of beginning ch. End Color C. (32 sts, 8 ch sps.)

- A: 3 yds/2.7 m
- B: 11 yds/10 m
- C: 6 yds/5.5 m
- D: 10 yds/9.1 m
- E: 7 yds/6.4 m

**ROUND 5:** Join Color D, ch 3 (counts as 1 dc), dc, tr, 2 dc in same st, * 2 dc in ch-2 sp, dc in next 7 sts, 2 dc in ch-2 sp **, (2 dc, tr, 2 dc) in corner dc; rep from * twice more, then from * to ** once more, join with slip st into top of beginning ch. End Color D. (64 sts.)

**ROUND 6:** Join Color B, ch 1 and sc in same sp, sc in next st, * (sc, hdc, sc) in tr **, sc in each dc to tr; rep from * twice more, then from * to ** once more, sc in each st to end of round, join with slip st into first sc made. End Color B. (72 sts.)

**ROUND 7:** Join Color E, ch 1 and sc in same sp, sc in next 2 sts, * (sc, hdc, sc) in hdc **, sc in each sc to hdc; rep from * twice more, then from * to ** once more, sc in each st to end of round, join with slip st into first sc made. End Color E. (80 sts.)

## Yarn requirement for throws

**NOTE:** *All yarn requirements are estimated using an H-size (5 mm) crochet hook and worsted/10-ply yarn. Measurements and yarn requirements do not include joining and edging.*

### Flower in Web

|   | BABY | LAP | BED |
|---|------|-----|-----|
| A | 360 yds/329 m | 630 yds/576 m | 1540 yds/1408 m |
| B | 144 yds/132 m | 252 yds/230 m | 616 yds/563 m |
| C | 396 yds/362 m | 693 yds/634 m | 1694 yds/1549 m |
| D | 360 yds/329 m | 630 yds/576 m | 1540 yds/1408 m |

### Flower in Web 2

|   | BABY | LAP | BED |
|---|------|-----|-----|
| A | 360 yds/329 m | 630 yds/576 m | 1540 yds/1408 m |
| B | 144 yds/132 m | 252 yds/230 m | 616 yds/563 m |
| C | 180 yds/165 m | 315 yds/288 m | 770 yds/704 m |
| D | 360 yds/329 m | 630 yds/576 m | 1540 yds/1408 m |
| E | 216 yds/198 m | 378 yds/346 m | 924 yds/845 m |

### Webbed Flower

|   | BABY | LAP | BED |
|---|------|-----|-----|
| A | 108 yds/99 m | 189 yds/173 m | 462 yds/422 m |
| B | 396 yds/362 m | 693 yds/634 m | 1694 yds/1549 m |
| C | 216 yds/198 m | 378 yds/346 m | 924 yds/845 m |
| D | 360 yds/329 m | 630 yds/576 m | 1540 yds/1408 m |
| E | 252 yds/230 m | 441 yds/403 m | 1078 yds/986 m |

# Bobble Heart

- **SKILL LEVEL:** *Intermediate*

A: 28 yds/25.6 m
B: 11 yds/10 m

## Method

**SPECIAL STITCH:**

- Bobble—B: Work 5 dc in same st, leaving last loop of each st on hook (6 loops on hook), yo and draw through all loops on hook.

**FOUNDATION ROW:** Using Color A, ch 22. (21 sts + 1 turning ch.)

**ROW 1:** Begin with 2nd ch from hook and sc in each ch across, turn. (21 sts.)

**ROW 2:** Ch 1, sc in each st across, turn. (21 sts.)

**ROW 3:** Repeat Row 2.

**ROW 4:** Ch 1, sc in next 10 sts, join Color B, make B, end Color B, with Color A, sc in next 10 sts, turn.

**ROW 5:** Repeat Row 2.

**ROW 6:** Ch 1, sc in next 8 sts, join Color B, make B, end Color B, with Color A, sc in next 3 sts, join Color B, make B, end Color B, with Color A sc in next 8 sts, turn.

**ROW 7:** Repeat Row 2.

**ROW 8:** Ch 1, sc in next 6 sts, join Color B, make B, end Color B, with Color A, sc in next 7 sts, join Color B, make B, end Color B, with Color A sc in next 6 sts, turn.

**ROW 9:** Repeat Row 2.

**ROW 10:** Ch 1, sc in next 4 sts, join Color B, make B, end Color B, with Color A, sc in next 11 sts, join Color B, make B, end Color B, with Color A sc in next 4 sts, turn.

**ROW 11:** Repeat Row 2.

**ROW 12:** Ch 1, sc in next 2 sts, join Color B, make B, end Color B, with Color A, sc in next 15 sts, join Color B, make B, end Color B, with Color A sc in next 2 sts, turn.

**ROW 13:** Repeat Row 2.

**ROW 14:** Repeat Row 12.

**ROW 15:** Repeat Row 2.

**ROW 16:** Ch 1, sc in next 2 sts, join Color B, make B, end Color B, [with Color A, sc in next 7 sts, join Color B, make B, end Color B] twice, with Color A, sc in next 2 sts, turn.

**ROW 17:** Repeat Row 2.

**ROW 18:** Ch 1, sc in next 3 sts, [join Color B, make B, end Color B, with Color A, sc in next 4 sts, join Color B, make B, end Color B, with Color A sc in next 3 sts] twice, turn.

**ROW 19:** Repeat Row 2.

**ROW 20:** Ch 1, [sc in next 4 sts, join Color B, make B, end Color B, with Color A, sc in next 1 st, join Color B, make B, end Color B, with Color A sc in next 3 sts] twice, sc in last st, turn.

**ROWS 21–23:** Repeat Row 2.

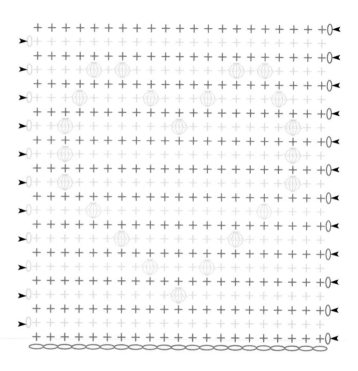

## Yarn requirement for throws

**NOTE:** *All yarn requirements are estimated using an H-size (5 mm) crochet hook and worsted/10-ply yarn. Measurements and yarn requirements do not include joining and edging.*

| Bobble Heart | | | |
|---|---|---|---|
| | BABY | LAP | BED |
| A | 1008 yds/922 m | 1764 yds/1613 m | 4312 yds/3943 m |
| B | 396 yds/362 m | 693 yds/634 m | 1694 yds/1549 m |

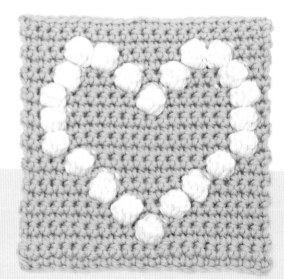

## Project Notes

- A: 117 yds/107 m
- B: 117 yds/107 m
- C: 117 yds/107 m
- D: 117 yds/107 m
- E: 117 yds/107 m
- F: 117 yds/107 m
- G: 198 yds/181 m
- H: 84 yds/77 m
- I: 84 yds/77 m
- J: 84 yds/77 m
- K: 84 yds/77 m
- L: 84 yds/77 m
- M: 84 yds/77 m
- N: 150 yds/137 m

Make three squares in each of the following colors:
Colors A–F

Make three squares in each of the following colors and working the Bobbles in Color G:
Colors H–M

Lay blocks out randomly, or following the photograph for reference, in six rows of six squares. Using Color N and holding squares so wrong sides are facing, join with single-crochet method.

### EDGING
**ROUND 1:** Using Color N, sc in each stitch around, working 3 sc in corner stitches, join to first sc made.
Repeat Round 1 three times.

# Traditional Granny

- ● A: 2 yds/1.8 m
- ◐ B: 3 yds/2.7 m
- ○ C: 6 yds/5.5 m
- ◕ D: 8 yds/7.3 m
- ○ E: 9 yds/8.2 m

• **SKILL LEVEL:** *Beginner*

## Method

**FOUNDATION RING:** Using Color A, ch 4 and join with slip st to form a ring.

**ROUND 1:** Ch 3 (counts as 1 dc), 2 dc into ring, ch 2, * 3 dc into ring, ch 2; rep from * twice more, join with slip st into top of beginning ch. End Color A. (12 sts, 4 ch sps.)

**ROUND 2:** Join Color B in any ch-2 sp, ch 3 (counts as 1 dc), 2 dc, ch 2, 3 dc into same sp, * ch 1, (3 dc, ch 2, 3 dc) into next ch-2 sp; rep from * twice more, ch 1, join with slip st into top of beginning ch. End Color B. (24 sts, 8 ch sps.)

**ROUND 3:** Join Color C in any ch-2 sp, 2 dc, ch 2, 3 dc into same sp, * ch 1, 3 dc into ch-1 sp, ch 1 ** (3 dc, ch 2, 3 dc) into next corner ch-2 sp; rep from * twice more, then from * to ** once more, join with slip st into top of beginning ch. End Color C. (36 sts, 12 ch sps.)

**ROUND 4:** Join Color D in any ch-2 sp, 2 dc, ch 2, 3 dc into same sp, * [ch 1, 3 dc] into next ch-1 sp twice, ch 1, ** (3 dc, ch 2, 3 dc) into next corner ch-2 sp; rep from * twice more, then from * to ** once more, join with slip st into top of beginning ch. End Color D. (48 sts, 16 ch sps.)

**ROUND 5:** Join Color E in any ch-2 sp, 2 dc, ch 2, 3 dc into same sp, * [ch 1, 3 dc] into next ch-1 sp 3 times, ch 1, ** (3 dc, ch 2, 3 dc) into next corner ch-2 sp; rep from * twice more, then from * to ** once more, join with slip st into top of beginning ch. End Color E. (60 sts, 20 ch sps.)

**COLOR VARIATION**

## Traditional Granny 2

Follow the written instructions or the chart, using colors as follows:

- ○ A: 2 yds/1.8 m
- ◐ B: 3 yds/2.7 m
- ● C: 6 yds/5.5 m
- ○ D: 8 yds/7.3 m
- ● E: 9 yds/8.2 m

Traditional Granny

Traditional Granny 2

Treble Granny

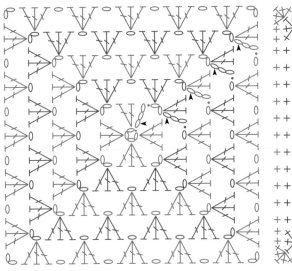

Traditional Granny Square

Treble Granny

---

## STITCH VARIATION

## Treble Granny

• **SKILL LEVEL:** *Beginner*

## Method

**FOUNDATION RING:** Using Color A, ch 4 and join with slip st to form a ring.
**ROUND 1:** Ch 4 (counts as 1 tr), 2 tr into ring, ch 3, * 3 tr into ring, ch 3; rep from * twice more, join with slip st into top of beginning ch. End Color A. (12 sts, 4 ch sps.)
**ROUND 2:** Join Color B in any ch-3 sp, ch 4 (counts as 1 tr), 2 tr, ch 3, 3 tr into same sp, * ch 1, (3 tr, ch 3, 3 tr) into next ch-3 sp; rep from * twice more, ch 1, join with slip st into top of beginning ch. End Color B. (24 sts, 8 ch sps.)
**ROUND 3:** Join Color C in any ch-3 sp, ch 4 (counts as 1 tr), 2 tr, ch 3, 3 tr into same sp, * ch 1, 3 tr into ch-1 sp, ch 1 ** (3 tr, ch 3, 3 tr) into next corner ch-3 sp; rep from * twice more, then from * to ** once more, join with slip st into top of beginning ch. End Color C.

(36 sts, 12 ch sps.)
**ROUND 4:** Join Color A in same place as join, ch 1 and sc in same space, sc in next 2 sts, (2 sc, hdc, 2 sc) in ch-3 sp, * sc in each st and ch sp to next corner ch-3 sp, (2 sc, hdc, 2 sc) in ch-3 sp; rep from * twice more, sc in each st and ch sp to end of round, join with slip st into first sc made. End Color A. (64 sts.)
**ROUND 5:** Join Color B, ch 1 and sc in same sp, * sc in each st to hdc, (2 sc, hdc, 2 sc) in hdc; rep from * 3 more times, sc in each st to end of round, join with slip st into first sc made. End Color B. (80 sts.)

◐ A: 8 yds/7.3 m
● B: 12 yds/11 m
○ C: 8 yds/7.3 m

## Yarn requirement for throws

**NOTE:** *All yarn requirements are estimated using an H-size (5 mm) crochet hook and worsted/10-ply yarn. Measurements and yarn requirements do not include joining and edging.*

### Traditional Granny

| | BABY | LAP | BED |
|---|---|---|---|
| A | 72 yds/66 m | 126 yds/115 m | 308 yds/282 m |
| B | 108 yds/99 m | 189 yds/173 m | 462 yds/422 m |
| C | 216 yds/198 m | 378 yds/346 m | 924 yds/845 m |
| D | 288 yds/263 m | 504 yds/461 m | 1232 yds/1127 m |
| E | 324 yds/296 m | 567 yds/518 m | 1386 yds/1267 m |

### Traditional Granny 2

| | BABY | LAP | BED |
|---|---|---|---|
| A | 72 yds/66 m | 126 yds/115 m | 308 yds/282 m |
| B | 108 yds/99 m | 189 yds/173 m | 462 yds/422 m |
| C | 216 yds/198 m | 378 yds/346 m | 924 yds/845 m |
| D | 288 yds/263 m | 504 yds/461 m | 1232 yds/1127 m |
| E | 324 yds/296 m | 567 yds/518 m | 1386 yds/1267 m |

### Treble Granny

| | BABY | LAP | BED |
|---|---|---|---|
| A | 288 yds/263 m | 504 yds/461 m | 1232 yds/1127 m |
| B | 432 yds/395 m | 756 yds/691 m | 1848 yds/1690 m |
| C | 288 yds/263 m | 504 yds/461 m | 1232 yds/1127 m |

# Miter Box

• **SKILL LEVEL:** *Beginner*

| | | |
|---|---|---|
| ◐ | A: | 5 yds/4.6 m |
| ● | B: | 7 yds/6.4 m |
| ◔ | C: | 10 yds/9.1 m |
| ● | D: | 13 yds/11.9 m |

## Method

**FOUNDATION RING:** Using Color A, make a Magic Ring.

**ROUND 1:** Ch 1, 8 sc in ring, join with slip st into first sc made. End Color A. (8 sts.)

**ROUND 2:** Join Color B, ch 3 (counts as 1 dc), * (dc, tr, dc) in next st **, dc in next st; rep from * twice more, then from * to ** once more, join with slip st into top of beginning ch. End Color B. (16 sts.)

**ROUND 3:** Join Color C, ch 3 (counts as 1 dc), dc in next st, * (2 dc, tr, 2 dc) in tr **, dc in each st to next tr; rep from * twice more, then from * to ** once more, dc in next st, join with slip st into top of beginning ch. End Color C. (32 sts.)

**ROUND 4:** Join Color D, ch 3 (counts as 1 dc), dc in next 3 sts, * (2 dc, tr, 2 dc) in tr **, dc in each st to next tr; rep from * twice more, then from* to ** once more, dc in next 3 sts, join with slip st into top of beginning ch. End Color D. (48 sts.)

**ROW 5:** Join Color A in corner tr, ch 3 (counts as 1 dc), dc in each st to next tr, (2 dc, tr, 2 dc) in tr, dc in next 12 sts, turn. End Color A. (29 sts.)

**ROW 6:** Join Color B, ch 3 (counts as 1 dc), dc in each st to tr, (2 dc, tr, 2 dc) in tr, dc in each st to end of row, turn. End Color B. (33 sts.)

**ROW 7:** Join Color C and rep Row 6. End Color C. (37 sts.)

**ROUND 8:** Join Color D in corner tr of Row 7, ch 1, (sc, hdc, sc) in tr, sc in each st to last st of row, (sc, hdc, sc) in last st, (sc around post of dc, sc in base of same dc) 3 times, sc in each sc of square, (sc, hdc, sc) in tr, sc in each sc of square, (sc in base of dc, sc around post of same dc) 3 times, sc in each dc, join with slip st into first sc made. End Color D. (80 sts.)

Miter Box

Miter Box 2

## COLOR VARIATION

## Miter Box 2

Follow the written instructions or the chart, using colors as follows:

| | | |
|---|---|---|
| ○ | A: | 5 yds/4.6 m |
| ● | B: | 7 yds/6.4 m |
| ◔ | C: | 10 yds/9.1 m |
| ● | D: | 13 yds/11.9 m |

Stars and Stripes

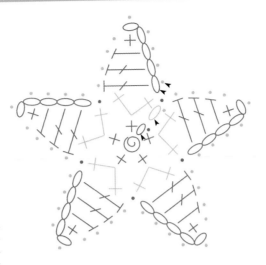

Miter Box

Stars and Stripes

## Yarn requirement for throws

**NOTE:** *All yarn requirements are estimated using an H-size (5 mm) crochet hook and worsted/10-ply yarn. Measurements and yarn requirements do not include joining and edging.*

### Miter Box
| | BABY | LAP | BED |
|---|---|---|---|
| A | 180 yds/165 m | 315 yds/288 m | 770 yds/704 m |
| B | 252 yds/230 m | 441 yds/403 m | 1078 yds/986 m |
| C | 360 yds/329 m | 630 yds/576 m | 1540 yds/1408 m |
| D | 468 yds/428 m | 819 yds/749 m | 2002 yds/1831 m |

### Miter Box 2
| | BABY | LAP | BED |
|---|---|---|---|
| A | 180 yds/165 m | 315 yds/288 m | 770 yds/704 m |
| B | 252 yds/230 m | 441 yds/403 m | 1078 yds/986 m |
| C | 360 yds/329 m | 630 yds/576 m | 1540 yds/1408 m |
| D | 468 yds/428 m | 819 yds/749 m | 2002 yds/1831 m |

### Stars and Stripes
| | BABY | LAP | BED |
|---|---|---|---|
| A | 540 yds/494 m | 945 yds/864 m | 2310 yds/2112 m |
| B | 576 yds/527 m | 1008 yds/922 m | 2464 yds/2253 m |
| C | 396 yds/362 m | 693 yds/634 m | 1694 yds/1549 m |

## STITCH VARIATION

## Stars and Stripes

- A: 15 yds/13.7 m
- B: 16 yds/14.6 m
- C: 11 yds/10 m

- **SKILL LEVEL:** *Beginner*

## Method
### BLOCK
Follow instructions and chart for Miter Box, opposite, alternating colors as follows:

**ROUNDS 1–4:** Color A
**ROW 5:** Color B
**ROW 6:** Color C
**ROW 7:** Color B
**ROUND 8:** Color C

### STAR
**FOUNDATION RING:** With Color B, make a Magic Ring.
**ROUND 1:** Ch 1, work 5 sc in ring, join with slip st into first sc made. (5 sts.)
**ROUND 2:** Ch 1, 2 sc in each sc around, join with slip st into first sc made. (10 sts.)
**ROUND 3:** * Ch 5, sc in 2nd ch from hook, hdc in next ch, dc in next 2 ch, skip 1 sc of previous round, slip st in next st; rep from * 4 more times. (20 sts.)
**ROUND 4:** * Slip st in next 5 ch, slip st in next 4 sts, skip slip st; rep from * 4 more times. End Color B.
### JOINING
Using Color C, sew Star to Block using overcast stitch.

# Bobble Row

● A: 20 yds/18.3 m
● B: 9 yds/8.2 m
● C: 4 yds/3.7 m
○ D: 4 yds/3.7 m

• **SKILL LEVEL:** *Beginner*

## Method

**SPECIAL STITCH:**

• Bobble—B: Work 5 tr in same st, leaving last loop of each st on hook (6 loops on hook), yo and draw through all loops on hook.

**FOUNDATION ROW:** Using Color A, ch 22. (19 sts + 3 turning chs.)

**ROW 1:** Begin with 5th ch from hook and dc in each ch across, turn. (19 sts.)

**ROW 2:** Ch 3 (counts as 1 dc), dc in each st across, turn. (19 sts.)

**ROW 3:** Repeat Row 2. End Color A.

**ROW 4:** Join Color B, ch 1, sc in each st across, turn. End Color B.

**ROW 5:** Join Color C and repeat Row 4.

**ROW 6:** Join Color A and repeat Row 4.

**ROW 7:** Join Color D and repeat Row 4.

**ROW 8:** Join Color B, ch 3 (counts as 1 dc), dc in next st, [ch 1, skip 1 st, make B in next st, ch 1, skip 1 st, dc in next st] 4 times, dc in next st, turn. End Color B.

**ROW 9:** Join Color D, ch 1, sc in next 2 dc, [sc over ch-1 sp into sc of Round 6, sc in B, sc over ch-1 sp into sc of Round 6, sc in dc] 4 times, sc in dc, turn. End Color D.

**ROW 10:** Join Color A, ch 1, sc in each st across, turn. End Color A.

**ROW 11:** Join Color C and repeat Row 10. End Color C.

**ROW 12:** Join Color B and repeat Row 10. End Color B.

**ROW 13:** Join Color A, ch 3 (counts as 1 dc), dc in each st across, turn.

**ROW 14:** Repeat Row 13.

**ROW 15:** Repeat Row 13.

Bobble Row

Bobble Row 2

## COLOR VARIATION

### Bobble Row 2

Follow the written instructions or the chart, using colors as follows:

● A: 20 yds/18.3 m
○ B: 9 yds/8.2 m
● C: 4 yds/3.7 m
● D: 4 yds/3.7 m

Double Bobble Row

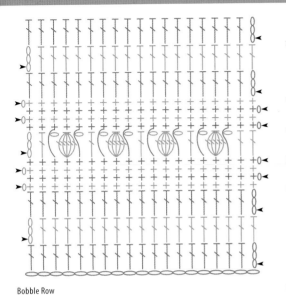

Bobble Row

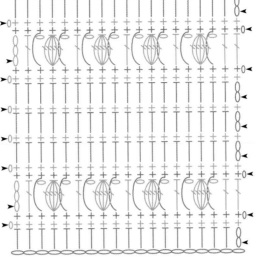

Double Bobble Row

## Yarn requirement for throws

**NOTE:** *All yarn requirements are estimated using an H-size (5 mm) crochet hook and worsted/10-ply yarn. Measurements and yarn requirements do not include joining and edging.*

| Bobble Row | | | |
|---|---|---|---|
| | BABY | LAP | BED |
| A | 720 yds/658 m | 1260 yds/1152 m | 3080 yds/2816 m |
| B | 324 yds/296 m | 567 yds/518 m | 1386 yds/1267 m |
| C | 144 yds/132 m | 189 yds/173 m | 462 yds/422 m |
| D | 144 yds/132 m | 189 yds/173 m | 462 yds/422 m |

| Bobble Row 2 | | | |
|---|---|---|---|
| | BABY | LAP | BED |
| A | 720 yds/658 m | 1260 yds/1152 m | 3080 yds/2816 m |
| B | 324 yds/296 m | 567 yds/518 m | 1386 yds/1267 m |
| C | 144 yds/132 m | 189 yds/173 m | 462 yds/422 m |
| D | 144 yds/132 m | 189 yds/173 m | 462 yds/422 m |

| Double Bobble Row | | | |
|---|---|---|---|
| | BABY | LAP | BED |
| A | 288 yds/263 m | 504 yds/461 m | 1232 yds/1127 m |
| B | 288 yds/263 m | 504 yds/461 m | 1232 yds/1127 m |
| C | 576 yds/527 m | 1008 yds/922 m | 2464 yds/2253 m |
| D | 504 yds/461 m | 882 yds/807 m | 2156 yds/1971 m |

**STITCH VARIATION**

## Double Bobble Row

• **SKILL LEVEL:** *Beginner*

- A: 8 yds/7.3 m
- B: 8 yds/7.3 m
- C: 16 yds/14.7 m
- D: 14 yds/12.8 m

## Method

**SPECIAL STITCH:**
• Bobble—B: Work 5 tr in same st, leaving last loop of each st on hook (6 loops on hook), yo and draw through all loops on hook.

**FOUNDATION ROW:** Using Color A, ch 21. (19 sts + 2 turning chs.)

**ROW 1:** Begin in 4th ch from hook and hdc in each ch across, turn. End Color A. (19 sts.)

**ROW 2:** Join Color B, ch 1, sc in each st across, turn. End Color B. (19 sts.)

**ROW 3:** Join Color C, repeat Row 2. End Color C.

**ROW 4:** Join Color D, ch 3 (counts as 1 dc), dc in next st, [ch 1, skip 1 st, make B in next st, ch 1, skip 1 st, dc in next st] 4 times, dc in last st, turn. End Color D.

**ROW 5:** Join Color C, ch 1, sc in next 2 dc, [sc over ch-1 sp into sc of Round 6, sc in B, sc over ch-1 sp into sc of Round 6, sc in dc] 4 times, sc in last st, turn. End Color C.

**ROW 6:** Join Color B, ch 1, sc in each st across, turn. End Color B.

**ROW 7:** Join Color A, ch 2 (counts as 1 hdc), hdc in each st across, turn. End Color A.

**ROW 8:** Join Color C, ch 1, sc in each st across, turn. End Color C.

**ROW 9:** Join Color D, ch 2 (counts as 1 hdc), hdc in each st across, turn. End Color D.

**ROW 10:** Join Color C, repeat Row 2. End Color C.

**ROWS 11–17:** Repeat Rows 1–7.

# Octagon Tile

| | | |
|---|---|---|
| | A: | 10 yds/9.1 m |
| | B: | 5 yds/4.6 m |
| | C: | 5 yds/4.6 m |
| | D: | 6 yds/5.5 m |
| | E: | 9 yds/8.2 m |

• **SKILL LEVEL:** *Intermediate*

## Method

**FOUNDATION RING:** Using Color A, ch 8, join with slip st to make a ring.

**ROUND 1:** Ch 3 (counts as 1 dc), dc into ring, [ch 1, 2 dc into ring] 7 times, ch 1, join with slip st into top of beginning ch. End Color A. (16 sts, 8 ch sps.)

**ROUND 2:** Join Color B, ch 3 (counts as 1 dc), dc in next st, [(dc, ch 2, dc) in ch-1 sp, dc in next 2 sts] 7 times, (dc, ch 2, dc) in next ch-1 sp, join with slip st into top of beginning ch. End Color B. (32 sts, 8 ch sps.)

**ROUND 3:** Join Color C, ch 1 and sc in same st, (sc in each st to ch-2 sp, 3 sc in ch-2 sp) 8 times, sc in next st, join with slip st into first sc made. End Color C. (56 sts.)

**ROUND 4:** Join Color D, ch 1 and sc in same st, sc in next 3 sts, [3 sc in next st, sc in next 6 sts] 7 times, 3 sc in next st, sc in next 2 sts, join with slip st into first sc made. End Color D. (72 sts.)

**ROUND 5:** Join Color E, ch 1 and sc in same st, sc in next 5 sts, hdc in next st, dc in next 2 sts, * 2 tr in next st, ch 2, 2 tr in next st, dc in next 2 sts, hdc in next st **, sc in next 10 sts, hdc in next st, dc in next 2 sts; rep from * twice more, then from * to ** once more, sc in next 4 sts, join with slip st into first sc made. End Color E. (80 sts, 4 ch sps.)

**ROUND 6:** Join Color A, ch 1 and sc in same st, * sc in each st to corner, (sc, hdc, sc) in corner ch-2 sp; rep from * 3 more times, sc in each st to end of round, join with slip st into first sc made. End Color A. (92 sts.)

Octagon Tile

**COLOR VARIATION**

## Octagon Tile 2

Follow the written instructions or the chart, using colors as follows:

| | | |
|---|---|---|
| | A: | 10 yds/9.1 m |
| | B: | 5 yds/4.6 m |
| | C: | 5 yds/4.6 m |
| | D: | 6 yds/5.5 m |
| | E: | 9 yds/8.2 m |

Octagon Tile 2

Octagon Ridged Tile

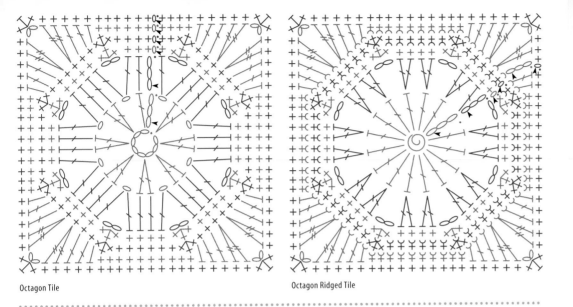

Octagon Tile

Octagon Ridged Tile

## Yarn requirement for throws

**NOTE:** *All yarn requirements are estimated using an H-size (5 mm) crochet hook and worsted/10-ply yarn. Measurements and yarn requirements do not include joining and edging.*

| Octagon Tile | | | |
|---|---|---|---|
| | BABY | LAP | BED |
| A | 360 yds/329 m | 630 yds/576 m | 1540 yds/1408 m |
| B | 180 yds/165 m | 315 yds/288 m | 770 yds/704 m |
| C | 180 yds/165 m | 315 yds/288 m | 770 yds/704 m |
| D | 216 yds/198 m | 378 yds/346 m | 924 yds/845 m |
| E | 324 yds/296 m | 567 yds/518 m | 1386 yds/1267 m |

| Octagon Tile 2 | | | |
|---|---|---|---|
| | BABY | LAP | BED |
| A | 360 yds/329 m | 630 yds/576 m | 1540 yds/1408 m |
| B | 180 yds/165 m | 315 yds/288 m | 770 yds/704 m |
| C | 180 yds/165 m | 315 yds/288 m | 770 yds/704 m |
| D | 216 yds/198 m | 378 yds/346 m | 924 yds/845 m |
| E | 324 yds/296 m | 567 yds/518 m | 1386 yds/1267 m |

| Octagon Ridged Tile | | | |
|---|---|---|---|
| | BABY | LAP | BED |
| A | 360 yds/329 m | 630 yds/576 m | 1540 yds/1408 m |
| B | 180 yds/165 m | 315 yds/288 m | 770 yds/704 m |
| C | 180 yds/165 m | 315 yds/288 m | 770 yds/704 m |
| D | 216 yds/198 m | 378 yds/346 m | 924 yds/845 m |
| E | 324 yds/296 m | 567 yds/518 m | 1386 yds/1267 m |

## STITCH VARIATION

## Octagon Ridged Tile

• **SKILL LEVEL:** *Advanced*

- A: 10 yds/9.1 m
- B: 5 yds/4.6 m
- C: 5 yds/4.6 m
- D: 6 yds/5.5 m
- E: 9 yds/8.2 m

## Method

**FOUNDATION RING:** Using Color A, make a Magic Ring.

**ROUND 1:** Ch 3 (counts as 1 dc), 15 dc into ring, join with slip st into top of beginning ch. End Color A. (16 sts.)

**ROUND 2:** Join Color B, ch 3 (counts as 1 dc), dc in same st, (2 dc in next st, ch 2, 2 dc in next st) 7 times, 2 dc in next st, ch 2, join with slip st into top of beginning ch. End Color B. (32 sts, 8 ch sps.)

**ROUND 3:** Join Color C, ch 1 and sc in same st, (sc in each st to ch-2 sp, 3 sc in ch-2 sp) 7 times, join with slip st into first sc made. End Color C. (56 sts.)

**ROUND 4:** Join Color D in horizontal bar at back of st, ch 1 and sc in same st, sc into horizontal bar in next 4 sts, [3 sc into horizontal bar in next st, sc into horizontal bar in next 6 sts] 7 times, 3 sc in next st, sc into horizontal bar in next st, join with slip st into first sc made. End Color D. (72 sts.)

**ROUND 5:** Join Color E in horizontal bar at back of st, ch 3 (counts as 1 dc), * 2 tr into horizontal bar in next st, ch 2, 2 tr into horizontal bar in next st, dc into horizontal bar in next 2 sts, hdc into horizontal bar in next st, sc into horizontal bar in next 10 sts, hdc into horizontal bar in next st **, dc into horizontal bar in next 2 sts; rep from * twice more, then from * to ** once more, dc into horizontal bar in next st, join with slip st into top of beginning ch. End Color E. (80 sts, 4 ch sps.)

**ROUND 6:** Join Color A, ch 1 and sc in same st, * sc in each st to corner, (sc, hdc, sc) in corner ch-2 sp; rep from * 3 more times, sc in each st to end of round, join with slip st into first sc made. End Color A. (92 sts.)

# Simple Waves

● A: 19 yds/17.4 m
〰 B: 15 yds/13.7 m

• **SKILL LEVEL:** *Beginner*

## Method

**FOUNDATION ROW:** Using Color A, work a multiple of 21 + 1 turning ch.

**ROW 1:** Begin in 2nd ch from hook, work sc in next 3 ch, hdc in next 3 ch, dc in next 3 ch, tr in next 3 ch, dc in next 3 ch, hdc in next 3 ch, sc in next 3 ch, do not turn. End Color A.

**ROW 2:** Join Color B in first st of last row (right-hand side), ch 4 (counts as tr), tr in next 2 sts, dc in next 3 sts, hdc in next 3 sts, sc in next 3 sts, hdc in next 3 sts, dc in next 3 sts, tr in next 3 sts, do not turn. End Color B. (21 sts.)

**ROW 3:** Join Color A in first st of last row (right-hand side), ch 1, sc in next 3 sts, hdc in next 3 sts, dc in next 3 sts, tr in next 3 sts, dc in next 3 sts, hdc in next 3 sts, sc in next 3 sts, do not turn. End Color A.

Rows 2 and 3 form the pattern.

Simple Waves

## COLOR VARIATION

### Simple Waves 2

● A: 19 yds/17.4 m
〰 B: 15 yds/13.7 m

Follow the written instructions or the chart, using colors as follows:

Simple Waves 2

Simple Ridged Waves

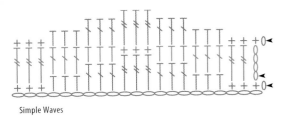

Simple Waves

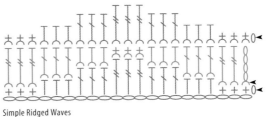

Simple Ridged Waves

## Yarn requirement for throws

**NOTE:** *All yarn requirements are estimated using an H-size (5 mm) crochet hook and worsted/10-ply yarn. Measurements and yarn requirements do not include joining and edging.*

### STITCH VARIATION

## Simple Ridged Waves

- ● A: 19 yds/17.4 m
- ● B: 15 yds/13.7 m

• **SKILL LEVEL:** *Beginner*

## Method

**FOUNDATION ROW:** Using Color A, work a multiple of 21 + 1 turning ch.

**ROW 1:** Begin in 2nd ch from hook, work sc in next 3 ch, * hdc in next 3 ch, dc in next 3 ch, tr in next 3 ch, dc in next 3 ch, hdc in next 3 ch, sc in next 3 ch; rep from * to end, do not turn. End Color A.

**ROW 2:** Join Color B in Back Loop of first st on last row (right-hand side), ch 4 (counts as tr), tr tbl in next 2 sts, * dc tbl in next 3 sts, hdc tbl in next 3 sts, sc tbl in next 3 sts, hdc tbl in next 3 sts, dc tbl in next 3 sts, tr tbl in next 3 sts; rep from * to end, do not turn. End Color B.

**ROW 3:** Join Color A in Back Loop of first st on last row (right-hand side), ch 1, sc tbl in next 2 sts, * hdc tbl in next 3 sts, dc tbl in next 3 sts, tr tbl in next 3 sts, dc tbl in next 3 sts, hdc tbl in next 3 sts, sc tbl in next 3 sts; rep from * to end, do not turn. End Color A.
Rows 2 and 3 form the pattern.

### Simple Waves

| | BABY | LAP | BED |
|---|---|---|---|
| A | 684 yds/625 m | 1197 yds/1095 m | 2926 yds/2676 m |
| B | 540 yds/494 m | 945 yds/864 m | 2310 yds/2112 m |

**Baby:** Ch 127, work 25 repeats.
**Lap:** Ch 148, work 37 repeats.
**Bed:** Ch 232, work 57 repeats.

### Simple Waves 2

| | BABY | LAP | BED |
|---|---|---|---|
| A | 684 yds/625 m | 1197 yds/1095 m | 2926 yds/2676 m |
| B | 540 yds/494 m | 945 yds/864 m | 2310 yds/2112 m |

### Simple Ridged Waves

| | BABY | LAP | BED |
|---|---|---|---|
| A | 684 yds/625 m | 1197 yds/1095 m | 2926 yds/2676 m |
| B | 540 yds/494 m | 945 yds/864 m | 2310 yds/2112 m |

**Baby:** Ch 127, work 25 repeats.
**Lap:** Ch 148, work 37 repeats.
**Bed:** Ch 232, work 57 repeats.

# Back Post

• **SKILL LEVEL:** *Beginner*

| | | |
|---|---|---|
| ● | A: | 3 yds/2.7 m |
| ● | B: | 4 yds/3.7 m |
| ● | C: | 6 yds/5.5 m |
| ● | D: | 8 yds/7.3 m |
| ● | E: | 10 yds/9.1 m |

## Method

**FOUNDATION RING:** Using Color A, ch 4 and join with slip st to form a ring.

**ROUND 1:** Ch 3 (counts as 1 dc), 2 dc into ring, ch 2, [3 dc into ring, ch 2] twice, 3 dc into ring, join with hdc to top of beginning ch (counts as ch 2). End Color A. (4 groups of 3 dc, 4 ch sps.)

**ROUND 2:** Join Color B, ch 3 (counts as 1 dc), 1 dc into same ch sp, * 1 BPdc around each stitch across to corner ch sp, (2 dc ** , ch 2, 2 dc) into ch-2 sp; rep from * twice more, then from * to ** once more, join with hdc into top of beginning ch (counts as ch 2). End Color B. (24 sts, 4 ch sps.)

**ROUND 3:** Using Color C, rep Round 2. End Color C. (44 sts, 4 ch sps.)

**ROUND 4:** Using Color D, rep Round 2. End Color D. (60 sts, 4 ch sps.)

**ROUND 5:** Using Color E, rep Round 2. End Color E. (76 sts, 4 ch sps.)

Back Post

---

**COLOR VARIATION**

## Back Post 2

Follow the written instructions or the chart, using colors as follows:

| | | |
|---|---|---|
| ● | A: | 3 yds/2.7 m |
| ● | B: | 4 yds/3.7 m |
| ● | C: | 6 yds/5.5 m |
| ● | D: | 8 yds/7.3 m |
| ● | E: | 10 yds/9.1 m |

Back Post 2

Back and Front

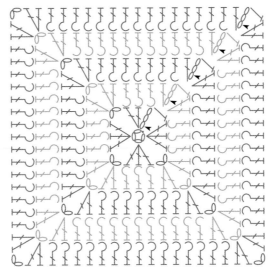

Back Post

Back and Front

## Yarn requirement for throws

**NOTE:** All yarn requirements are estimated using an H-size (5 mm) crochet hook and worsted/10-ply yarn. Measurements and yarn requirements do not include joining and edging.

### Back Post Square

|   | BABY | LAP | BED |
|---|------|-----|-----|
| A | 108 yds/99 m | 189 yds/173 m | 462 yds/422 m |
| B | 144 yds/132 m | 252 yds/230 m | 616 yds/563 m |
| C | 216 yds/198 m | 378 yds/346 m | 924 yds/845 m |
| D | 288 yds/263 m | 504 yds/461 m | 1232 yds/1127 m |
| E | 360 yds/329 m | 630 yds/576 m | 1540 yds/1408 m |

### Back Post Square 2

|   | BABY | LAP | BED |
|---|------|-----|-----|
| A | 108 yds/99 m | 189 yds/173 m | 462 yds/422 m |
| B | 144 yds/132 m | 252 yds/230 m | 616 yds/563 m |
| C | 216 yds/198 m | 378 yds/346 m | 924 yds/845 m |
| D | 288 yds/263 m | 504 yds/461 m | 1232 yds/1127 m |
| E | 360 yds/329 m | 630 yds/576 m | 1540 yds/1408 m |

### Back and Front

|   | BABY | LAP | BED |
|---|------|-----|-----|
| A | 468 yds/428 m | 819 yds/749 m | 2002 yds/1831 m |
| B | 144 yds/132 m | 252 yds/230 m | 616 yds/563 m |
| C | 216 yds/198 m | 378 yds/346 m | 924 yds/845 m |
| D | 288 yds/263 m | 504 yds/461 m | 1232 yds/1127 m |

## STITCH VARIATION

## Back and Front

• **SKILL LEVEL:** *Beginner*

- A: 13 yds/11.9 m
- B: 4 yds/3.7 m
- C: 6 yds/5.5 m
- D: 8 yds/7.3 m

## Method

**FOUNDATION RING:** Using Color A, ch 4 and join with slip st to form a ring.

**ROUND 1:** Ch 3 (counts as 1 dc), 2 dc into ring, ch 2, [3 dc into ring, ch 2] twice, 3 dc into ring, join with hdc to top of beginning ch (counts as ch 2). End Color A. (4 groups of 3 dc, 4 ch sps.)

**ROUND 2:** Join Color B, ch 3 (counts as 1 dc), 1 dc into same ch-sp, * 1 FPdc around each stitch across to corner ch sp, (2 dc **, ch 2, 2 dc) into ch-2 sp; rep from * twice more, then from * to ** once more, join with hdc into top of beginning ch (counts as ch 2). End Color B. (24 sts, 4 ch sps.)

**ROUND 3:** Join Color C, ch 3 (counts as 1 dc), 1 dc into same ch sp, * 1 BPdc around each stitch across to corner ch sp, (2 dc **, ch 2, 2 dc) into ch sp; rep from * twice more, then from * to ** once more, join with hdc into top of beginning ch (counts as ch 2). End Color C. (44 sts, 4 ch sps.)

**ROUND 4:** Using Color D, rep Round 2. End Color D. (60 sts, 4 ch sps.)

**ROUND 5:** Using Color A, rep Round 3. End Color A. (76 sts, 4 ch sps.)

# Mitered Flower

● A:  5 yds/4.6 m
◐ B:  11 yds/10 m
○ C:  11 yds/10 m
  D:  11 yds/10 m

• SKILL LEVEL: *Intermediate*

## Method

**SPECIAL STITCH:**
• Picot: Ch 3, slip st in first ch.
**FOUNDATION RING:** Using Color A, make a Magic Ring.
**ROW 1 (RS):** Ch 1, 3 sc into ring, turn. (3 sts.)
**ROW 2:** Ch 1, sc in same st, 2 sc in next st, 1 sc in last st, turn. (4 sts.)
**ROW 3:** Ch 1 and sc in same st, 2 sc in next 2 sts, sc in last st, turn. End Color A. (6 sts.)
**ROW 4:** Join Color B, ch 1 and 2 sc in same st, sc in next 4 sts, 2 sc in last st, turn. (8 sts.)
**ROW 5:** Ch 3 (counts as 1 dc), dc in same st, dc in next 6 sts, 2 dc in last st, turn. (10 sts.)
**ROW 6:** Ch 3 (counts as 1 dc), dc in same st, dc in next st, 2 dc in next st, dc in next 4 sts, 2 dc in next st, dc in next st, 2 dc in last st, turn. End Color B. (14 sts.)
**ROW 7:** Join Color C, ch 1, sc in each st, turn. (14 sts.)
**ROW 8:** Ch 1 and sc in same st, skip 1 st, (2 dc, tr, picot, tr, 2 dc) in next st, skip 1 st, sc in next st, skip 1 st, (2 dc, 2 tr, picot) in next st, (2 tr, 2 dc) in next st, skip 1 st, sc in next st, skip 1 st, (2 dc, tr, picot, tr, 2 dc) in next st, skip 1 st, sc in last st. End Color C. (24 sts, 3 picots.)

**ROW 9:** Join Color D, ch 3 (counts as 1 dc), 2 dc in same st, sc in picot, [(2 tr, 2 dc, 2 tr) in next sc, sc in picot] twice, 3 dc in last sc, turn. (21 sts.)
**ROW 10:** Ch 1, sc in same st, sc in next 2 sts, hdc in next 3 sts, dc in next 2 sts, tr in next 2 sts, (2 dtr, ch 2, 2 dtr) in next st, tr in next 2 sts, dc in next 2 sts, hdc in next 3 sts, sc in next 3 sts, turn. (24 sts.)
**ROW 11:** Ch 1, sc in each st to corner ch-2 sp, (2 sc, hdc, 2 sc) in ch-2 sp, sc in each st to end, turn. End Color D. (29 sts.)
**ROW 12:** Join Color B, ch 1 and sc in same st, sc in each st to hdc, (sc, hdc, sc) in hdc, sc in each st to end, turn. End Color B. (31 sts.)
**ROW 13:** Join Color C and rep Row 12. End Color C. (33 sts.)
**ROW 14:** Join Color A and rep Row 12. End Color A. (35 sts.)
**ROW 15:** Join Color C and rep Row 12. End Color C. (37 sts.)
**ROW 16:** Join Color B and rep Row 12. End Color B. (39 sts.)
**ROW 17**: Join Color D and rep Row 12. End Color D. (41 sts.)

Mitered Flower

Mitered Flower 2

## COLOR VARIATION

### Mitered Flower 2

Follow the written instructions or the chart, using colors as follows:

○ A:  5 yds/4.6 m
○ B:  11 yds/10 m
◐ C:  11 yds/10 m
● D:  11 yds/10 m

Mighty Mitered Flower

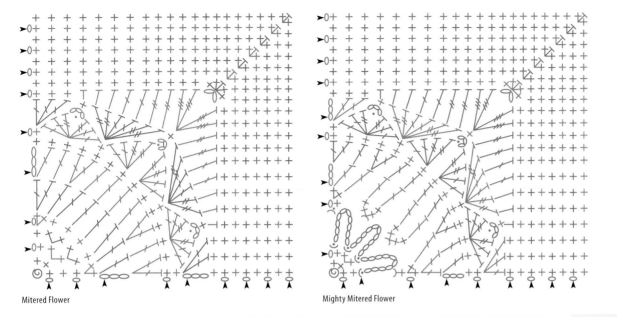

Mitered Flower

Mighty Mitered Flower

........................................................................................................

## STITCH VARIATION

## Mighty Mitered Flower

• **SKILL LEVEL:** *Advanced*

## Method

**SPECIAL STITCH:**

• Picot: Ch 3, slip st in first ch.

**FOUNDATION RING:** Using Color A, make a Magic Ring.

**ROW 1 (RS):** Ch 1, 3 sc into ring, turn. (3 sts.)

**ROW 2:** Ch 1, sc in same sp, 2 sc in next st, 1 sc in last st, turn. (4 sts.)

**ROW 3:** Slip st into Front Loop of first st, * ch 10, slip st into Front Loop of next st; rep from * twice more, turn. (4 sts, 3 ch sps.)

**ROW 4:** Slip st into Back Loop of first st on Row 2, ch 1 and sc in same sp, 2 sc in Back Loop of next 2 sts, sc in Back Loop of last st, turn. End Color A. (6 sts.)

**ROW 5:** Join Color B, ch 1 and 2 sc in same sp, sc in next 4 sts, 2 sc in last st, turn. (8 sts.)

**ROW 6:** Ch 3 (counts as 1 dc), dc in same st, dc in next 6 sts, 2 dc in last st, turn. (10 sts.)

**ROW 7:** Ch 3 (counts as 1 dc), dc in same st, dc in next st, 2 dc in next st, dc in next 4 sts, 2 dc in next st, dc in next st, 2 dc in last st, turn. End Color B. (14 sts.)

**ROW 8:** Join Color C, ch 1, sc in each st, turn. (14 sts.)

**ROW 9:** Ch 1 and sc in same st, skip 1 st, (2 dc, tr, picot, tr, 2 dc) in next st, skip 1 st, sc in next st, skip 1 st, (2 dc, 2 tr, picot) in next st, (2 tr, 2 dc) in next st, skip 1 st, sc in next st, skip 1 st, (2 dc, tr, picot, tr, 2 dc) in next st, skip 1 st, sc in last st. End Color C. (24 sts, 3 picots.)

**ROW 10:** Join Color D, ch 3 (counts as 1 dc), 2 dc in same st, sc in picot, [(2 tr, 2 dc, 2 tr) in next sc, sc in picot] twice, 3 dc in last sc, turn. (21 sts.)

**ROW 11:** Ch 1, sc in same st, sc in next 2 sts, hdc in next 3 sts, dc in next 2 sts, tr in next 2 sts, (2 dtr, ch 2, 2 dtr) in next st, tr in next 2 sts, dc in next 2 sts, hdc in next 3 sts, sc in next 3 sts, turn. (24 sts, 1 ch sp.)

**ROW 12:** Ch 1, sc in each st to corner ch-2 sp, (2 sc, hdc, 2 sc) in ch-2 sp, sc in each st to end, turn. End Color D. (29 sts.)

**ROW 13:** Join Color B, ch 1 and sc in same st, sc in each st to hdc, (sc, hdc, sc) in hdc, sc in each st to end, turn. End Color B. (31 sts.)

**ROW 14:** Join Color C and rep Row 13. End Color C. (33 sts.)

**ROW 15:** Join Color A and rep Row 13. End Color A. (35 sts.)

**ROW 16:** Join Color C and rep Row 13. End Color C. (37 sts.)

**ROW 17:** Join Color B and rep Row 13. End Color B. (39 sts.)

**ROW 18:** Join Color D and rep Row 13. End Color D. (41 sts.)

○ A: 6 yds/5.5 m
◑ B: 11 yds/10 m
● C: 11 yds/10 m
○ D: 11 yds/10 m

## Yarn requirement for throws

**NOTE:** *All yarn requirements are estimated using an H-size (5 mm) crochet hook and worsted/10-ply yarn. Measurements and yarn requirements do not include joining and edging.*

........................................................................................................

**Mitered Flower**

| | BABY | LAP | BED |
|---|---|---|---|
| A | 180 yds/165 m | 315 yds/288 m | 770 yds/704 m |
| B | 396 yds/362 m | 693 yds/634 m | 1694 yds/1549 m |
| C | 396 yds/362 m | 693 yds/634 m | 1694 yds/1549 m |
| D | 396 yds/362 m | 693 yds/634 m | 1694 yds/1549 m |

**Mitered Flower 2**

| | BABY | LAP | BED |
|---|---|---|---|
| A | 180 yds/165 m | 315 yds/288 m | 770 yds/704 m |
| B | 396 yds/362 m | 693 yds/634 m | 1694 yds/1549 m |
| C | 396 yds/362 m | 693 yds/634 m | 1694 yds/1549 m |
| D | 396 yds/362 m | 693 yds/634 m | 1694 yds/1549 m |

**Mighty Mitered Flower**

| | BABY | LAP | BED |
|---|---|---|---|
| A | 216 yds/198 m | 378 yds/346 m | 924 yds/845 m |
| B | 396 yds/362 m | 693 yds/634 m | 1694 yds/1549 m |
| C | 396 yds/362 m | 693 yds/634 m | 1694 yds/1549 m |
| D | 396 yds/362 m | 693 yds/634 m | 1694 yds/1549 m |

# Home

• **SKILL LEVEL:** *Beginner*

A: 39 yds/35.7 m
B: 5 yds/4.6 m
C: 2 yds/1.8 m
D: 3 yds/2.7 m

## Method

**FOUNDATION ROW:** Using Color A, ch 22, turn. (21 sts + 1 turning ch.)

**ROW 1:** Begin with 2nd ch from hook, 1 sc in each ch across, turn. (21 sts.)

**ROW 2:** Ch 1, sc in each st across, turn. (21 sts.) Repeat Row 2 for 21 more rows. End Color A.

**CROSS-STITCH EMBROIDERY:** Using one strand of each color, follow the chart, working in cross stitch.

## COLOR VARIATION

### Home 2

A: 39 yds/35.7 m
B: 5 yds/4.6 m
C: 2 yds/1.8 m
D: 3 yds/2.7 m

Follow the written instructions and the chart, using colors as follows:

Home

Home 2

Sweet

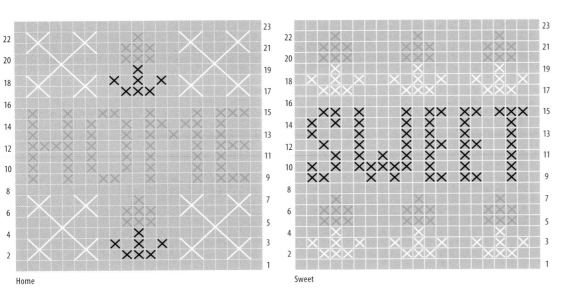

Home

Sweet

## Yarn requirement for throws

**NOTE:** *All yarn requirements are estimated using an H-size (5 mm) crochet hook and worsted/10-ply yarn. Measurements and yarn requirements do not include joining and edging.*

| Home | | | |
|---|---|---|---|
| | BABY | LAP | BED |
| **A** | 1404 yds/1284 m | 2457 yds/2247 m | 6006 yds/5492 m |
| **B** | 180 yds/165 m | 315 yds/288 m | 770 yds/704 m |
| **C** | 72 yds/66 m | 126 yds/115 m | 308 yds/282 m |
| **D** | 108 yds/99 m | 189 yds/173 m | 462 yds/422 m |

| Home 2 | | | |
|---|---|---|---|
| | BABY | LAP | BED |
| **A** | 1404 yds/1284 m | 2457 yds/2247 m | 6006 yds/5492 m |
| **B** | 180 yds/165 m | 315 yds/288 m | 770 yds/704 m |
| **C** | 72 yds/66 m | 126 yds/115 m | 308 yds/282 m |
| **D** | 108 yds/99 m | 189 yds/173 m | 462 yds/422 m |

| Sweet | | | |
|---|---|---|---|
| | BABY | LAP | BED |
| **A** | 1404 yds/1284 m | 2457 yds/2247 m | 6006 yds/5492 m |
| **B** | 180 yds/165 m | 315 yds/288 m | 770 yds/704 m |
| **C** | 108 yds/99 m | 189 yds/173 m | 462 yds/422 m |
| **D** | 108 yds/99 m | 189 yds/173 m | 462 yds/422 m |
| **E** | 36 yds/33 m | 63 yds/58 m | 154 yds/141 m |

## STITCH VARIATION

## Sweet

- **SKILL LEVEL:** *Beginner*

## Method

**FOUNDATION ROW:** Using Color A, ch 22, turn. (21 sts + 1 turning ch.)

**ROW 1:** Begin with 2nd ch from hook, 1 sc in each ch across, turn. (21 sts.)

**ROW 2:** Ch 1, sc in each st across, turn. (21 sts.) Repeat Row 2 for 21 more rows. End Color A.

**CROSS-STITCH EMBROIDERY:** Using one strand of each color, follow the chart, working in cross stitch.

- A: 39 yds/35.7 m
- B: 5 yds/4.6 m
- C: 3 yds/2.7 m
- D: 3 yds/2.7 m
- E: 1 yd/1 m

# Eye-popping Popcorn

- **SKILL LEVEL:** *Intermediate*

## Method

### SPECIAL STITCHES:

- Beginning Popcorn—Beg-PC: Ch 3, work 4 dc into the same place. Take the hook out of the working loop and insert it into 3rd ch of ch 3. Pick up working loop with hook and draw it through to fold the group of stitches, ch 1 pulling tightly to close the group of stitches.
- Popcorn—PC: Work a group of 5 dc into the same place. Take the hook out of the working loop and insert it under both loops at top of the first dc of the group. Pick up working loop with hook and draw it through to fold the group of stitches, ch 1 pulling tightly to close the group.

**FOUNDATION RING:** Using Color A, make a Magic Ring.

**ROUND 1:** Ch 3 (counts as 1 dc), 15 dc into ring, join with slip st into top of beginning ch. (16 sts.)

**ROUND 2:** Work Beg-PC in first st, [2 dc in next st, PC in next st] 7 times, 2 dc in next st, join with slip st into top of beginning ch. End Color A. (8 PC, 16 dc.)

**ROUND 3:** Join Color B, ch 3 (counts as 1 dc), dc in same st, [1 dc in next st, 2 dc in next st] 11 times, 1 dc in next st, join with slip st into top of beginning ch. End Color B. (36 sts.)

● A: 21 yds/19.2 m
▥ B: 8 yds/7.3 m
● C: 20 yds/18.3 m

**ROUND 4:** Join Color C, ch 1 and sc in same sp, * sc in next st, hdc in next 2 sts, dc in next st, ch 2, PC in next st, ch 2, dc in next st, hdc in next 2 sts **, sc in next st; rep from * twice more, then from * to ** once more, join with slip st into first sc made. (4 PC, 32 sts, 8 ch sps.)

**ROUND 5:** Ch 3 (counts as 1 dc), [dc in each st to ch-2 sp, 2 dc in ch-2 sp, (dc, tr, dc) in PC, 2 dc in ch-2 sp] 4 times, dc in each st to end of round, join with slip st into top of beginning ch. End Color C. (60 sts.)

**ROUND 6:** Join Color A, ch 1 and sc in same sp, [sc in each st to corner tr, (sc, hdc, sc) in tr] 4 times, sc in each st to end of round, join with slip st into first sc made. End Color A. (68 sts.)

**ROUND 7:** Join Color B, ch 1 and sc in same sp, [sc in each st to corner hdc, (sc, hdc, sc) in corner hdc] 4 times, sc in each st to end of round, join with slip st into first sc made. End Color B. (76 sts.)

Eye-popping Popcorn

Eye-popping Popcorn 2

## COLOR VARIATION

### Eye-popping Popcorn 2

Follow the written instructions or the chart, using colors as follows:

▥ A: 21 yds/19.2 m
● B: 8 yds/7.3 m
● C: 20 yds/18.3 m

Eye-popping Lace

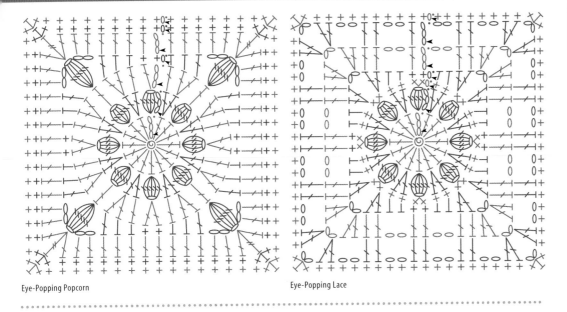

Eye-Popping Popcorn

Eye-Popping Lace

## Yarn requirement for throws

**NOTE:** *All yarn requirements are estimated using an H-size (5 mm) crochet hook and worsted/10-ply yarn. Measurements and yarn requirements do not include joining and edging.*

### Eye-popping Popcorn

|   | BABY | LAP | BED |
|---|---|---|---|
| A | 756 yds/691 m | 1323 yds/1210 m | 3234 yds/2957 m |
| B | 288 yds/263 m | 504 yds/461 m | 1232 yds/1127 m |
| C | 720 yds/658 m | 1260 yds/1152 m | 3080 yds/2816 m |

### Eye-popping Popcorn 2

|   | BABY | LAP | BED |
|---|---|---|---|
| A | 756 yds/691 m | 1323 yds/1210 m | 3234 yds/2957 m |
| B | 288 yds/263 m | 504 yds/461 m | 1232 yds/1127 m |
| C | 720 yds/658 m | 1260 yds/1152 m | 3080 yds/2816 m |

### Eye-popping Lace

|   | BABY | LAP | BED |
|---|---|---|---|
| A | 360 yds/329 m | 630 yds/576 m | 1540 yds/1408 m |
| B | 288 yds/263 m | 504 yds/461 m | 1232 yds/1127 m |
| C | 612 yds/560 m | 1071 yds/979 m | 2618 yds/2394 m |

## STITCH VARIATION

## Eye-popping Lace

● A:  10 yds/9.1 m
◐ B:  8 yds/7.3 m
◑ C:  17 yds/15.5 m

• **SKILL LEVEL:** *Intermediate*

## Method

**SPECIAL STITCHES:**

• Beginning Popcorn—Beg-PC: Ch 3, work 4 dc into the same place. Take the hook out of the working loop and insert it into 3rd ch of ch 3. Pick up working loop with hook and draw it through to fold the group of stitches, ch 1 pulling tightly to close the group of stitches.

• Popcorn—PC: Work a group of 5 dc into the same place. Take the hook out of the working loop and insert it under both loops at top of the first dc of the group. Pick up working loop with hook and draw it through to fold the group of stitches, ch 1 pulling tightly to close the group.

**FOUNDATION RING:** Using Color A, make a Magic Ring.

**ROUND 1:** Ch 4 (counts as 1 dc), 15 dc into ring, join with slip st into top of beginning ch. (16 sts.)

**ROUND 2:** Work Beg-PC in first st, [2 dc in next st, PC in next st] 7 times, 2 dc in next st, join with slip st into top of beginning ch. End Color A. (8 PC, 16 dc.)

**ROUND 3:** Join Color B, ch 1 and 2 sc in same st, [sc in next 2 sts, 2 sc in PC] 7 times, sc in next 2 sts, join with slip st into first sc made. End Color B. (32 sts.)

**ROUND 4:** Join Color C, ch 1 and sc in same st, sc in next sc, hdc in next 2 sts, * 2 dc in next st, ch 2, 2 dc in next st, hdc in next 2 sts **, sc in next 2 sts, hdc in next 2 sts; rep from * twice more, then from * to ** once more, join with slip st into first sc made. (40 sts, 4 ch sps.)

**ROUND 5:** Ch 3 (counts as 1 dc), dc in next st, ch 2, skip 2 sts, dc in next 2 sts, * (2 dc, ch 2, 2 dc) in ch-2 sp, dc in next 2 sts, ch 2, skip 2 sts **, dc in next 2 sts, ch 2, skip 2 sts, dc in next 2 sts; rep from * twice more, then from * to ** once more, join with slip st into top of beginning ch. (40 sts, 12 ch sps.)

**ROUND 6:** Ch 3 (counts as 1 dc), dc in next st, ch 2, dc in next 2 dc, * ch 2, skip 2 dc, (2 dc, ch 2, 2 dc) in ch-2 sp, ch 2, skip 2 dc, dc in next 2 sts **, [ch 2, dc in next 2 dc] twice; rep from * twice more, then from * to ** once more, ch 2, join with slip st into top of beginning ch. End Color C. (40 sts, 20 ch sps.)

**ROUND 7:** Join Color B, ch 1 and sc in same sp, sc in next st, [2 sc in ch-2 sp, sc in next 2 sts] twice, * (sc, hdc, sc) in corner ch-2 sp **, [sc in next 2 sts, 2 sc in ch-2 sp] 4 times, sc in next 2 sts; rep from * twice more, then from * to ** once more, [sc in next 2 sts, 2 sc in ch-2 sp] twice, join with slip st into first sc made. End Color B. (84 sts.)

# Platinum, Purple, and Pink

- **SKILL LEVEL:** *Intermediate*

## Method

**SPECIAL STITCH:**
- Puff Stitch—PS: Yo, insert hook into st indicated, (yo, pull up a loop to the height of hdc) 3 times (7 loops on hook), yo and pull through all 7 loops on hook.

**FOUNDATION RING:** Using Color A, make a Magic Ring.

**ROUND 1:** Ch 4 (counts as 1 tr), [5 dc into ring, tr into ring] 3 times, 5 dc into ring, join with slip st into top of beginning ch. End Color A. (24 sts.)

**ROUND 2:** Join Color B, ch 1 and sc in same st, * skip 2 sts, (3 dc, ch 3, 3 dc) in next st, skip 2 sts **, sc in next st; rep from * twice more, then from * to ** once more, join with slip st into first sc made. End Color B. (28 sts, 4 ch sps.)

**ROUND 3:** Join Color C with slip st, * skip 3 sts, (2 tr, 3 dc, ch 2, 3 dc, 2 tr) in ch-3 sp, skip 3 sts **, slip st in next sc; rep from * twice more, then from * to ** once more, join with slip st into beginning slip st. End Color C. (40 sts, 4 slip sts, 4 ch sps.)

**ROUND 4:** Join Color D in ch-2 sp, ch 1, *3 sc in ch-2 sp, sc in next 5 sts, sc into sc of Round 2, sc in next 5 sts; rep from * 3 more times, join with slip st into first sc made. End Color D. (56 sts.)

**ROUND 5:** Join Color E, ch 1 and sc in same st, * 3 sc in next st, sc in next 3 sts, hdc in next

2 sts, dc in next 3 sts, hdc in next 2 sts **, sc in next 3 sts; rep from * twice more, then from * to ** once more, sc in next 2 sts, join with slip st into first sc made. End Color E. (64 sts.)

**ROUND 6:** Join Color A in 2nd sc of corner, ch 4 (counts as 1 hdc, ch 2), hdc in same st, * [ch 1, skip 1 st, PS in next st] 7 times, ch 1 **, skip 1 st, (hdc, ch 2, hdc) in next st; rep from * twice more, then from * to ** once more, join with slip st into 2nd ch of beginning ch. End Color A. (36 sts, 36 ch sps.)

**ROUND 7:** Join Color E in ch-2 sp, ch 1, * 3 sc in ch-2 sp, sc in hdc, [sc over ch-sp and into st of Round 5, sc in PS] 7 times, sc over ch-sp and into st of Round 5 **, sc in hdc; rep from * twice more, then from * to ** once more, sc in top of 2nd ch from beginning of Round 6, join with slip st into first sc made. End Color E. (80 sts.)

- ● A: 13 yds/11.9 m
- ◐ B: 4 yds/3.7 m
- ● C: 7 yds/6.4 m
- ○ D: 5 yds/4.6 m
- ◑ E: 14 yds/12.8 m

## Yarn requirement for throws

**NOTE:** *All yarn requirements are estimated using an H-size (5 mm) crochet hook and worsted/10-ply yarn. Measurements and yarn requirements do not include joining and edging.*

| Platinum, Purple, and Pink | | | |
|---|---|---|---|
| | BABY | LAP | BED |
| **A** | 468 yds/428 m | 819 yds/749 m | 2002 yds/1831 m |
| **B** | 144 yds/132 m | 252 yds/230 m | 616 yds/563 m |
| **C** | 252 yds/230 m | 441 yds/403 m | 1078 yds/986 m |
| **D** | 180 yds/165 m | 315 yds/288 m | 770 yds/704 m |
| **E** | 504 yds/461 m | 882 yds/807 m | 2156 yds/1971 m |

## Project Notes

### YOU WILL NEED:

- 12 in. (30 cm) pillow form (or 14 in./35 cm for a plumper pillow)
- 12 in. (30 cm) zipper

- ● A: 104 yds/95 m
- ● B: 32 yds/29 m
- ● C: 56 yds/51 m
- ○ D: 40 yds/37 m
- ● E: 112 yds/102 m

Make 8 squares.

For the front panel, join four squares using Color E and mattress stitch with wrong sides facing.

Repeat for the back panel.

Sew the zipper along front edge and back panels on one side.

### EDGING

**ROUND 1:** Join panels together on three sides by holding wrong sides facing and using Color D, sc tbls of each stitch, working 3sc tbl in each corner stitch. Work only into the stitches of the front panel on the fourth side to allow for the zipper. Join to first sc made and end Color D.

**ROUND 2:** Join Color E, 1ch and sc in each stitch around working 3sc in corner stitches, join to first stitch made, and end Color E.

# Pretty in Pink

○ A: 6 yds/5.5 m
◐ B: 9 yds/8.2 m
● C: 18 yds/16.5 m

• **SKILL LEVEL:** *Intermediate*

## Method

**SPECIAL STITCHES:**

• Beg 4-st Cluster—Beg 4-Cl: Ch 2 *(counts as 1 dc)*, work 3 dc leaving last loop of each stitch on hook (4 loops on hook), yo, pull through all 4 loops on hook, ch 1 pulling tight to close group.

• 4-st Cluster—4-Cl: Work 4 dc in space indicated, leaving last loop of each stitch on hook (5 loops on hook), yo, pull through all 5 loops on hook, ch 1 pulling tight to close group.

• 3-st Cluster—3-Cl: Work 1 dc in each of next 3 sts, leaving last loop of each stitch on hook (4 loops on hook), yo, pull through all 4 loops on hook, ch 1 pulling tight to close group.

**FOUNDATION RING:** Using Color A, make a Magic Ring.

**ROUND 1:** Ch 5 (counts as 1 dc, ch 2), [dc into ring, ch 2] 7 times, join with slip st into 3rd ch of beginning ch. End Color A. (8 sts, 8 ch sps.)

**ROUND 2:** Join Color B in ch-2 sp, Beg 4-Cl in ch-2 sp, [ch 3, 4-Cl in next ch-2 sp] 7 times, ch 3, join with slip st into top of Beg 4-Cl. End Color B. (8 4-Cl, 8 ch sps.)

**ROUND 3:** Join Color C, ch 1 and sc in same st, [3 sc in ch-3 sp, sc in top of next 4-Cl] 7 times, 3 sc in ch-3 sp, join with slip st into first sc made. End Color C. (32 sts.)

**ROUND 4:** Join Color A, ch 1 and sc in same st, * ch 2, work 3-Cl over next 3 sts, ch 2 **, sc in next st; rep from * six more times, then from * to ** once more, join with slip st into first sc made. End Color A. (8 3-Cl, 8 sc, 16 ch sps.)

**ROUND 5:** Join Color B, ch 3 (counts as 1 dc), 3 dc in same st, [sc in 3-Cl, 4 dc in next sc] 7 times, sc in top of 3-Cl, join with slip st into top of beginning ch. End Color B. (40 sts.)

**ROUND 6:** Join Color C, ch 1 and sc in same st, sc in next 2 sts, * hdc in next st, dc in next st, (2 tr, ch 2, 2 tr) in next st, dc in next st, hdc in next st **, sc in next 5 sts; rep from * twice more, then from * to ** once more, sc in next 2 sts, join with slip st into first sc made. (52 sts, 4 ch sps.)

**ROUND 7:** Ch 3 (counts as 1 dc), [dc in each st to ch-2 sp, (2 dc, ch 2, 2 dc) in ch-2 sp] 4 times, dc in each st to end of round, join with slip st into top of beginning ch. End Color C. (68 sts, 4 ch sps.)

Pretty in Pink

## COLOR VARIATION

## Pretty in Pink 2

Follow the written instructions or the chart, using colors as follows:

○ A: 6 yds/5.5 m
◕ B: 9 yds/8.2 m
● C: 18 yds/16.5 m

Pretty in Pink 2

Pretty Pink Popcorn Flower

Pretty in Pink

Pretty Pink Popcorn Flower

## STITCH VARIATION

## Pretty Pink Popcorn Flower

• **SKILL LEVEL:** *Intermediate*

## Method

**SPECIAL STITCHES:**

• Beginning Popcorn—Beg PC: Ch 3, work 4 dc in same space. Take the hook out of the working loop and insert it into 3rd ch of ch-3. Pick up working loop with hook and draw it through to fold the group of stitches, ch 1 pulling tightly to close the group of stitches.

• Popcorn—PC: Work 5 dc into the same space. Take the hook out of the working loop and insert it under both loops at top of first dc of the group. Pick up working loop with hook and draw it through to fold the group of stitches, ch 1 pulling tightly to close the group of stitches.

• 3-st Cluster—3-Cl: Work 1 tr in each of next 3 sts, leaving last loop of each stitch on hook (4 loops on hook), yo, pull through all 4 loops on hook, ch 1 pulling tight to close group.

**FOUNDATION RING:** Using Color A, make a Magic Ring.

**ROUND 1:** Ch 5 (counts as 1 dc, ch 2), [dc into ring, ch 2] 7 times, join with slip st into 3rd ch of beginning ch. End Color A. (8 sts, 8 ch sps.)

- ○ A: 20 yds/18.3 m
- ○ B: 4 yds/3.7 m
- ● C: 3 yds/2.7 m
- ● D: 6 yds/5.5 m

**ROUND 2:** Join Color B in ch-2 sp, work Beg PC in same sp, ch 3, [work PC in next ch-2 sp, ch 3] 7 times, join with slip st into top of Beg PC. End Color B. (8 PC, 8 ch sps.)

**ROUND 3:** Join Color C, ch 1 and sc in same st, [3 sc in ch-3 sp, sc in top of next PC] 7 times, 3 sc in ch-3 sp, join with slip st into first sc made. End Color C. (32 sts.)

**ROUND 4:** Join Color D, ch 1 and sc in same st, * ch 3, work 3-Cl over next 3 sts, ch 3 **, sc in next st; rep from * 6 more times, then from * to ** once more, join with slip st into first sc made. End Color A. (8 3-Cl, 8 sc, 16 ch sps.)

**ROUND 5:** Join Color A, ch 5 (counts as 1 dc, ch 2), * sc in top of next 3-Cl, ch 2, (dc, ch 3, dc) in next sc, ch 2, sc in top of next 3-Cl, ch 2 **, dc in next sc, ch 2; rep from * twice more, then from * to ** once more, join with slip st into top of beginning ch. (20 sts, 20 ch sps.)

**ROUND 6:** Slip st into ch-2 sp, ch 3 (counts as 1 dc), 2 dc in same sp, ch 1, 3 dc in next ch-2 sp, ch 1, * (2 dc, ch 2, 2 dc) in next ch-3 sp **, [ch 1, 3 dc in next ch-2 sp] 4 times, ch 1; rep from * twice more, then from * to ** once more, (ch 1, 3 dc in next ch-2 sp) twice, ch 1, join with slip st into top of beginning ch. End Color A. (64 sts, 24 ch sps.)

## Yarn requirement for throws

**NOTE:** *All yarn requirements are estimated using an H-size (5 mm) crochet hook and worsted/10-ply yarn. Measurements and yarn requirements do not include joining and edging.*

### Pretty in Pink

|   | BABY | LAP | BED |
|---|------|-----|-----|
| A | 216 yds/198 m | 378 yds/346 m | 924 yds/845 m |
| B | 324 yds/296 m | 567 yds/518 m | 1386 yds/1267 m |
| C | 648 yds/593 m | 1134 yds/1037 m | 2772 yds/2535 m |

### Pretty in Pink 2

|   | BABY | LAP | BED |
|---|------|-----|-----|
| A | 216 yds/198 m | 378 yds/346 m | 924 yds/845 m |
| B | 324 yds/296 m | 567 yds/518 m | 1386 yds/1267 m |
| C | 648 yds/593 m | 1134 yds/1037 m | 2772 yds/2535 m |

### Pretty Pink Popcorn Flower

|   | BABY | LAP | BED |
|---|------|-----|-----|
| A | 720 yds/660 m | 1260 yds/1150 m | 3080 yds/2820 m |
| B | 144 yds/132 m | 252 yds/230 m | 616 yds/563 m |
| C | 108 yds/99 m | 189 yds/173 m | 462 yds/422 m |
| D | 216 yds/198 m | 378 yds/346 m | 924 yds/845 m |

# She Sells Seashells

A: 5 yds/4.6 m
B: 5 yds/4.6 m
C: 5 yds/4.6 m
D: 5 yds/4.6 m
E: 5 yds/4.6 m
F: 5 yds/4.6 m

• **SKILL LEVEL:** *Intermediate*

## Method

**SPECIAL STITCH:**

• Shell: (3 dc, ch 1, 3 dc) in same st.

**FOUNDATION ROW:** Using Color A, work a multiple of 6 + 7 + 1 turning ch.

**ROW 1:** Work sc in 2nd ch from hook, * skip 2 ch, Shell in next ch, skip 2 ch, sc in next ch; rep from * to last 7 ch, sc in next ch, skip 2 ch, Shell in next ch, skip 2 ch, sc in last ch, turn. End Color A.

**ROW 2:** Join Color B, ch 5 (counts as 1 dc, ch 2), * sc in ch-1 sp of Shell, ch 2, dc in sc, ch 2; rep from * to last Shell, sc in ch-1 sp of Shell, ch 2, dc in last sc, turn.

**ROW 3:** Ch 3 (counts as 1 dc), 2 dc in same st, * sc in sc, Shell in next dc; rep from * to last sc, sc in sc, 3 dc in 3rd ch of beginning ch of previous row, turn. End Color B.

**ROW 4:** Join Color C, ch 1, sc in same st, ch 2, * dc in sc, ch 2, sc in ch-1 sp of Shell, ch 2; rep from * last sc, dc in sc, ch 2, sc in top of beginning ch of previous row, turn.

**ROW 5:** Ch 1 and sc in same st, * Shell in dc, sc in sc; rep from * to last dc, Shell in dc, sc in last sc, turn. End Color C.

**ROWS 6–7:** Repeat Rows 2 and 3 using Color D.

**ROWS 8–9:** Repeat Rows 4 and 5 using Color E.

**ROWS 10–11:** Repeat Rows 2 and 3 using Color F.

Continue repeating Rows 2–5 throughout, alternating Colors A, B, C, D, E, then F.

She Sells Seashells

She Sells Seashells 2

## COLOR VARIATION

### She Sells Seashells 2

A: 10 yds/9.1 m
B: 10 yds/9.1 m
C: 10 yds/9.1 m

Follow the written instructions or the chart, using colors as follows:

**FOUNDATION ROW, ROWS 1, 6, AND 7:** Color A.
**ROWS 2, 3, 8, AND 9:** Color B.
**ROWS 4, 5, 10, AND 11:** Color C.

By the Seashore

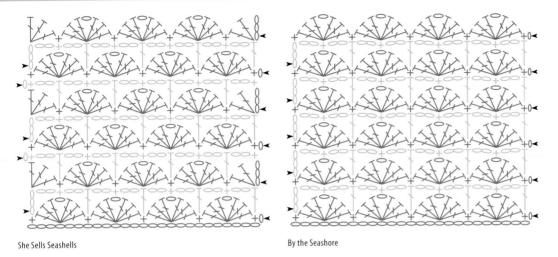

She Sells Seashells

By the Seashore

---

## Yarn requirement for throws

**NOTE:** *All yarn requirements are estimated using an H-size (5 mm) crochet hook and worsted/10-ply yarn. Measurements and yarn requirements do not include joining and edging.*

### She Sells Seashells

|   | BABY | LAP | BED |
|---|---|---|---|
| A | 180 yds/165 m | 315 yds/288 m | 770 yds/704 m |
| B | 180 yds/165 m | 315 yds/288 m | 770 yds/704 m |
| C | 180 yds/165 m | 315 yds/288 m | 770 yds/704 m |
| D | 180 yds/165 m | 315 yds/288 m | 770 yds/704 m |
| E | 180 yds/165 m | 315 yds/288 m | 770 yds/704 m |
| F | 180 yds/165 m | 315 yds/288 m | 770 yds/704 m |

**Baby:** Ch 122, work 6 repeats of color sequence.
**Lap:** Ch 194, work 9 repeats of color sequence.
**Bed:** Ch 470, work 14 repeats of color sequence.

### She Sells Seashells 2

|   | BABY | LAP | BED |
|---|---|---|---|
| A | 360 yds/329 m | 630 yds/576 m | 1540 yds/1408 m |
| B | 360 yds/329 m | 630 yds/576 m | 1540 yds/1408 m |
| C | 360 yds/329 m | 630 yds/576 m | 1540 yds/1408 m |

### By the Seashore

|   | BABY | LAP | BED |
|---|---|---|---|
| A | 360 yds/329 m | 630 yds/576 m | 1540 yds/1408 m |
| B | 360 yds/329 m | 630 yds/576 m | 1540 yds/1408 m |
| C | 360 yds/329 m | 630 yds/576 m | 1540 yds/1408 m |

---

## STITCH VARIATION

## By the Seashore

○ A: 10 yds/9.1 m
● B: 10 yds/9.1 m
◐ C: 10 yds/9.1 m

• **SKILL LEVEL:** *Intermediate*

## Method

**SPECIAL STITCH:**
• Shell: Work (3 dc, ch 1, 3 dc) in same chain or stitch.

**FOUNDATION ROW:** Using Color A, work a multiple of 6 + 1 + 1 turning ch.

**ROW 1:** Work 1 sc in 2nd ch from hook, * skip 2 ch, Shell in next ch, skip 2 ch, sc in next ch; rep from * to last 6 ch, skip 2 ch, Shell in next ch, skip 2 ch, sc in last ch. End Color A.

**ROW 2:** Join Color B, ch 5 (counts as 1 dc, ch 2), * sc in ch-1 sp of Shell, ch 2, dc in sc, ch 2; rep from * to last Shell, ch 2, sc in ch-1 sp of Shell, ch 2, dc in last sc.

**ROW 3:** Ch 1 and sc in same st, * Shell in sc, sc in dc; rep from * to last 3 sts and ch-2 sps, sc in dc, Shell in sc, sc in first st made. End Color B.

**ROWS 4–5:** Repeat Rows 2 and 3 using Color C.

**ROWS 6–7:** Repeat Rows 2 and 3 using Color A.

**ROWS 8–9:** Repeat Rows 2 and 3 using Color B.

**ROWS 10–11:** Repeat Rows 2 and 3 using Color C.

Continue repeating Rows 2 and 3, alternating Color A, B, then C throughout.

# Fluffy Flower

○ A: 8 yds/7.3 m
◐ B: 13 yds/11.9 m
● C: 22 yds/20.1 m
● D: 6 yds/5.5 m

• **SKILL LEVEL:** *Advanced*

## Method

**FOUNDATION RING:** Using Color A, make a Magic Ring.

**ROUND 1:** Ch 2 (counts as 1 hdc), 5 hdc in ring, join with slip st through front loop of beginning ch. (6 sts.)

**ROUND 2:** *Ch 7, slip st in front loop of next st; rep from * 4 more times, ch 7, join with slip st through back loop of Round 1 beginning ch. (6 ch sps.)

**ROUND 3:** Ch 2 (counts as 1 hdc), hdc tbl in same space, 2 hdc tbl in each st around, join with slip st through front loop of beginning ch. (12 sts.)

**ROUND 4:** *Ch 7, slip st in front loop of next st; rep from * 10 more times, ch 7, join with slip st through both loops of Round 3 beginning ch. End Color A. (12 slip sts, 12 ch sps.)

**ROUND 5:** Join Color B, ch 1 and sc in same sp, * ch 3, skip 1 slip st **, sc tbl in next slip st; rep from * 4 more times, then from * to ** once more, join with slip st into first sc made. (6 sc, 6 ch sps.)

**ROUND 6:** Slip st into ch sp, ch 1, * (sc, hdc, dc, tr, dc hdc, sc) in ch sp **, slip st in sc; rep from * 4 more times, then from * to ** once more, join with slip st into beginning slip st. (6 petals.)

**ROUND 7:** *Slip st in next st, sc in next st, hdc in next st, (2 dc, ch 2, 2 dc) in next st, hdc in next st, sc in next st, slip st in next 2 sts; rep from * 5 more times. End Color B. (6 petals.)

**ROUND 8:** Join Color C by slip st around a sc of Round 5, * [ch 4, slip st around next sc of

Round 5] twice, ch 3, slip st around next sc of Round 5; rep from * once more, join with slip st into first slip st made. (6 ch sps.)

**ROUND 9:** Slip st into ch-4 sp, ch 3 (counts as 1 dc), (dc, ch 2, 4 dc) in same ch sp, (4 dc, ch 2, 2 dc) in next ch-4 sp, 4 dc in next ch-3 sp, (2 dc, ch 2, 4 dc) in next ch-4 sp, (4 dc, ch 2, 2 dc) in next ch-4 sp, 4 dc in next ch-3 sp, join with slip st into top of beginning ch. (32 sts, 4 ch sps.)

**ROUND 10:** Ch 3 (counts as 1 dc), * dc in each st to corner ch sp, (2 dc, ch 2, 2 dc) in corner ch sp; rep from * 3 more times, dc in each st to end of round, join with slip st into top of beginning ch. (48 sts, 4 ch sps.)

**ROUND 11:** Ch 3 (counts as 1 dc), dc in next 3 sts, * (2 dc, ch 2, 2 dc) in ch sp, dc in next st, dc through ch-2 of Round 7 petal and into next st, dc in next 8 sts, dc through ch-2 of Round 7 petal and into next st, dc in next st, (2 dc, ch 2, 2 dc) in ch sp, dc in next 5 sts, dc through ch-2 of Round 7 petal and into next st **, dc in next 6 sts; rep from * to ** once more, dc in next 2 sts, join with slip st into top of beginning ch. End Color C. (64 sts, 4 ch sps.)

**ROUND 12:** Join Color D, ch 1 and sc in same sp, * sc in each st to corner ch sp, (sc, hdc, sc) in ch sp; rep from * 3 more times, sc in each st to end of round, join with slip st into first sc made. End Color D. (76 sts.)

Fluffy Flower

Fluffy Flower 2

## COLOR VARIATION

### Fluffy Flower 2

Follow the written instructions or the chart, using colors as follows:

◐ A: 8 yds/7.3 m
○ B: 13 yds/11.9 m
● C: 22 yds/20.1 m
● D: 6 yds/5.5 m

Dutch Flower

Fluffy Flower

Dutch Flower

## STITCH VARIATION

## Dutch Flower

• **SKILL LEVEL:** *Advanced*

- ● A: 3 yds/2.7 m
- ◕ B: 7 yds/6.4 m
- ● C: 6 yds/5.5 m
- ○ D: 22 yds/20.1 m

## Method

**FOUNDATION RING:** Using Color A, make a Magic Ring.

**ROUND 1:** Ch 2 (counts as 1 hdc), 5 hdc in ring, join with slip st into top of beginning ch. (6 sts.)

**ROUND 2:** Ch 2 (counts as 1 hdc), hdc in same sp, 2 hdc in each st around, join with slip st into top of beginning ch. End Color A. (12 sts.)

**ROUND 3:** Join Color B, ch 1 and sc in same sp, * ch 3, skip 1 st **, sc in next st; rep from * 4 more times, then from * to ** once more, join with a slip st into first sc made. (6 sc, 6 ch sps.)

**ROUND 4:** Slip st into ch sp, * (sc, hdc, dc, tr, dc, hdc, sc) all in ch sp **, slip st in sc; rep from * 4 more times, then from * to ** once more, join with slip st into slip st. End Color B. (6 petals.)

**ROUND 5:** Join Color C, * slip st in next st, sc in next st, hdc in next st, (2 dc, ch 2, 2 dc) in next st, hdc in next st, sc in next st, slip st in next st and in slip st; rep from * 5 more times. End Color C. (6 petals.)

**ROUND 6:** Join Color D with slip st around a sc of Round 3, * ch 3, slip st around next sc of Round 3, [ch 4, slip st around next sc of Round 3] twice; rep from * once, join with slip st to first slip st made. (6 ch sps.)

**ROUND 7:** Slip st into ch sp, ch 3 (counts as 1 dc), 3 dc in same ch sp, (2 dc, ch 2, 4 dc) in next ch sp, (4 dc, ch 2, 2 dc) in next ch sp, 4 dc in next ch sp, (2 dc, ch 2, 4 dc) in next ch sp, (4 dc, ch 2, 2 dc) in next ch sp, join with slip st into top of beginning ch. (32 sts, 4 ch sps.)

**ROUND 8:** Ch 3 (counts as 1 dc), * dc in each st to corner ch sp, (2 dc, ch 2, 2 dc) in corner ch sp; rep from * 3 more times, dc in each st to end of round, join with slip st into top of beginning ch. (48 sts, 4 ch sps.)

**ROUND 9:** Ch 3 (counts as 1 dc), dc in next st, * dc through ch 2 of Round 5 petal and into next st of Round 8, dc in next 5 sts, (2 dc, ch 2, 2 dc) in ch sp, dc in next st, dc through ch of Round 5 petal and into next st of Round 8, dc in next 8 sts, dc through ch of Round 5 petal and into next st of Round 8, dc in next st, (2 dc, ch 2, 2 dc) in ch sp **, dc in next 6 sts; rep from * to ** once more, dc in next 4 sts, join with slip st into top of beginning ch. End Color D. (64 sts, 4 ch sps.)

**ROUND 10:** Join Color B, ch 1 and sc in same space, * sc in each st to corner ch sp, (sc, hdc, sc) in ch sp; rep from * 3 more times, sc in each st to end of round, join with slip st into first sc made. End Color B. (76 sts.)

## Yarn requirement for throws

**NOTE:** *All yarn requirements are estimated using an H-size (5 mm) crochet hook and worsted/10-ply yarn. Measurements and yarn requirements do not include joining and edging.*

### Fluffy Flower

| | BABY | LAP | BED |
|---|---|---|---|
| A | 288 yds/263 m | 504 yds/461 m | 1232 yds/1127 m |
| B | 468 yds/428 m | 819 yds/749 m | 2002 yds/1831 m |
| C | 792 yds/724 m | 1386 yds/1267 m | 3388 yds/3098 m |
| D | 216 yds/198 m | 378 yds/346 m | 924 yds/845 m |

### Fluffy Flower 2

| | BABY | LAP | BED |
|---|---|---|---|
| A | 288 yds/263 m | 504 yds/461 m | 1232 yds/1127 m |
| B | 468 yds/428 m | 819 yds/749 m | 2002 yds/1831 m |
| C | 792 yds/724 m | 1386 yds/1267 m | 3388 yds/3098 m |
| D | 216 yds/198 m | 378 yds/346 m | 924 yds/845 m |

### Dutch Flower

| | BABY | LAP | BED |
|---|---|---|---|
| A | 108 yds/99 m | 189 yds/173 m | 462 yds/422 m |
| B | 252 yds/230 m | 441 yds/403 m | 1078 yds/986 m |
| C | 216 yds/198 m | 378 yds/346 m | 924 yds/845 m |
| D | 792 yds/724 m | 1386 yds/1267 m | 3388 yds/3098 m |

# Pink Lavender

● A:  14 yds/12.8 m
○ B:  4 yds/3.7 m
◐ C:  7 yds/6.4 m
◑ D:  7 yds/6.4 m

• **SKILL LEVEL:** *Beginner*

## Method

**FOUNDATION RING:** Using Color A, make a Magic Ring.

**ROUND 1:** Ch 4 (counts as 1 tr), * 5 dc **, tr; rep from * twice more, then from * to ** once more, join with slip st in top of beginning ch. End Color A. (24 sts.)

**ROUND 2:** Join Color B, ch 5 (counts as 1 dc, ch 2), dc in same sp, ch 1, * [skip 1 dc, dc in next dc, ch 1] twice, skip 1 dc **, (dc, ch 2, dc) in next tr, ch 1; rep from * twice more, then from * to ** once more, join with slip st into 3rd ch of beginning ch. End Color B. (16 sts, 16 ch sps.)

**ROUND 3:** Join Color C, ch 3 (counts as 1 dc), * (2 dc, tr, 2 dc) in next ch-2 sp, [dc in dc, dc in ch-1 sp] 3 times **, dc in dc; rep from * twice more, then from * to ** once more, join with slip st into top of beginning ch. End Color C. (48 sts.)

**ROUND 4:** Join Color D, ch 4 (counts as 1 dc, ch 1), * skip 1 dc, dc in next dc, (dc, ch 2, dc) in tr, dc in next st, ch 1 **, [skip 1 dc, dc in next dc, ch 1] 4 times; rep from * twice more, then from * to ** once more, [skip 1 dc, dc in next dc, ch 1] 3 times, join with slip st into 3rd ch of beginning ch. End Color D. (32 sts, 24 ch sps.)

**ROUND 5:** Join Color A, ch 3 (counts as 1 dc), dc in ch-1 sp, * dc in next 2 dc, (2 dc, tr, 2 dc) in corner ch-2 sp, dc in next 2 dc **, [dc in ch-1 sp, dc in next dc] 4 times, dc in ch-1 sp; rep from * twice more, then from * to ** once more, [dc in ch-1 sp, dc in next dc] 3 times, dc in ch-1 sp, join with slip st into top of beginning ch. End Color A. (72 sts.)

Pink Lavender

Pink Lavender 2

Lavender Haze

## COLOR VARIATION

### Pink Lavender 2

Follow the written instructions or the chart, using colors as follows:

● A:  14 yds/12.8 m
○ B:  4 yds/3.7 m
◐ C:  7 yds/6.4 m
◑ D:  7 yds/6.4 m

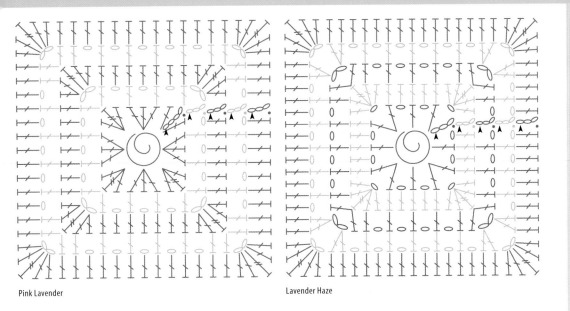

Pink Lavender

Lavender Haze

## Yarn requirement for throws

**NOTE:** *All yarn requirements are estimated using an H-size (5 mm) crochet hook and worsted/10-ply yarn. Measurements and yarn requirements do not include joining and edging.*

| Pink Lavender | | | |
|---|---|---|---|
| | BABY | LAP | BED |
| A | 504 yds/461 m | 882 yds/807 m | 2156 yds/1971 m |
| B | 144 yds/132 m | 252 yds/230 m | 616 yds/563 m |
| C | 252 yds/230 m | 441 yds/403 m | 1078 yds/986 m |
| D | 252 yds/230 m | 441 yds/403 m | 1078 yds/986 m |

| Pink Lavender 2 | | | |
|---|---|---|---|
| | BABY | LAP | BED |
| A | 504 yds/461 m | 882 yds/807 m | 2156 yds/1971 m |
| B | 144 yds/132 m | 252 yds/230 m | 616 yds/563 m |
| C | 252 yds/230 m | 441 yds/403 m | 1078 yds/986 m |
| D | 252 yds/230 m | 441 yds/403 m | 1078 yds/986 m |

| Lavender Haze | | | |
|---|---|---|---|
| | BABY | LAP | BED |
| A | 756 yds/691 m | 1323 yds/1210 m | 3234 yds/2957 m |
| B | 504 yds/461 m | 882 yds/807 m | 2156 yds/1971 m |

## STITCH VARIATION

## Lavender Haze

● A: 21 yds/19.2 m
● B: 14 yds/12.8 m

• **SKILL LEVEL:** *Beginner*

## Method

**FOUNDATION RING:** Using Color A, make a Magic Ring.

**ROUND 1:** Ch 4 (counts as 1 dc, ch 1), * dc into ring, ch 1; rep from * 10 more times, join with slip st in 3rd ch of beginning ch. End Color A. (12 sts, 12 ch sps.)

**ROUND 2:** Join Color B, ch 3 (counts as 1 dc), * (2 dc, tr, 2 dc) in next ch sp, [dc in next st, dc in ch sp] twice **, dc in dc; rep from * twice more, then from * to ** once more, join with slip st into top of beginning ch. End Color B. (40 sts.)

**ROUND 3:** Join Color A, ch 4 (counts as 1 dc, 1ch), skip 1 st, dc in next st, * (dc, ch 2, dc) in next tr, dc in next st **, [ch 1, skip 1 st, dc in next st] 3 times, ch 1, skip 1 st, dc in next st; rep from * twice more, then from * to ** once more, [ch 1, skip 1 st, dc in next st] twice, ch 1, join with slip st into top of beginning ch. End Color A. (28 sts, 20 ch sps.)

**ROUND 4:** Join Color B, ch 4 (counts as 1 dc, ch 1), skip 1 st, dc in next st, 1ch, skip 1 st, * (2 dc, ch 2, 2 dc) in ch-2 sp **, [ch 1, skip 1 st, dc in next st] 5 times, ch 1, skip 1 st; rep from * 2 more times, then from * to ** once more, [ch 1, skip 1 st, dc in next st] 3 times, ch 1, join with slip st into 3rd ch of beginning ch. End Color B. (36 sts, 28 ch sps.)

**ROUND 5:** Join Color A, ch 3 (counts as 1 dc), * dc in each st and ch sp to corner ch-2 sp, (2 dc, tr, 2 dc) in corner ch-2 sp; rep from * 3 more times, dc in each st to end of round, join with slip st into top of beginning ch. End Color A. (80 sts.)

# Love

• **SKILL LEVEL:** *Beginner*

## Method

**FOUNDATION ROW:** Using Color A, ch 10, with Color B, ch 11. (20 sts + 1 turning ch.)

**ROW 1:** Begin with 2nd ch from hook, with Color B 1 sc in 10 ch, change to Color A and 1 sc in rem 10 ch, turn. (20 sts.)

**ROW 2:** With Color A, ch 1, 1 sc in 10 sts, change to Color B and 1 sc in rem 10 sts, turn.

**ROW 3:** With Color B, ch 1, 1 sc in 10 sts, change to Color A and 1 sc in rem 10 sts, turn. Rep Rows 2 and 3 four more times, then rep Row 2 once more.

**NEXT ROW:** Change to Color C, ch 1, 1 sc in 10 sts, change to Color D and 1 sc in rem 10 sts, turn.

**NEXT ROW:** With Color D, ch 1, 1 sc in 10 sts, change to Color C and 1 sc in rem 10 sts, turn. Rep last 2 rows 5 more times. End both colors.

**WORKING THE PATTERN:** Starting at the bottom right-hand corner of the chart, work the 24-row pattern in sc.

A: 16 yds/14.6 m
B: 10 yds/9.1 m
C: 10 yds/9.1 m
D: 10 yds/9.1 m
E: 4 yds/3.7 m

When following the chart, read odd-numbered rows (right-side rows) from right to left and even-numbered rows (wrong-side rows) from left to right. Make sure to twist yarns when changing colors in the middle of every row to prevent leaving a hole.

**EDGING:** Using Color A, 1 sc in each st and row around, working 3 sc in each corner st. (92 sts.)

**CROSS STITCH:** Using one strand of Color E, follow the chart working in cross stitch.

Love

## COLOR VARIATION

### Love 2

Follow the written instructions and the chart, using colors as follows, and using Color E for the edging:

A: 10 yds/9.1 m
B: 10 yds/9.1 m
C: 10 yds/9.1 m
D: 10 yds/9.1 m
E: 10 yds/9.1 m

Love 2

Love Heart

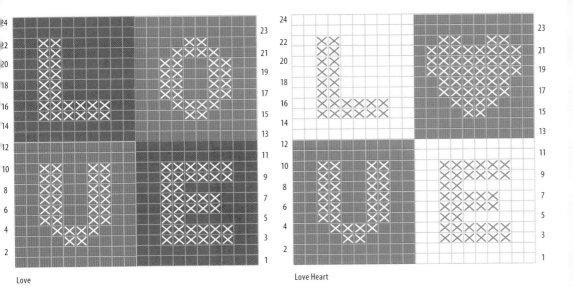

Love

Love Heart

## Yarn requirement for throws

**NOTE:** *All yarn requirements are estimated using an H-size (5 mm) crochet hook and worsted/10-ply yarn. Measurements and yarn requirements do not include joining and edging.*

| Love | | | |
|---|---|---|---|
| | **BABY** | **LAP** | **BED** |
| **A** | 576 yds/527 m | 1008 yds/922 m | 2464 yds/2253 m |
| **B** | 360 yds/329 m | 630 yds/576 m | 1540 yds/1408 m |
| **C** | 360 yds/329 m | 630 yds/576 m | 1540 yds/1408 m |
| **D** | 360 yds/329 m | 630 yds/576 m | 1540 yds/1408 m |
| **E** | 144 yds/132 m | 252 yds/230 m | 616 yds/563 m |

| Love 2 | | | |
|---|---|---|---|
| | **BABY** | **LAP** | **BED** |
| **A** | 360 yds/329 m | 630 yds/576 m | 1540 yds/1408 m |
| **B** | 360 yds/329 m | 630 yds/576 m | 1540 yds/1408 m |
| **C** | 360 yds/329 m | 630 yds/576 m | 1540 yds/1408 m |
| **D** | 360 yds/329 m | 630 yds/576 m | 1540 yds/1408 m |
| **E** | 360 yds/329 m | 630 yds/576 m | 1540 yds/1408 m |

| Love Heart | | | |
|---|---|---|---|
| | **BABY** | **LAP** | **BED** |
| **A** | 360 yds/329 m | 630 yds/576 m | 1540 yds/1408 m |
| **B** | 504 yds/461 m | 882 yds/807 m | 2156 yds/1971 m |
| **C** | 612 yds/560 m | 1071 yds/979 m | 2618 yds/2394 m |
| **D** | 360 yds/329 m | 630 yds/576 m | 1540 yds/1408 m |

## STITCH VARIATION

## Love Heart

• **SKILL LEVEL:** *Beginner*

- A: 10 yds/9.1 m
- B: 14 yds/12.8 m
- C: 17 yds/15.5 m
- D: 10 yds/9.1 m

## Method

**FOUNDATION ROW:** Using Color A, ch 10, with B, ch 11. (20 sts + 1 turning ch.)

**ROW 1:** Begin with 2nd ch from hook, with B 1 sc in 10 ch, change to A and 1 sc in rem 10 ch, turn. (20 sts.)

**ROW 2:** With A, ch 1, 1 sc in 10 sts, change to B and 1 sc in rem 10 sts, turn.

**ROW 3:** With B, ch 1, 1 sc in 10 sts, change to A and 1 sc in rem 10 sts, turn.

Rep Rows 2 and 3 four more times, then rep Row 2 once more.

**NEXT ROW:** Change to C, ch 1, 1 sc in 10 sts, change to D and 1 sc in rem 10 sts turn.

**NEXT ROW:** With D, ch 1, 1 sc in 10 sts, change to C and 1 sc in rem 10 sts, turn.

Rep last 2 rows 5 more times. End both colors.

**WORKING THE PATTERN:** Starting at the bottom right-hand corner of the chart, work the 24-row pattern in sc.

When following the chart, read odd-numbered rows (right-side rows) from right to left and even-numbered rows (wrong-side rows) from left to right. Make sure to twist yarns when changing colors in the middle of every row to prevent leaving a hole.

**EDGING:** Using Color C, sc in each st and row around, working 3 sc in each corner st. (92 sts.)

**CROSS STITCH:** Using one strand of Color C and Color B follow the chart working in cross stitch.

# Framed Primrose

● A:  1 yd/0.9 m
○ B:  5 yds/4.6 m
◐ C:  10 yds/9.1 m
● D:  9 yds/8.2 m

• **SKILL LEVEL:** *Intermediate*

## Method

**FOUNDATION RING:** With Color A, make a Magic Ring.

**ROUND 1:** Ch 1, work 6 sc into ring, join with slip st into first sc made. End Color A. (6 sts.)

**ROUND 2:** Join Color B in same place, ch 2 (counts as 1 hdc), hdc in same sp, 2 hdc in each st around, join with slip st into top of beginning ch. End Color B. (12 sts.)

**ROUND 3:** Join Color C, [ch 4, skip 2 hdc, slip st in next hdc] 3 times, ch 4, join with slip st to beginning of round. (4 slip sts, 4 ch sp.)

**ROUND 4:** * slip st into ch-4 sp, (ch 2, 3 dc, ch 1, 3 dc, ch 2, slip st) in same ch-4 sp; rep from * 3 more times. End Color C.

**ROUND 5:** Join Color D in any ch-1 sp of previous round, ch 1 and sc in same sp, * ch 4, skip petal stitches, dc in slip st between two petals, ch 4 **, sc in ch-1 sp; rep from * twice more, then from * to ** once more, join with slip st into first sc made. (8 sts, 8 ch sps.)

**ROUND 6:** Ch 3 (counts as 1 dc), tr, dc in same st, * 4 dc in ch-4 sp, dc in next dc, 4 dc in ch-4 sp **, (dc, tr, dc) in sc; rep from * twice more, then from * to ** once more, join with slip st into top of beginning ch. End Color D. (48 sts.)

**ROUND 7:** Join Color B, ch 1 and sc in same st, [(sc, hdc, sc) in next st, sc in next 11 sts] 3 times, (sc, hdc, sc) in next st, sc in next 10 sts, join with slip st into first sc made. End Color B. (56 sts.)

**ROUND 8:** Join Color C, ch 1 and sc in same st, sc in next st, [(sc, hdc, sc) in next st, sc in next 13 sts] 3 times, (sc, hdc, sc) in next st, sc in next 11 sts, join with slip st into first sc made. End Color C. (64 sts.)

**ROUND 9:** Join Color D, ch 2 (counts as 1 hdc), hdc in next 2 sts, [(hdc, dc, hdc) in next st, hdc in next 15 sts] 3 times, (hdc, dc, hdc) in next st, hdc in next 12 sts, join with slip st into top of beginning ch. End Color D. (72 sts.)

Framed Primrose

Framed Primrose 2

## COLOR VARIATION

## Framed Primrose 2

Follow the written instructions or the chart, using colors as follows:

◐ A:  1 yd/0.9 m
◐ B:  5 yds/4.6 m
○ C:  10 yds/9.1 m
● D:  9 yds/8.2 m

Pretty Primrose

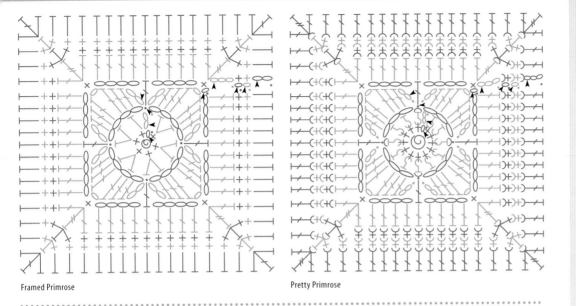

Framed Primrose

Pretty Primrose

## Yarn requirement for throws

**NOTE:** *All yarn requirements are estimated using an H-size (5 mm) crochet hook and worsted/10-ply yarn. Measurements and yarn requirements do not include joining and edging.*

| Framed Primrose | | | |
|---|---|---|---|
| | BABY | LAP | BED |
| A | 36 yds/33 m | 63 yds/58 m | 154 yds/141 m |
| B | 180 yds/165 m | 315 yds/288 m | 770 yds/704 m |
| C | 360 yds/329 m | 630 yds/576 m | 1540 yds/1408 m |
| D | 324 yds/296 m | 567 yds/518 m | 1386 yds/1267 m |

| Framed Primrose 2 | | | |
|---|---|---|---|
| | BABY | LAP | BED |
| A | 36 yds/33 m | 63 yds/58 m | 154 yds/141 m |
| B | 180 yds/165 m | 315 yds/288 m | 770 yds/704 m |
| C | 360 yds/329 m | 630 yds/576 m | 1540 yds/1408 m |
| D | 324 yds/296 m | 567 yds/518 m | 1386 yds/1267 m |

| Pretty Primrose | | | |
|---|---|---|---|
| | BABY | LAP | BED |
| A | 180 yds/165 m | 315 yds/288 m | 770 yds/704 m |
| B | 216 yds/198 m | 378 yds/346 m | 924 yds/845 m |
| C | 216 yds/198 m | 378 yds/346 m | 924 yds/845 m |
| D | 324 yds/296 m | 567 yds/518 m | 1386 yds/1267 m |
| E | 324 yds/296 m | 567 yds/518 m | 1386 yds/1267 m |

## STITCH VARIATION

## Pretty Primrose

- **SKILL LEVEL:** *Advanced*

## Method

**FOUNDATION RING:** With Color A, make a Magic Ring.
**ROUND 1:** Ch 1, 12 sc into ring, join with slip st into first sc made. End Color A. (12 sts.)
**ROUND 2:** With Color B, join by slip st around back post of sc, ch 2 (counts as 1 bp-hdc), 1bp-hdc around next 11 sc, join with slip st into top of beginning ch. End Color B. (12 sts.)
**ROUND 3:** With Color C, join with * slip st around bp-hdc of previous round, ch 3, skip 2 hdc; rep from * 3 more times, join with slip st in first slip st made. (4 slip sts, 4 ch sps.)
**ROUND 4:** Slip st into ch-3 sp, * (ch 2, 3 dc, ch 1, 3 dc, ch 2, slip st) into same ch-3 sp **, slip st into next ch-3 sp; rep from * twice more, then from * to ** once more. End Color C. (4 petals.)
**ROUND 5:** Join Color D in ch-1 sp, ch 1 and sc in same sp, * ch 4, skip petal stitches, dc in slip st between 2 petals, ch 4 **, sc in ch-1 sp; rep from * twice more, then from * to ** once more, join with slip st into first sc made. (8 sts, 8 ch sps.)

- A: 5 yds/4.6 m
- B: 6 yds/5.5 m
- C: 6 yds/5.5 m
- D: 9 yds/8.2 m
- E: 9 yds/8.2 m

**ROUND 6:** Ch 3 (counts as 1 dc), tr, dc in same sp, * 4 dc in ch-4 sp, dc in dc, 4 dc in ch-4 sp **, (dc, tr, dc) in sc; rep from * twice more, then from * to ** once more, join with slip st into top of beginning ch. End Color D. (48 sts.)
**ROUND 7:** With Color A, join through the horizontal bar at the back of st, ch 1 and sc in same st, * (sc, hdc, sc) through horizontal bar of tr **, sc through horizontal bar in each st to next tr; rep from * twice more, then from * to ** once more, sc through horizontal bar in each st to end of round, join with slip st into first sc made. End Color A. (56 sts.)
**ROUND 8:** With Color B, join through the horizontal bar at the back of st, ch 1 and sc in same st, sc through horizontal bar in next st, * (sc, hdc, sc) through horizontal bar of hdc **, sc through horizontal bar in each st to next hdc; rep from * twice more, then from * to ** once more, sc through horizontal bar in each st to end of round, join with slip st into first sc made. End Color B. (64 sts.)
**ROUND 9:** With Color E, join through the horizontal bar at the back of st, ch 3 (counts as 1 dc), dc through horizontal bar of each st around working (dc, tr, dc) in corner hdc st, join with slip st into top of beginning ch. End Color E. (72 sts.)

# Wildfire

• **SKILL LEVEL:** *Beginner*

## Method

**FOUNDATION RING:** Using Color A, ch 4 and join with slip st to form a ring.

**ROUND 1:** Ch 3 (counts as 1 dc), 2 dc into ring, ch 2, [3 dc into ring, ch 2] twice, 3 dc into ring, join with hdc to top of beginning ch (counts as ch 2). End Color A. (12 sts, 4 ch sps.)

**ROUND 2:** Join Color B, ch 3 (counts as 1 dc), 1 dc into same ch sp, * 1 dc in each stitch across to corner ch sp, (2 dc **, ch 2, 2 dc) into ch sp; rep from * twice more, then from * to ** once more, join with hdc into top of beginning ch (counts as ch 2). End Color B. (28 sts, 4 ch sps.)

**ROUND 3:** Using Color C, rep Round 2. End Color C. (44 sts, 4 ch sps.)

**ROUND 4:** Using Color D, rep Round 2. End Color D. (60 sts, 4 ch sps.)

**ROUND 5:** Using Color E, rep Round 2 to **, ch 2, join with slip st into top of beginning ch. End Color E. (76 sts, 4 ch sps.)

A: 3 yds/2.7 m
B: 4 yds/3.7 m
C: 6 yds/5.5 m
D: 8 yds/7.3 m
E: 10 yds/9.1 m

Wildfire

**COLOR VARIATION**

## Wildfire 2

Follow the written instructions or the chart, using colors as follows:

A: 3 yds/2.7 m
B: 4 yds/3.7 m
C: 6 yds/5.5 m
D: 8 yds/7.3 m
E: 10 yds/9.1 m

Wildfire 2

Embers

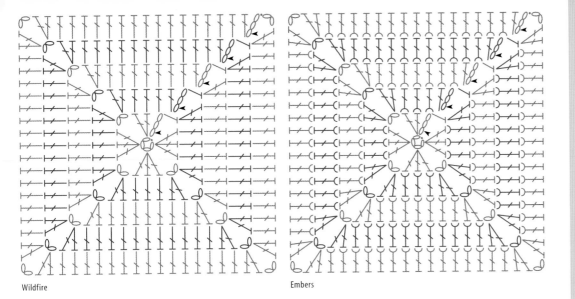

Wildfire            Embers

## Yarn requirement for throws

**NOTE:** All yarn requirements are estimated using an H-size (5 mm) crochet hook and worsted/10-ply yarn. Measurements and yarn requirements do not include joining and edging.

| Wildfire | | | |
|---|---|---|---|
| | **BABY** | **LAP** | **BED** |
| **A** | 108 yds/99 m | 189 yds/173 m | 462 yds/422 m |
| **B** | 144 yds/132 m | 252 yds/230 m | 616 yds/563 m |
| **C** | 216 yds/198 m | 378 yds/346 m | 924 yds/845 m |
| **D** | 288 yds/263 m | 504 yds/461 m | 1232 yds/1127 m |
| **E** | 360 yds/329 m | 630 yds/576 m | 1540 yds/1408 m |

| Wildfire 2 | | | |
|---|---|---|---|
| | **BABY** | **LAP** | **BED** |
| **A** | 108 yds/99 m | 189 yds/173 m | 462 yds/422 m |
| **B** | 144 yds/132 m | 252 yds/230 m | 616 yds/563 m |
| **C** | 216 yds/198 m | 378 yds/346 m | 924 yds/846 m |
| **D** | 288 yds/263 m | 504 yds/461 m | 1232 yds/1127 m |
| **E** | 360 yds/329 m | 630 yds/576 m | 1540 yds/1408 m |

| Embers | | | |
|---|---|---|---|
| | **BABY** | **LAP** | **BED** |
| **A** | 108 yds/99 m | 189 yds/173 m | 462 yds/422 m |
| **B** | 144 yds/132 m | 252 yds/230 m | 616 yds/563 m |
| **C** | 216 yds/198 m | 378 yds/346 m | 924 yds/846 m |
| **D** | 288 yds/263 m | 504 yds/461 m | 1232 yds/1127 m |
| **E** | 360 yds/329 m | 630 yds/576 m | 1540 yds/1408 m |

## STITCH VARIATION

## Embers

• **SKILL LEVEL:** *Beginner*

- A: 3 yds/2.7 m
- B: 4 yds/3.7 m
- C: 6 yds/5.5 m
- D: 8 yds/7.3 m
- E: 10 yds/9.1 m

## Method

**FOUNDATION RING:** Using Color A, ch 4 and join with slip st to form a ring.

**ROUND 1:** Ch 3 (counts as 1 dc), 2 dc into ring, ch 2, [3 dc into ring, ch 2] twice, 3 dc into ring, join with hdc into top of beginning ch (counts as ch 2). End Color A. (4 groups of 3 dc, 4 ch sps.)

**ROUND 2:** Join Color B, ch 3 (counts as 1 dc), 1 dc into same ch sp, * 1 dc tbl in each st across to corner ch sp, (2 dc ** , ch 2, 2 dc) into ch sp; rep from * twice more, then from * to ** once more, join with hdc into top of beginning ch (counts as ch 2). End Color B. (28 sts, 4 ch sps.)

**ROUND 3:** Using Color C, rep Round 2. End Color C. (44 sts, 4 ch sps.)

**ROUND 4:** Using Color D, rep Round 2. End Color D. (60 sts, 4 ch sps.)

**ROUND 5:** Using Color E, rep Round 2 to ** , ch 2, join with slip st into top of beginning ch. End Color E. (76 sts, 4 ch sps.)

# Rainbow Ripple

A:  6 yds/5.5 m
B:  6 yds/5.5 m
C:  6 yds/5.5 m
D:  6 yds/5.5 m
E:  6 yds/5.5 m

• **SKILL LEVEL:** *Beginner*

## Method

**FOUNDATION ROW:** Using Color A, work the required number of ch. (Multiple of 13 + 11 + 3 turning ch.)

**ROW 1:** Work dc in 4th ch from hook, dc in next 3 ch, * (dc, ch 2, dc) in next ch, dc in next 5 ch, skip 2 ch, dc in next 5 ch; rep from * to last 6 ch, (dc, ch 2, dc) in next ch, dc in last 5 ch, turn. End Color A.

**ROW 2:** Join Color B, sl st into next st, ch 3 (counts as 1 dc), dc into next 4 sts, * (dc, ch 2, dc) in ch-2 sp, dc in next 5 sts, skip 2 sts, dc into next 5 sts; rep from * to last ch-2 sp, (dc, ch 2, dc) in ch-2 sp, dc in next 5 sts, turn. End Color B.

**ROW 3:** Repeat Row 2 with Color C.
**ROW 4:** Repeat Row 2 with Color D.
**ROWS 5–6:** Repeat Row 2 with Color E.
**ROW 7:** Repeat Row 2 with Color D.
**ROW 8:** Repeat Row 2 with Color C.
**ROW 9:** Repeat Row 2 with Color B.
**ROWS 10–11:** Repeat Row 2 with Color A.
Rows 2–11 form the pattern.

Rainbow Ripple

## COLOR VARIATION

### Rainbow Ripple 2

Follow the written instructions or the chart, using colors as follows:

A:  6 yds/5.5 m
B:  6 yds/5.5 m
C:  6 yds/5.5 m
D:  6 yds/5.5 m
E:  6 yds/5.5 m

**ROWS 1–2:** Color E
**ROWS 3–4:** Color D
**ROWS 5–6:** Color C
**ROWS 7–8:** Color B
**ROWS 9–10:** Color A

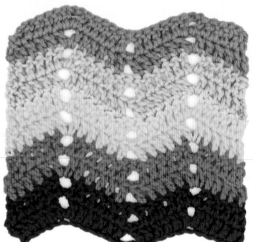

Rainbow Ripple 2

Rainbow Stripes

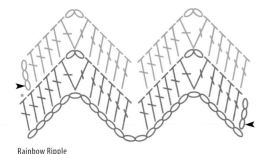

Rainbow Ripple

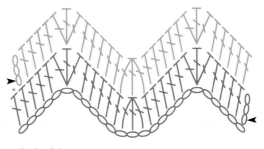

Rainbow Stripes

## STITCH VARIATION

## Rainbow Stripes

• **SKILL LEVEL:** *Beginner*

## Method

**SPECIAL STITCH:**

• Decrease dc—Dec dc: (Yo, insert hook into next st, yo and draw through a loop, yo and draw through 2 loops on hook) 3 times (4 loops on hook), yo and pull through all loops on hook.

**FOUNDATION ROW:** Using Color A, work the required number of ch. (Multiple of 14 + 10 + 4 turning ch.)

**ROW 1:** Work dc in 5th ch from hook, dc in next 3 ch, * 3 dc in next ch, dc in next 5 ch, Dec dc in next 3 sts, dc in next 5 ch; rep from * to last 6 ch, 3 dc in next st, dc in next 5 ch, turn. End Color A.

● A: 6 yds/5.5 m
◐ B: 6 yds/5.5 m
● C: 6 yds/5.5 m
◐ D: 6 yds/5.5 m
● E: 6 yds/5.5 m

**ROW 2:** Join Color B, slip st into next st, ch 3 (counts as 1 dc), dc in next 4 sts, * 3 dc in next st, dc in next 5 sts, Dec dc over next 3 sts, dc in next 5 sts; rep from * to last 6 sts, 3 dc in next st, dc in next 5 sts, turn. End Color B.

**ROW 3:** Repeat Row 2 with Color C.

**ROW 4:** Repeat Row 2 with Color D.

**ROWS 5–6:** Repeat Row 2 with Color E.

**ROW 7:** Repeat Row 2 with Color D.

**ROW 8:** Repeat Row 2 with Color C.

**ROW 9:** Repeat Row 2 with Color B.

**ROWS 10–11:** Repeat Row 2 with Color A. Continue repeating Row 2 throughout, changing colors as established in Rows 2–11.

## Yarn requirement for throws

**NOTE:** *All yarn requirements are estimated using an H-size (5 mm) crochet hook and worsted/10-ply yarn. Measurements and yarn requirements do not include joining and edging.*

### Rainbow Ripple

| | BABY | LAP | BED |
|---|---|---|---|
| **A** | 216 yds/198 m | 378 yds/346 m | 924 yds/845 m |
| **B** | 216 yds/198 m | 378 yds/346 m | 924 yds/845 m |
| **C** | 216 yds/198 m | 378 yds/346 m | 924 yds/845 m |
| **D** | 216 yds/198 m | 378 yds/346 m | 924 yds/845 m |
| **E** | 216 yds/198 m | 378 yds/346 m | 924 yds/845 m |

**Baby:** Ch 118, work 6 repeats of Rows 2–11.
**Lap:** Ch 196, work 9 repeats of Rows 2–11.
**Bed:** Ch 495, work 14 repeats of Rows 2–11.

### Rainbow Ripple 2

| | BABY | LAP | BED |
|---|---|---|---|
| **A** | 216 yds/198 m | 378 yds/346 m | 924 yds/845 m |
| **B** | 216 yds/198 m | 378 yds/346 m | 924 yds/845 m |
| **C** | 216 yds/198 m | 378 yds/346 m | 924 yds/845 m |
| **D** | 216 yds/198 m | 378 yds/346 m | 924 yds/845 m |
| **E** | 216 yds/198 m | 378 yds/346 m | 924 yds/845 m |

### Rainbow Stripes

| | BABY | LAP | BED |
|---|---|---|---|
| **A** | 216 yds/198 m | 378 yds/346 m | 924 yds/845 m |
| **B** | 216 yds/198 m | 378 yds/346 m | 924 yds/845 m |
| **C** | 216 yds/198 m | 378 yds/346 m | 924 yds/845 m |
| **D** | 216 yds/198 m | 378 yds/346 m | 924 yds/845 m |
| **E** | 216 yds/198 m | 378 yds/346 m | 924 yds/845 m |

**Baby:** Ch 126, work six repeats.
**Lap:** Ch 210, work nine repeats.
**Bedspread:** Ch 532, work 14 repeats.

# Frilly Circle

- A: 2 yds/1.8 m
- B: 4 yds/3.7 m
- C: 5 yds/4.6 m
- D: 10 yds/9.1 m
- E: 16 yds/14.6 m

• **SKILL LEVEL:** *Intermediate*

## Method

**FOUNDATION RING:** Using Color A, make a Magic Ring.

**ROUND 1:** Ch 3 (counts as 1 dc), 11 dc into ring, join with slip st into top of beginning ch. End Color A. (12 sts.)

**ROUND 2:** Join Color B, ch 3 (counts as 1 dc), dc in same place, 2 dc in each dc around, join with slip st into top of beginning ch. End Color B. (24 sts.)

**ROUND 3:** Join Color C, ch 3 (counts as 1 dc), dc in same space, * dc in next dc, 2 dc in next dc; rep from * 11 more times, join with slip st into top of beginning ch. End Color C. (36 sts.)

**ROUND 4:** Join Color D, ch 1 and sc in same space, * ch 3, skip 2 sts, sc in next st; rep from * 10 more times, ch 3, join with slip st into first sc made. (12 sc, 12 ch sps.)

**ROUND 5:** * In next ch-3 sp work (sc, hdc, dc, ch 3, dc, hdc, sc), in next 2 ch-3 sps work (sc, hdc, 2 dc, hdc, sc); rep from * 3 more times, join with slip st into first sc made. End Color D. (72 sts, 4 ch sps.)

**ROUND 6:** Join Color E in corner ch-3 sp, ch 1 and sc in same space, * ch 2, [bpdc around sc of Round 4, ch 3] twice, bpdc around next sc of Round 4, ch 2 **, in ch-3 sp of Round 5 work (sc, hdc, dc, hdc, sc); rep from * twice more, then from * to ** once more, (sc, hdc, dc, hdc) in ch-3 sp of Round 5, join with slip st into first sc made. (32 sts, 16 ch sps.)

**ROUND 7:** Ch 3 (counts as 1 dc), * 2 dc in ch-2 sp, dc in dc, [3 dc in ch-3 sp, dc in dc] twice, 2 dc in ch-2 sp, dc in next 2 sts, (dc, tr, dc) in next st **, dc in next 2 sts; rep from * twice more, then from * to ** once more, dc in next st, join with slip st into top of beginning ch. End Color E. (80 sts.)

Frilly Circle

Frilly Circle 2

## Frilly Circle 2

Follow the written instructions or the chart, using colors as follows:

- A: 12 yds/11 m
- B: 4 yds/3.7 m
- C: 5 yds/4.6 m
- D: 16 yds/14.6 m

**ROUND 1:** Color A
**ROUND 2:** Color B
**ROUND 3:** Color C
**ROUND 4:** Color A
**ROUND 5:** Color A
**ROUND 6:** Color D
**ROUND 7:** Color D

Frilly Granny Circle

Frilly Circle

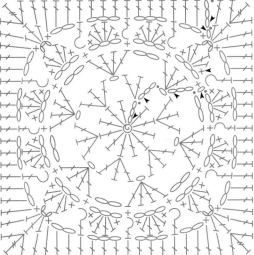

Frilly Granny Circle

## Yarn requirement for throws

**NOTE:** *All yarn requirements are estimated using an H-size (5 mm) crochet hook and worsted/10-ply yarn. Measurements and yarn requirements do not include joining and edging.*

### Frilly Circle

|   | BABY | LAP | BED |
|---|------|-----|-----|
| A | 72 yds/66 m | 126 yds/115 m | 308 yds/282 m |
| B | 144 yds/132 m | 252 yds/230 m | 616 yds/563 m |
| C | 180 yds/165 m | 315 yds/288 m | 770 yds/704 m |
| D | 360 yds/329 m | 630 yds/576 m | 1540 yds/1408 m |
| E | 576 yds/527 m | 1008 yds/922 m | 2464 yds/2253 m |

### Frilly Circle 2

|   | BABY | LAP | BED |
|---|------|-----|-----|
| A | 432 yds/395 m | 756 yds/691 m | 1848 yds/1690 m |
| B | 144 yds/132 m | 252 yds/230 m | 616 yds/563 m |
| C | 180 yds/165 m | 315 yds/288 m | 770 yds/704 m |
| D | 576 yds/527 m | 1008 yds/922 m | 2464 yds/2253 m |

### Frilly Granny Circle

|   | BABY | LAP | BED |
|---|------|-----|-----|
| A | 72 yds/66 m | 126 yds/115 m | 308 yds/282 m |
| B | 108 yds/99 m | 315 yds/288 m | 770 yds/704 m |
| C | 144 yds/132 m | 252 yds/230 m | 616 yds/563 m |
| D | 360 yds/329 m | 630 yds/576 m | 1540 yds/1408 m |
| E | 576 yds/527 m | 1008 yds/922 m | 2464 yds/2253 m |

## STITCH VARIATION

## Frilly Granny Circle

• **SKILL LEVEL:** *Intermediate*

## Method

**FOUNDATION RING:** Using Color A, make a Magic Ring.

**ROUND 1:** Ch 3 (counts as 1 dc), 11 dc into ring, join with slip st into top of beginning ch. End Color A. (12 sts.)

**ROUND 2:** Join Color B, ch 3 (counts as 1 dc), 2 dc in same space, * ch 1, skip 1 st, 3 dc in next st; rep from * 4 more times, ch 1, join with slip st into top of beginning ch. End Color B. (18 sts, 6 ch sps.)

**ROUND 3:** Join Color C in ch-1 sp, ch 3 (counts as 1 dc), 3 dc in same space, * ch 2, 4 dc in next ch-1 sp; rep from * 4 more times, ch 2, join with slip st into top of beginning ch. End Color C. (24 sts, 6 ch sps.)

**ROUND 4:** Join Color D, ch 1 and sc in same space, * ch 3, skip 2 sts, sc in next st, ch 3 **, skip ch-2 sp, sc in next st; rep from * 4 more times, then from * to ** once more, join with slip st into first sc made. (12 sts, 12 ch sps.)

**ROUND 5:** * In next ch-3 sp work (sc, hdc, dc, ch 3, dc, hdc, sc), in next 2 ch-3 sps work (sc, hdc, 2 dc, hdc, sc); rep from * 3 more times, join with slip st into first sc made. End Color D. (72 sts, 4 ch sps.)

**ROUND 6:** Join Color E in corner ch-3 sp, ch 1 and sc in same space, * ch 2, [bpdc around sc of Round 4, ch 3] twice, bpdc around sc of Round 4, ch 2 **, in corner ch-3 sp of Round 5 work (sc, hdc, dc, hdc, sc); rep from * twice more, then from * to ** once more, (sc, hdc, dc, hdc) in corner ch-3 sp of Round 5, join with slip st into first sc made. (32 sts, 16 ch sps.)

**ROUND 7:** Ch 3 (counts as 1 dc), * 2 dc in ch-2 sp, dc in bpdc, [3 dc in ch-3 sp, dc in bpdc] twice, 2 dc in ch-2 sp, dc in next 2 sts, (dc, tr, dc) in next st **, dc in next 2 sts; rep from * twice more, then from * to ** once more, dc in next st, join with slip st into top of beginning ch. End Color E. (80 sts.)

• A: 2 yds/1.8 m
• B: 3 yds/2.7 m
• C: 4 yds/3.7 m
• D: 10 yds/9.1 m
• E: 16 yds/14.6 m

# Big Bloom

● A: 15 yds/13.7 m
B: 14 yds/12.8 m
● C: 26 yds/23.8 m

• **SKILL LEVEL:** *Advanced*

## Method

**FOUNDATION ROW:** Using Color A, make a Magic Ring.

**ROUND 1:** Ch 2 (counts as 1 hdc), 11 hdc into ring, join with slip st through Front Loop only of top of beginning ch. (12 sts.)

**ROUND 2:** * Ch 7, slip st through Front Loop of next hdc; rep from * 10 more times, ch 7, join with slip st into Back Loop only of top of Round 1 beginning ch. (12 ch sps.)

**ROUND 3:** Ch 2 (counts as 1 hdc), hdc tbl in same place, 2 hdc tbl in each st around, join with slip st into Front Loop of top of beginning ch. (24 sts.)

**ROUND 4:** * Ch 7, slip st through Front Loop of next hdc; rep from * 22 more times, ch 7, join with slip st into Back Loop only of top of Round 3 beginning ch. End Color A. (24 ch sps.)

**ROUND 5:** Join Color B, ch 2 (counts as 1 hdc), * 2 hdc tbl in next st, 1 hdc tbl in next st; rep from * 11 more times, 2 hdc tbl in next st, join with slip st into Front Loop only of top of beginning ch. (36 sts.)

**ROUND 6:** * Ch 7, slip st through Front Loop of next hdc; rep from * 34 more times, ch 7, join with slip st into Back Loop only of top of Round 5 beginning ch. End Color B. (36 ch sps.)

**ROUND 7:** Join Color C through Back Loop only, ch 1 and sc tbl in same space, * sc tbl in next st, hdc tbl in next st, dc tbl in next 2 sts, (dc, tr, dc) tbl in next st, dc tbl in next 2 sts, hdc tbl in next st **, sc tbl in next st; rep from * twice more, then from * to ** once more, join with slip st in first sc made. (44 sts.)

**ROUND 8:** Ch 3 (counts as 1 dc), * dc in each st across to corner tr, work (dc, tr, dc) in tr; rep from * 3 more times, dc in each st to end of round, join with slip st in top of beginning ch. (52 sts.)

**ROUND 9:** Ch 3 (counts as 1 dc), * dc in each st across to corner tr, work (dc, tr, dc) in tr; rep from * 3 more times, dc in each st to end of round, join with slip st in top of beginning ch. (60 sts.)

**ROUND 10:** Ch 1, sc in same space, sc in each st across to corner tr, work (sc, hdc, sc) in tr; rep from * 3 more times, sc in each st to end of round, join with slip st into first sc made. End Color C. (68 sts.)

## Yarn requirement for throws

**NOTE:** *All yarn requirements are estimated using an H-size (5 mm) crochet hook and worsted/10-ply yarn. Measurements and yarn requirements do not include joining and edging.*

| Big Bloom | | | |
|---|---|---|---|
| | BABY | LAP | BED |
| A | 540 yds/494 m | 945 yds/864 m | 2310 yds/2112 m |
| B | 504 yds/461 m | 882 yds/807 m | 2156 yds/1971 m |
| C | 936 yds/856 m | 1638 yds/1498 m | 4004 yds/3661 m |

## Project Notes

**YOU WILL NEED:**
- 18 in. (46 cm) pillow form (or 20 in./51 cm for a plumper pillow)
- 18 in. (46 cm) zipper

- A: 90 yds/82 m
- B: 252 yds/230 m
- C: 336 yds/307 m
- D: 52 yds/48 m
- E: 52 yds/48 m
- F: 52 yds/48 m
- G: 52 yds/48 m
- H: 52 yds/48 m
- I: 60 yds/55 m

Make 6 squares in the following colors:
**ROUNDS 1–4:** Color A
**ROUNDS 5–6:** Color B
**ROUNDS 7–11:** Color C

Make 2 squares in the following colors:
**ROUNDS 1–4:** Color C
**ROUNDS 5–6:** Color B
**ROUNDS 7–11:** Colors D, E, F, G, H, I

Lay out the squares following the photograph for reference: nine squares for the front panel and nine squares for the back panel. Join the squares using Color I and mattress stitch. Attach an 18 in. (46 cm) zip along one edge of the front and back panels. Sew three sides together using Color I and woven seam method. Stuff with an 18 or 20 in. (46 or 51 cm) pillow inner.

# Spiky Square

• **SKILL LEVEL:** *Beginner*

● A:  11 yds/10 m
○ B:  5 yds/4.6 m
◐ C:  7 yds/6.4 m
◑ D:  12 yds/11 m

## Method

**FOUNDATION RING:** Using Color A, ch 4 and join with slip st to form a ring.

**ROUND 1:** Ch 3 (counts as 1 dc), 2 dc into ring, ch 2, [3 dc into ring, ch 2] twice, 3 dc into ring, join with hdc to top of beginning ch (counts as ch 2). End Color A. (12 sts, 4 ch sps.)

**ROUND 2:** Join Color B, ch 3 (counts as 1 dc), 1 dc into same ch sp, * 1 dc in each stitch across to corner ch-2 sp, (2 dc **, ch 2, 2 dc) into ch-2 sp; rep from * twice more, then from * to ** once more, join with hdc into top of beginning ch (counts as ch 2). End Color B. (28 sts, 4 ch sps.)

**ROUND 3:** Join Color C, ch 3 (counts as 1 dc), 1 dc into same ch sp, * 1 dc in next st, ch 2, skip 1 st, 1 dc in next st, 1 bptr around middle dc of 3 dc in Round 1, skip 1 st, dc in next st, ch 1, skip 1 st, dc in next st **, (2 dc, ch 2, 2 dc) in ch-2 sp; rep from * twice more, then from * to ** once more, 2 dc in ch-2 sp, join with hdc (counts as ch 2) into top of beginning ch. End Color C. (36 sts, 12 ch sps.)

**ROUND 4:** Join Color A, ch 3 (counts as 1 dc), dc into same ch sp, * dc in next st, ch 1, skip 1 st, dc in next st, 1 bptr around 2nd dc of Round 2, skip ch sp, dc in next dc, ch 1, skip 1 st, dc in next dc, 1 bptr around 6th dc of Round 2, skip ch sp, dc in next dc, ch 1, skip 1 st, dc in next dc **, (2 dc, ch 2, 2 dc) in ch-2 sp; rep from * twice more, then from * to ** once more, 2 dc in ch-2 sp, join with hdc (counts as ch 2) into top of beginning ch. End Color A. (48 sts, 16 sps.)

**ROUND 5:** Join Color D, ch 3 (counts as 1 dc), dc into same ch sp, * dc in next 3 sts, 1 bptr around 2nd dc of Round 3, skip ch sp, dc in next 3 sts, 1 bptr around bptr of Round 3, skip ch sp, dc in next 3 sts, 1 bptr around 8th dc of Round 3, skip ch sp, dc in next 3 sts **, (2 dc, ch 2, 2 dc) in ch-2 sp; rep from * twice more, then from * to ** once more, 2 dc in ch-2 sp, ch 2, join with slip st into top of beginning ch. End Color D. (76 sts, 4 ch sps.)

Spiky Square

Spiky Square 2

---

**COLOR VARIATION**

## Spiky Square 2

● A:  11 yds/10 m
○ B:  17 yds/15.5 m
◐ C:  7 yds/6.4 m

Follow the written instructions or the chart, using colors as follows:

**FOUNDATION RING AND ROUND 1:** Color A
**ROUND 2:** Color B
**ROUND 3:** Color C
**ROUND 4:** Color A
**ROUND 5:** Color B

Side Spikes

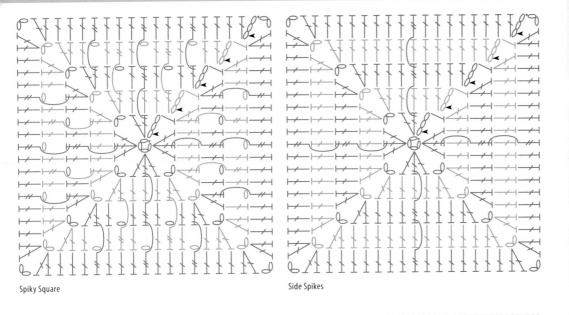

Spiky Square

Side Spikes

## STITCH VARIATION

## Side Spikes

- **SKILL LEVEL:** *Beginner*

## Method

**FOUNDATION RING:** Using Color A, ch 4 and join with slip st to form a ring.

**ROUND 1:** Ch 3 (counts as 1 dc), 2 dc into ring, ch 2, [3 dc into ring, ch 2] twice, 3 dc into ring, join with hdc to top of beginning ch (counts as ch 2). End Color A. (12 sts, 4 ch sps.)

**ROUND 2:** Join Color B, ch 3 (counts as 1 dc), 1 dc into same ch sp, * 1 dc in each stitch across to corner ch-2 sp, 2 dc **, ch 2, 2 dc into ch-2 sp; rep from * twice more, then from * to ** once more, join with hdc into top of beginning ch (counts as ch 2). End Color B. (28 sts, 4 ch sps.)

**ROUND 3:** Join Color C, ch 3 (counts as 1 dc), 1 dc into same ch sp, * 1 dc in next 3 sts, 1 bptr around middle dc of 3-dc in Round 1, dc in next 3 sts **, (2 dc, ch 2, 2 dc) in ch-2 sp; rep from * twice more, then from * to ** once more, 2 dc in ch-2 sp, join with hdc (counts as ch 2) into top of beginning ch. End Color C. (44 sts, 4 ch sps.)

**ROUND 4:** Join Color D, ch 3 (counts as 1 dc), dc into same ch sp, * dc in next 11 sts **, (2 dc, ch 2, 2 dc) in ch-2 sp; rep from * twice more, then from * to ** once more, 2 dc in ch-2 sp, join with hdc (counts as ch 2) into top of beginning ch. End Color D. (60 sts, 4 ch sps.)

**ROUND 5:** Join Color B, ch 3 (counts as 1 dc), dc into same ch sp, * dc in next 7 sts, 1 bptr around bptr of Round 3, dc in next 7 sts **, [2 dc, ch 2, 2 dc] in ch-2 sp; rep from * twice more, then from * to ** once more, 2 dc in ch-2 sp, ch 2, join with slip st into top of beginning ch. End Color B. (76 sts, 4 ch sps.)

- A: 3 yds/2.7 m
- B: 17 yds/15.5 m
- C: 7 yds/6.4 m
- D: 8 yds/7.3 m

## Yarn requirement for throws

**NOTE:** *All yarn requirements are estimated using an H-size (5 mm) crochet hook and worsted/10-ply yarn. Measurements and yarn requirements do not include joining and edging.*

### Spiky Square

|   | BABY | LAP | BED |
|---|------|-----|-----|
| A | 396 yds/362 m | 693 yds/634 m | 1694 yds/1549 m |
| B | 180 yds/165 m | 315 yds/288 m | 770 yds/704 m |
| C | 252 yds/230 m | 441 yds/403 m | 1078 yds/986 m |
| D | 432 yds/395 m | 756 yds/691 m | 1848 yds/1690 m |

### Spiky Square 2

|   | BABY | LAP | BED |
|---|------|-----|-----|
| A | 396 yds/362 m | 693 yds/634 m | 1694 yds/1549 m |
| B | 612 yds/560 m | 1071 yds/979 m | 2618 yds/2394 m |
| C | 252 yds/230 m | 441 yds/403 m | 1078 yds/986 m |

### Side Spikes

|   | BABY | LAP | BED |
|---|------|-----|-----|
| A | 108 yds/99 m | 189 yds/173 m | 462 yds/422 m |
| B | 612 yds/560 m | 1071 yds/979 m | 2618 yds/2394 m |
| C | 252 yds/230 m | 441 yds/403 m | 1078 yds/986 m |
| D | 288 yds/263 m | 504 yds/461 m | 1232 yds/1127 m |

# Bright Flower

• **SKILL LEVEL:** *Beginner*

- ● A: 4 yds/3.7 m
- ● B: 2 yds/1.8 m
- ● C: 3 yds/2.7 m
- ● D: 9 yds/8.2 m
- ● E: 22 yds/20 m

## Method

**FOUNDATION RING:** Using Color A, make a Magic Ring.

**ROUND 1:** Ch 1, 8 sc into ring, join with slip st into first sc made. End Color A. (8 sts.)

**ROUND 2:** Join Color B, ch 1 and 2 sc in same place, * 2 sc into next st; rep from * 6 more times, join with slip st into first sc made. End Color B. (16 sts.)

**ROUND 3:** Join Color C, ch 1 and 2 sc in same place, * sc in next st, 2 sc in next st; rep from * 6 more times, sc in next st, join with slip st into first sc made. End Color C. (24 sts.)

**ROUND 4:** Join Color A, ch 1 and sc in same place, * sc in next st, 2 sc in next st, sc in next st; rep from * 6 more times, sc in next st, 2 sc in next st, join with slip st into first sc made. End Color A. (32 sts.)

**ROUND 5:** Join Color D, * ch 4 (counts as 1 tr), [2 tr in next st] twice, ch 4 (counts as 1 tr), slip st in next st **, slip st in next st; rep from * 6 more times, then from * to ** once more, slip st in base of beginning ch. End Color D. (48 sts.)

**ROUND 6:** Join Color E into Back Loop of slip st between two petals of Round 5, ch 6 (counts as 1 dc, ch 3), dc tbl in same place, * ch 3, sc tbl in next slip st between two petals, ch 3 **, (dc, ch 3, dc) in Back Loop of slip st between next two petals; rep from * twice more, then from * to ** once more, join with slip st into 3rd ch of beginning ch. (12 sts, 12 ch sps.)

**ROUND 7:** Ch 3 (counts as 1 dc), * (3 dc, tr, 3 dc) in corner ch-3 sp, dc in dc, 4 dc in ch-3 sp, dc in dc, 4 dc in ch-3 sp **, dc in dc; rep from * twice more, then from * to ** once more, join with slip st into top of beginning ch. (72 sts.)

**ROUND 8:** Ch 3 (counts as 1 dc), work dc in each dc and (dc, tr, dc) in each corner tr around, join with slip st into top of beginning ch. End Color E. (80 sts.)

Bright Flower

Bright Flower 2

## COLOR VARIATION

### Bright Flower 2

Follow the written instructions or the chart, using colors as follows:

- ● A: 4 yds/3.7 m
- ● B: 2 yds/1.8 m
- ● C: 3 yds/2.7 m
- ● D: 9 yds/8.2 m
- ● E: 22 yds/20 m

Cartwheel Flower

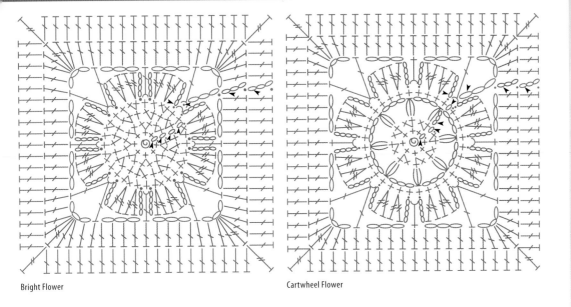

Bright Flower          Cartwheel Flower

## STITCH VARIATION

# Cartwheel Flower

- **SKILL LEVEL:** *Intermediate*

## Method
**SPECIAL STITCHES:**
- Beginning Puff Stitch—Beg PS: Made of 2ch, 2 hdc.
- Puff Stitch–PS: Made of 3 hdc.

**FOUNDATION RING:** Using Color A, make a Magic Ring.

**ROUND 1:** Ch 1, 8 sc into ring, join with slip st into first sc made. End Color A. (8 sts.)

**ROUND 2:** Join Color B, ch 1 and 2 sc in same space, * 2 sc into next st; rep from * 6 more times, join with slip st into first sc made. End Color B. (16 sts.)

**ROUND 3:** Join Color C, work Beg PS in same place, *ch 3, skip 1 st, work PS in next st; rep from * 6 more times, join with slip st into top of first PS made. End Color C. (8 PS, 8 ch sps.)

**ROUND 4:** Join Color A, ch 1 and sc in same space, * 3 sc in next ch-3 sp, sc in next PS; rep from * 6 more times, 3 sc in next ch-3 sp, join with slip st into first sc made. End Color A. (32 sts.)

● A:  1 yd/0.9 m
● B:  5 yds/4.6 m
○ C:  4 yds/3.7 m
● D:  9 yds/8.2 m
◍ E:  22 yds/20 m

**ROUND 5:** Join Color D, * ch 4, [2 tr in next st] twice, ch 4, slip st in next st **, slip st in next st; rep from * 6 more times, then from * to ** once more, slip st in base of beginning ch. End Color D. (8 petals.)

**ROUND 6:** Join Color E into Back Loop of slip st between two petals of Round 5, ch 6 (counts as 1 dc, ch 3), dc in same space, * ch 3, sc in next slip st between two petals, ch 3 **, (dc, ch 3, dc) in Back Loop of slip st between next two petals; rep from * twice more, then from * to ** once more, join with slip st into 3rd ch of beginning ch. (12 sts, 12 ch sps.)

**ROUND 7:** Ch 3 (counts as 1 dc), * (3 dc, tr, 3 dc) in corner ch-3 sp, dc in dc, 4 dc in ch-3 sp, dc in sc, 4 dc in ch-3 sp **, dc in dc; rep from * twice more, then from * to ** once more, join with slip st into top of beginning ch. (72 sts.)

**ROUND 8:** Ch 3 (counts as 1 dc), work dc in each dc and (dc, tr, dc) in each corner tr around, join with slip st into top of beginning ch. End Color E. (80 sts.)

## Yarn requirement for throws

**NOTE:** *All yarn requirements are estimated using an H-size (5 mm) crochet hook and worsted/10-ply yarn. Measurements and yarn requirements do not include joining and edging.*

### Bright Flower

|   | BABY | LAP | BED |
|---|------|-----|-----|
| A | 144 yds/132 m | 252 yds/230 m | 616 yds/563 m |
| B | 72 yds/66 m | 126 yds/115 m | 308 yds/282 m |
| C | 108 yds/99 m | 189 yds/173 m | 462 yds/422 m |
| D | 324 yds/296 m | 567 yds/518 m | 1386 yds/1267 m |
| E | 792 yds/724 m | 1386 yds/1267 m | 3388 yds/3098 m |

### Bright Flower 2

|   | BABY | LAP | BED |
|---|------|-----|-----|
| A | 144 yds/132 m | 252 yds/230 m | 616 yds/563 m |
| B | 72 yds/66 m | 126 yds/115 m | 308 yds/282 m |
| C | 108 yds/99 m | 189 yds/173 m | 462 yds/422 m |
| D | 324 yds/296 m | 567 yds/518 m | 1386 yds/1267 m |
| E | 792 yds/724 m | 1386 yds/1267 m | 3388 yds/3098 m |

### Cartwheel Flower

|   | BABY | LAP | BED |
|---|------|-----|-----|
| A | 36 yds/33 m | 63 yds/58 m | 154 yds/141 m |
| B | 180 yds/165 m | 315 yds/288 m | 770 yds/704 m |
| C | 144 yds/132 m | 252 yds/230 m | 616 yds/563 m |
| D | 324 yds/296 m | 567 yds/518 m | 1386 yds/1267 m |
| E | 792 yds/724 m | 1386 yds/1267 m | 3388 yds/3098 m |

# Simple Ripple

● A: 8 yds/7.3 m
◐ B: 16 yds/14.6 m
● C: 8 yds/7.3 m

• **SKILL LEVEL:** *Beginner*

## Method

**FOUNDATION ROW:** Using Color A, ch a multiple of 9 + 7 + 1 turning ch.

**ROW 1:** Sc in 2nd ch from hook, sc in next 2 ch, * 3 sc in next ch, sc in next 3 ch, skip 2 ch, sc in next 3 ch; rep from * to last 4 ch, 3 sc in next ch, sc in next 3 ch, turn.

**ROW 2:** Ch 1, skip first sc, sc in next 3 sts, * 3 sc in next st, sc in next 3 sts, skip 2 sts, sc in next 3 sts; rep from * to last 5 sts, 3 sc in next st, sc in next 2 sts, skip 1 st, sc in last st, turn. End Color A.

**ROWS 3–4:** Join Color B and repeat Row 2.
**ROWS 5–6:** Join Color C and repeat Row 2.
**ROWS 7–8:** Join Color B and repeat Row 2.
**ROWS 9–10:** Join Color A and repeat Row 2.
**ROWS 11–12:** Join Color B and repeat Row 2.
**ROWS 13–14:** Join Color C and repeat Row 2.
**ROWS 15–16:** Join Color B and repeat Row 2.
Continue repeating Row 2, alternating colors as established.

## COLOR VARIATION

## Simple Ripple 2

● A: 8 yds/7.3 m
● B: 8 yds/7.3 m
◐ C: 8 yds/7.3 m
● D: 8 yds/7.3 m

Follow the written instructions or the chart, using colors as follows:

**ROWS 1–2:** Color A
**ROWS 3–4:** Color B
**ROWS 5–6:** Color C
**ROWS 7–8:** Color D
**ROWS 9–10:** Color A
**ROWS 11–12:** Color B
**ROWS 13–14:** Color C
**ROWS 15–16:** Color D

Simple Ripple

Simple Ripple 2

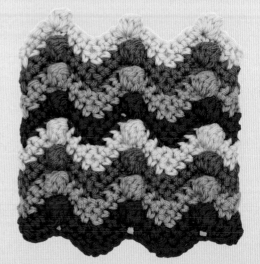

Simple Bobble Ripple

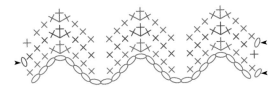

Simple Ripple

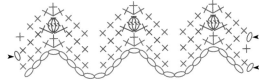

Simple Bobble Ripple

## STITCH VARIATION

## Simple Bobble Ripple

- **SKILL LEVEL:** *Beginner*

## Method

**SPECIAL STITCH:**

• Bobble—B: (Yo, insert hook into st, yo and draw through loop, yo and draw through 2 loops on hook) 4 times in same st (5 loops on hook), yo and draw through all loops on hook, ch 1 pulling tight to close stitch.

**FOUNDATION ROW:** Using Color A, ch a multiple of 9 + 7 + 1 turning ch.

**ROW 1:** Sc in 2nd ch from hook, sc in next 2 ch, * 3 sc in next ch, sc in next 3 ch, skip 2 ch, sc in next 3 ch; rep from * to last 4 ch, 3 sc in next ch, sc in next 3 ch, turn.

**ROW 2:** Ch 1, skip first sc, sc in next 3 sts, * (sc, make B, sc) in next st, sc in next 3 sts, skip 2 sts, sc in next 3 sts; rep from * to last 5 sts, (sc, make B, sc) in next st, sc in next 2 sts, skip 1 st, sc in last st, turn. End Color A.

- **A:** 10 yds/9.1 m
- **B:** 10 yds/9.1 m
- **C:** 10 yds/9.1 m
- **D:** 10 yds/9.1 m

**ROW 3:** Join Color B, ch 1, skip first sc, sc in next 3 sts, * 3 sc in top of B, sc in next 3 sts, skip 2 sts, sc in next 3 sts; rep from * to last 5 sts, 3 sc in top of B, sc in next 2 sts, skip 1 st, sc in last st, turn.

**ROW 4:** Repeat Row 2. End Color B.

**ROWS 5–6:** Join Color C and repeat Row 3, then Row 2. End Color C.

**ROWS 7–8:** Join Color D and repeat Row 3, then Row 2. End Color D.

**ROWS 9–10:** Join Color A and repeat Row 3, then Row 2. End Color A.

**ROWS 11–12:** Join Color B and repeat Row 3, then Row 2. End Color B.

**ROWS 13–14:** Join Color C and repeat Row 3, then Row 2. End Color C.

**ROWS 15–16:** Join Color D and repeat Row 3, then Row 2. End Color D.

Continue repeating Row 3, then Row 2 throughout, alternating colors as established.

## Yarn requirement for throws

**NOTE:** *All yarn requirements are estimated using an H-size (5 mm) crochet hook and worsted/10-ply yarn. Measurements and yarn requirements do not include joining and edging.*

### Simple Ripple

| | BABY | LAP | BED |
|---|---|---|---|
| **A** | 288 yds/263 m | 504 yds/461 m | 1232 yds/1127 m |
| **B** | 576 yds/527 m | 1008 yds/922 m | 2464 yds/2253 m |
| **C** | 288 yds/263 m | 504 yds/461 m | 1232 yds/1127 m |

### Simple Ripple 2

| | BABY | LAP | BED |
|---|---|---|---|
| **A** | 288 yds/263 m | 504 yds/461 m | 1232 yds/1127 m |
| **B** | 288 yds/263 m | 504 yds/461 m | 1232 yds/1127 m |
| **C** | 288 yds/263 m | 504 yds/461 m | 1232 yds/1127 m |
| **D** | 288 yds/263 m | 504 yds/461 m | 1232 yds/1127 m |

### Simple Bobble Ripple

| | BABY | LAP | BED |
|---|---|---|---|
| **A** | 360 yds/329 m | 630 yds/576 m | 1540 yds/1408 m |
| **B** | 360 yds/329 m | 630 yds/576 m | 1540 yds/1408 m |
| **C** | 360 yds/329 m | 630 yds/576 m | 1540 yds/1408 m |
| **D** | 360 yds/329 m | 630 yds/576 m | 1540 yds/1408 m |

**Baby:** Ch 170, work 12 repeats of color sequence.
**Lap:** Ch 278, work 18 repeats of color sequence.
**Bed:** Ch 692, work 28 repeats of color sequence.

# Orange Slices Flower

Orange Slices Flower

- **SKILL LEVEL:** *Advanced*

## Method

**SPECIAL STITCHES:**

- Beg Cluster—Beg Cl: Ch 2 (counts as 1 dc), work 2 dc leaving last loop of each st on hook (3 loops on hook), yo, pull through all 3 loops on hook, ch 1 pulling tight to close the group.
- Cluster—Cl: Work 3 dc leaving last loop of each st on hook (4 loops on hook), yo, pull through all 4 loops on hook, ch 1 pulling tight to close the group.

**FOUNDATION RING:** Using Color A, make a Magic Ring.

**ROUND 1:** Beg Cl into ring, * ch 2, Cl into ring; rep from * 6 more times, ch 3, join with slip st into first ch of ch-3 sp after Beg Cl. End Color A. (8 Cl, 8 ch sps.)

**ROUND 2:** Join Color B in ch-3 sp, ch 3 (counts as 1 dc), 3 dc in same ch-3 sp, * turn, ch 3 (counts as 1 dc), dc in same st, 2 dc in next 3 sts, ch 4, turn **, 4 dc in next ch-3 sp of Round 1; rep from * 6 more times, then from * to ** once more, join with slip st into first ch of ch-4 sp at beginning of round. End Color B. (96 sts, 8 ch sps.)

- A: 8 yds/7.3 m
- B: 18 yds/16.5 m
- C: 13 yds/11.9 m

**ROUND 3:** Join Color C in ch-4 sp, ch 3 (counts as 1 dc), 2 dc, ch 2, 3 dc in same sp, * ch 1, 3 dc in next ch-4 sp, ch 1 **, (3 dc, ch 2, 3 dc) in next ch-4 sp; rep from * twice more, then from * to ** once more, join with slip st into top of beginning ch. (36 sts, 12 ch sps.)

**ROUND 4:** Slip st in next 2 sts and into ch-2 sp, ch 3 (counts as 1 dc), 2 dc, ch 2, 3 dc in same ch-2 sp, * [ch 1, 3 dc in next ch-1 sp] twice, ch 1 **, (3 dc, ch 2, 3 dc) in next ch-2 sp; rep from * twice more, then from * to ** once more, join with slip st into top of beginning ch. End Color C. (48 sts, 16 ch sps.)

**ROUND 5:** Join Color A, ch 1 and sc in same st, sc in next 2 sts, * (sc, hdc, sc) in ch-2 sp **, sc in each st and ch-1 sp to next corner ch-2 sp; rep from * twice more, then from * to ** once more, sc in each st and ch-1 sp to end of round, join with slip st into first sc made. End Color A. (72 sts.)

**ROUND 6:** Join Color B tbl, ch 1 and sc tbl in same st, * sc tbl in each sc to hdc, (sc tbl, hdc tbl, sc tbl) in hdc; rep from * 3 more times, sc tbl in each st to end of round, join with slip st into first sc made. End Color B. (80 sts.)

Orange Slices Flower 2

**COLOR VARIATION**

## Orange Slices Flower 2

Follow the written instructions or the chart, using colors as follows:

- A: 8 yds/7.3 m
- B: 18 yds/16.5 m
- C: 13 yds/11.9 m

Lemon Slices Flower

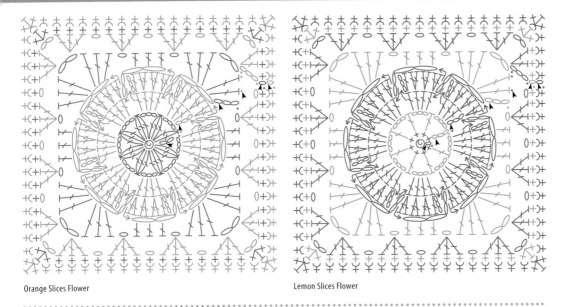

Orange Slices Flower　　　　　　　Lemon Slices Flower

## STITCH VARIATION

## Lemon Slices Flower

• **SKILL LEVEL:** *Advanced*

## Method

**FOUNDATION RING:** Using Color A, make a Magic Ring.

**ROUND 1:** Ch 1, 8 sc into ring, join with slip st into first sc made. End Color A. (8 sts.)

**ROUND 2:** Join Color B, ch 6 (counts as 1 dc, ch 3), [dc in next st, ch 3] 7 times, join with slip st into 3rd ch of beginning ch. End Color B. (8 sts, 8 ch sps.)

**ROUND 3:** Join Color C in ch-3 sp, ch 3 (counts as 1 dc), 3 dc in same ch-3 sp, * turn, ch 3 (counts as 1 dc), dc in same st, 2 dc in each of next 3 sts, ch 4, turn **, 4 dc in next ch-3 sp of Round 2; rep from * 6 more times, then from * to ** once more, join with slip st into first ch of ch-4 sp at beginning of round. End Color C. (96 sts, 8 ch sps.)

**ROUND 4:** Join Color D in ch-4 sp, ch 3 (counts as 1 dc), 2 dc, ch 2, 3 dc in same sp, * ch 1, 3 dc in next ch-4 sp, ch 1 **, (3 dc, ch 2, 3 dc) in next ch-4 sp; rep from * twice more, then from * to ** once more, join with slip st into top of beginning ch. End Color D. (36 sts, 12 ch sps.)

**ROUND 5:** Slip st in next 2 sts and into ch-2 sp, ch 3 (counts as 1 dc), 2 dc, ch 2, 3 dc in same sp, * [ch 1, 3 dc in next ch-1 sp] twice, ch 1 **, (3 dc, ch 2, 3 dc) in next ch-2 sp; rep from * twice more, then from * to ** once more, join with slip st into top of beginning ch. End Color C. (48 sts, 16 ch sps.)

**ROUND 6:** Join Color A, ch 1 and sc in same sp, sc in next 2 sts, * (sc, hdc, sc) in ch-2 sp **, sc in each st and ch-1 sp to next corner ch-2 sp; rep from * twice more, then from * to ** once more, sc in each st and ch-1 sp to end of round, join with slip st into first sc made. End Color A. (72 sts.)

**ROUND 7:** Join Color E tbl, ch 1 and sc tbl in same st, * sc tbl in each sc to hdc, (sc tbl, hdc tbl, sc tbl) in hdc; rep from * 3 more times, sc tbl in each st to end of round, join with slip st into first sc made. End Color E. (80 sts.)

● A:　5 yds/4.6 m
● B:　2 yds/1.8 m
○ C:　13 yds/11.9 m
● D:　13 yds/11.9 m
● E:　5 yds/4.6 m

## Yarn requirement for throws

**NOTE:** *All yarn requirements are estimated using an H-size (5 mm) crochet hook and worsted/10-ply yarn. Measurements and yarn requirements do not include joining and edging.*

| Orange Slices Flower | | | |
|---|---|---|---|
| | BABY | LAP | BED |
| A | 288 yds/263 m | 504 yds/461 m | 1232 yds/1127 m |
| B | 648 yds/593 m | 1134 yds/1037 m | 2772 yds/2535 m |
| C | 468 yds/428 m | 819 yds/749 m | 2002 yds/1831 m |

| Orange Slices Flower 2 | | | |
|---|---|---|---|
| | BABY | LAP | BED |
| A | 288 yds/263 m | 504 yds/461 m | 1232 yds/1127 m |
| B | 648 yds/593 m | 1134 yds/1037 m | 2772 yds/2535 m |
| C | 468 yds/428 m | 819 yds/749 m | 2002 yds/1831 m |

| Lemon Slices Flower | | | |
|---|---|---|---|
| | BABY | LAP | BED |
| A | 180 yds/165 m | 315 yds/288 m | 770 yds/704 m |
| B | 72 yds/66 m | 126 yds/115 m | 308 yds/282 m |
| C | 468 yds/428 m | 819 yds/749 m | 2002 yds/1831 m |
| D | 468 yds/428 m | 819 yds/749 m | 2002 yds/1831 m |
| E | 180 yds/165 m | 315 yds/288 m | 770 yds/704 m |

# Pastel Diamonds

○ A: 3 yds/2.7 m
● B: 13 yds/11.9 m
◐ C: 7 yds/6.4 m
◑ D: 8 yds/7.3 m

• **SKILL LEVEL:** *Beginner*

## Method

**FOUNDATION RING:** Using Color A, make a Magic Ring.

**ROUND 1:** Ch 4 (counts as 1 tr), [4 dc into ring, tr into ring] 3 times, 4 dc into ring, join with slip st into top of beginning ch. End Color A. (20 sts.)

**ROUND 2:** Join Color B, ch 1 and sc in same st, * skip 1 st, (2 dc, tr) in next st, ch 1, (tr, 2 dc) in next st, skip 1 st **, sc in next st; rep from * twice more, then from * to ** once more, join with slip st into first sc made. End Color B. (28 sts, 4 ch sps.)

**ROUND 3:** Join Color C, ch 4 (counts as 1 tr), 3 tr in same st, * sc in ch-1 sp, (4 tr, ch 1, 4 tr) in next sc; rep from * twice more, sc in next ch-1 sp, 4 tr in sc at beginning of round, ch 1, join with slip st into top of beginning ch. End Color C. (36 sts, 4 ch sps.)

**ROUND 4:** Join Color D, ch 2 (counts as 1 hdc), * dc in next 2 sts, tr in next st, (2 tr, ch 2, 2 tr) in next st, tr in next st, dc in next 2 sts, hdc in next st, sc in ch sp **, hdc in next st; rep from * twice more, then from * to ** once more, join with slip st into top of beginning ch. End Color D. (52 sts, 4 ch sps.)

**ROUND 5:** Join Color B, ch 3 (counts as 1 dc), [dc in each st to corner ch-2 sp, (2 dc, ch 2, 2 dc) in corner ch-2 sp] 4 times, dc in each st to end of round, join with slip st into top of beginning ch. End Color B. (68 sts, 4 ch sps.)

Pastel Diamonds

## COLOR VARIATION

### Pastel Diamonds 2

A: 3 yds/2.7 m
● B: 13 yds/11.9 m
○ C: 7 yds/6.4 m
● D: 8 yds/7.3 m

Follow the written instructions or the chart, using colors as follows:

Pastel Diamonds 2

3D Pastel Diamonds

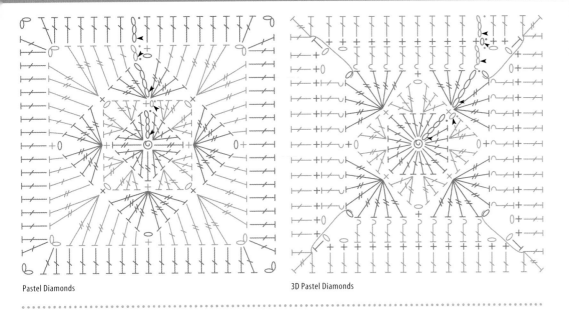

Pastel Diamonds

3D Pastel Diamonds

## STITCH VARIATION

## 3D Pastel Diamonds

• **SKILL LEVEL:** *Beginner*

## Method

**FOUNDATION RING:** Using Color A, make a Magic Ring.

**ROUND 1:** Ch 4 (counts as 1 tr), [4 dc into ring, tr into ring] 3 times, 4 dc into ring, join with slip st into top of beginning ch. End Color A. (20 sts.)

**ROUND 2:** Join Color B, ch 1 and sc in same sp, * skip 1 st, (2 dc, tr) in next st, ch 1, (tr, 2 dc) in next st, skip 1 st **, sc in next st; rep from * twice more, then from * to ** once more, join with slip st into first sc made. End Color B. (28 sts, 4 ch sps.)

**ROUND 3:** Join Color C, ch 4 (counts as 1 tr), 3 tr in same sp, * sc in ch-1 sp, (4 tr, ch 1, 4 tr) in next sc; rep from * twice more, sc in next ch-1 sp, 4 tr in next sc, ch 1, join with slip st into top of beginning ch. End Color C. (36 sts, 4 ch sps.)

**ROUND 4:** Join Color D by working a sl st around back post, ch 3 (counts as 1 dc), [bpdc around each st to ch-1 sp, ch 3] 4 times, join with slip st into top of beginning ch. End Color D. (36 sts, 4 ch sps.)

**ROUND 5:** Join Color A, ch 1, [sc in each st to corner ch-3 sp, work (2 sc, hdc, 2 sc) in corner ch-3 sp] 4 times, join with slip st into first sc made. End Color A. (56 sts.)

**ROUND 6:** Join Color B, ch 3 (counts as 1 dc), [dc in each st to corner hdc, dc in corner hdc, dtr into ch-1 sp of Round 3, dc in corner hdc] 4 times, dc in next 2 sts, join with slip st into top of beginning ch. End Color B. (64 sts.)

● A: 7 yds/6.4 m
○ B: 13 yds/11.9 m
● C: 7 yds/6.4 m
○ D: 6 yds/5.5 m

## Yarn requirement for throws

**NOTE:** *All yarn requirements are estimated using an H-size (5 mm) crochet hook and worsted/10-ply yarn. Measurements and yarn requirements do not include joining and edging.*

### Pastel Diamonds

|   | BABY | LAP | BED |
|---|------|-----|-----|
| A | 108 yds/99 m | 189 yds/173 m | 462 yds/422 m |
| B | 468 yds/428 m | 819 yds/749 m | 2002 yds/1831 m |
| C | 252 yds/230 m | 441 yds/403 m | 1078 yds/986 m |
| D | 288 yds/263 m | 504 yds/461 m | 1232 yds/1127 m |

### Pastel Diamonds 2

|   | BABY | LAP | BED |
|---|------|-----|-----|
| A | 108 yds/99 m | 189 yds/173 m | 462 yds/422 m |
| B | 468 yds/428 m | 819 yds/749 m | 2002 yds/1831 m |
| C | 252 yds/230 m | 441 yds/403 m | 1078 yds/986 m |
| D | 288 yds/263 m | 504 yds/461 m | 1232 yds/1127 m |

### 3D Pastel Diamonds

|   | BABY | LAP | BED |
|---|------|-----|-----|
| A | 252 yds/230 m | 441 yds/403 m | 1078 yds/986 m |
| B | 468 yds/428 m | 819 yds/749 m | 2002 yds/1831 m |
| C | 252 yds/230 m | 441 yds/403 m | 1078 yds/986 m |
| D | 216 yds/198 m | 378 yds/346 m | 924 yds/845 m |

# Circle Square

• **SKILL LEVEL:** *Beginner*

● A: 4 yds/3.7 m
◐ B: 7 yds/6.4 m
○ C: 5 yds/4.6 m
◐ D: 5 yds/4.6 m
● E: 11 yds/10 m
○ F: 7 yds/6.4 m

## Method

**FOUNDATION RING:** Using Color A, make a Magic Ring.

**ROUND 1:** Ch 1, 8 sc into ring, join with slip st into first sc made. End Color A. (8 sts.)

**ROUND 2:** Join Color B, ch 1 and sc in same sp, [ch 2, sc in next st] 7 times, ch 2, join with slip st into first sc made. End Color B. (8 sts, 8 ch sps.)

**ROUND 3:** Join Color C in ch-2 sp, ch 3 (counts as 1 dc), 2 dc in same sp, [ch 1, 3 dc in next ch-2 sp] 7 times, ch 1, join with slip st into top of beginning ch. End Color C. (24 sts, 8 ch sps.)

**ROUND 4:** Join Color D in ch-1 sp, ch 3 (counts as 1 dc), dc in same sp, [ch 1, skip 1 st, 2 dc in next st, ch 1, skip 1 st, 2 dc in ch-1 sp] 7 times, ch 1, skip 1 st, 2 dc in next st, ch 1, skip 1 st, join with slip st into top of beginning ch. End Color C. (32 sts, 16 ch sps.)

**ROUND 5:** Join Color E in ch-1 sp, ch 1 and sc in same sp, [ch 2, sc in next ch-1 sp] 15 times, ch 2, join with slip st into first sc made. End Color E. (16 sts, 16 ch sps.)

**ROUND 6:** Join Color F in ch-2 sp, ch 3 (counts as 1 dc), 2 dc in same sp, [ch 1, 3 dc in next ch-2 sp] 15 times, ch 1, join with slip st into top of beginning ch. End Color F. (48 sts, 16 ch sps.)

**ROUND 7:** Join Color A in ch-1 sp, ch 1 and sc in same sp, [ch 3, sc in next ch-1 sp] 15 times, ch 3, join with slip st into first sc made. End Color A. (16 sts, 16 ch sps.)

**ROUND 8:** Join Color E in ch-3 sp, ch 1, 4 sc in same sp, * (hdc, 3 dc) in next ch-3 sp, (tr, ch 2, tr) in next sc, (3 dc, hdc) in next ch-3 sp, 4 sc in next ch-3 sp **, 4 sc in next ch-3 sp; rep from * twice more, then from * to ** once more, join with slip st into first sc made. End Color E. (72 sts, 4 ch sps.)

**ROUND 9:** Join Color B, ch 1 and sc in same sp, [sc in each st to corner ch-2 sp, (sc, hdc, sc) in corner ch-2 sp] 4 times, sc in each st to end of round, join with slip st to first sc made. End Color B. (84 sts.)

Circle Square

---

**COLOR VARIATION**

## Circle Square 2

Follow the written instructions or the chart, using colors as follows:

**FOUNDATION RING:** Color A
**ROUND 1:** Color A
**ROUND 2:** Color B
**ROUND 3:** Color C
**ROUND 4:** Color D
**ROUND 5:** Color E
**ROUND 6:** Color F
**ROUND 7:** Color A
**ROUND 8:** Color B
**ROUND 9:** Color E

● A: 4 yds/3.7 m
○ B: 11 yds/10 m
◐ C: 5 yds/4.6 m
◐ D: 5 yds/4.6 m
● E: 9 yds/8.2 m
◐ F: 7 yds/6.4 m

Circle Square 2

Circle Granny

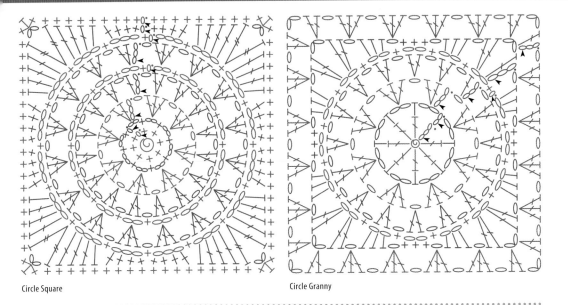

Circle Square

Circle Granny

## STITCH VARIATION

## Circle Granny

• **SKILL LEVEL:** *Beginner*

## Method

**FOUNDATION RING:** Using Color A, make a Magic Ring.

**ROUND 1:** Ch 3 (counts as 1 dc), 7 dc into ring, join with slip st into top of beginning ch. End Color A. (8 sts.)

**ROUND 2:** Join Color B, ch 4 (counts as 1 hdc, ch 2), [hdc in next st, ch 2] 7 times, join with slip st into 2nd ch of beginning ch. End Color B. (8 sts, 8 ch sps.)

**ROUND 3:** Join Color C in ch-2 sp, ch 3 (counts as 1 dc), 2 dc in same sp, [ch 1, 3 dc in next ch-2 sp] 7 times, ch 1, join with slip st into top of beginning ch. End Color C. (24 sts, 8 ch sps.)

**ROUND 4:** Join Color D in ch-1 sp, ch 3 (counts as 1 dc), 1 dc in same sp, [ch 1, skip 1 st, 2 dc in next st, ch 1, skip 1 st, 2 dc in ch-1 sp] 7 times, ch 1, skip 1 st, 2 dc in next st, ch 1, skip 1 st; join with slip st into top of beginning ch. End Color C. (32 sts, 16 ch sps.)

**ROUND 5:** Join Color E in ch-1 sp, ch 1 and sc in same sp, [ch 2, sc in next ch-1 sp] 15 times, ch 2, join with slip st into first sc made. End Color E. (16 sts, 16 ch sps.)

**ROUND 6:** Join Color F in ch-2 sp, ch 3 (counts as 1 dc), dc, ch 2, 2 dc in same ch-2 sp, ch 1, * 3 hdc in next ch-2 sp, ch 1, 3 sc in next ch-2 sp, ch 1, 3 hdc in next ch-2 sp, ch 1 **, (2 dc, ch 2, 2 dc) in next ch-2 sp, ch 1: rep from * twice more, then from * to ** once more, join with slip st into top of beginning ch. End Color F. (52 sts, 24 ch sps.)

**ROUND 7:** Join Color A in corner ch-2 sp, ch 3 (counts as 1 dc), 1 dc, ch 2, 2 dc in same sp, * [ch 1, 3 dc in next ch-1 sp] 4 times, ch 1 **, (2 dc, ch 2, 2 dc) in next ch-2 sp; rep from * twice more, then from * to ** once more, join with slip st into top of beginning ch. End Color A. (64 sts, 24 ch sps.))

● A: 11 yds/10 m
◐ B: 2 yds/1.8 m
○ C: 4 yds/3.7 m
◑ D: 5 yds/4.6 m
● E: 3 yds/2.7 m
○ F: 7 yds/6.4 m

## Yarn requirement for throws

**NOTE:** *All yarn requirements are estimated using an H-size (5 mm) crochet hook and worsted/10-ply yarn. Measurements and yarn requirements do not include joining and edging.*

### Circle Square

| | BABY | LAP | BED |
|---|---|---|---|
| A | 144 yds/132 m | 252 yds/230 m | 516 yds/472 m |
| B | 252 yds/230 m | 441 yds/403 m | 1078 yds/986 m |
| C | 180 yds/165 m | 315 yds/288 m | 770 yds/704 m |
| D | 180 yds/165 m | 315 yds/288 m | 770 yds/704 m |
| E | 396 yds/362 m | 693 yds/634 m | 1694 yds/1549 m |
| F | 252 yds/230 m | 441 yds/403 m | 1078 yds/986 m |

### Circle Square 2

| | BABY | LAP | BED |
|---|---|---|---|
| A | 144 yds/132 m | 252 yds/230 m | 516 yds/472 m |
| B | 396 yds/362 m | 693 yds/634 m | 1694 yds/1549 m |
| C | 180 yds/165 m | 315 yds/288 m | 770 yds/704 m |
| D | 180 yds/165 m | 315 yds/288 m | 770 yds/704 m |
| E | 324 yds/296 m | 567 yds/518 m | 1386 yds/1267 m |
| F | 252 yds/230 m | 441 yds/403 m | 1078 yds/986 m |

### Circle Granny

| | BABY | LAP | BED |
|---|---|---|---|
| A | 396 yds/362 m | 693 yds/634 m | 1694 yds/1549 m |
| B | 72 yds/66 m | 126 yds/115 m | 308 yds/282 m |
| C | 144 yds/132 m | 252 yds/230 m | 616 yds/563 m |
| D | 180 yds/165 m | 315 yds/288 m | 770 yds/704 m |
| E | 108 yds/99 m | 189 yds/173 m | 462 yds/422 m |
| F | 252 yds/230 m | 441 yds/403 m | 1078 yds/986 m |

# Baltic Sea

A: 4 yds/3.7 m
B: 6 yds/5.5 m
C: 10 yds/9.1 m
D: 13 yds/11.9 m
E: 16 yds/14.6 m

• **SKILL LEVEL:** *Intermediate*

## Method

**SPECIAL STITCHES:**

• Beg Popcorn—Beg PC: Ch 3 (counts as 1 dc), work 4 dc in same place. Take the hook out of the working loop and insert it into 3rd ch of ch 3. Pick up working loop with hook and draw it through to fold the group of stitches, ch 1 pulling tightly to close the group of stitches.

• Popcorn—PC: Work a group of 5 dc into the same place. Take the hook out of the working look and insert it under both loops at the top of the first dc of the group. Pick up working loop with hook and draw it through to fold the group of stitches, ch 1 pulling tightly to close the group.

**FOUNDATION RING:** Using Color A, ch 5, join to form a ring.

**ROUND 1:** Work Beg PC, (ch 4, PC) 3 times, ch 4, join with slip st into top of beginning ch. End Color A. (4 PC, 4 ch sps.)

**ROUND 2:** Join Color B in corner ch-4 sp, (Beg PC, ch 4, PC) in ch-4 sp, * ch 2, dc in PC, ch 2 **, (PC, ch 4, PC) in ch-4 sp; rep from * twice more, then from * to ** once more, join with slip st into top of first PC. End Color B. (8 PC, 4 dc, 12 ch sps.)

**ROUND 3:** Join Color C in corner ch-4 sp, work Beg PC, ch 4, PC in same ch-4 sp, * ch 2, dc in PC, 2 dc in ch-2 sp, dc in dc, 2 dc in ch-2 sp, dc in PC, ch 2 **, (PC, ch 4, PC) in corner ch-4 sp; rep from * twice more, then from * to ** once more, join with slip st into top of first PC. End Color C. (28 sts, 8 PC, 12 ch sps.)

**ROUND 4:** Join Color D in corner ch-4 sp, work Beg PC, ch 4, PC in ch-4 sp, * ch 2, dc in PC, 2 dc in ch-2 sp, dc in each dc to ch-2 sp, 2 dc in ch-2 sp, dc in PC, ch 2 **, (PC, ch 4, PC) in corner ch-4 sp; rep from * twice more, then from * to ** once more, join with slip st into top of first PC. End Color D. (52 sts, 8 PC, 12 ch sps.)

**ROUND 5:** Join Color E in Beg PC, ch 1, * work (2 sc, hdc, 2 sc) in ch-4 sp, sc in PC, 2 sc in ch-2 sp, sc in each st to next ch-2 sp, 2 sc in ch-2 sp, sc in PC; rep from * 3 more times, join with slip st into first sc made. End Color E. (96 sts.)

Baltic Sea

Baltic Sea 2

## COLOR VARIATION

## Baltic Sea 2

Follow the written instructions or the chart, using colors as follows:

A: 4 yds/3.7 m
B: 6 yds/5.5 m
C: 10 yds/9.1 m
D: 13 yds/11.9 m
E: 16 yds/14.6 m

Baltic Coast

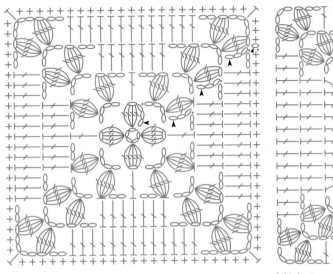

Baltic Sea

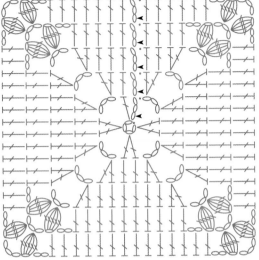

Baltic Coast

## STITCH VARIATION

## Baltic Coast

- **SKILL LEVEL:** *Intermediate*

## Method

**SPECIAL STITCH:**

- Popcorn—PC: Work a group of 5 dc into the same place. Take the hook out of the working loop and insert it under both loops at the top of the first dc of the group. Pick up working loop with hook and draw it through to fold the group of sts, ch 1 pulling tightly to close the group.

**FOUNDATION RING:** Using Color A, ch 4, join to form a ring.

**ROUND 1:** Ch 3 (counts as 1 dc), dc into ring, * ch 3, 2 dc into ring; rep from * twice more, ch 3, join with slip st into top of beginning ch. End Color A. (8 sts, 4 ch sps.)

**ROUND 2:** Join Color B, ch 3 (counts as 1 dc), dc in next st, * (2 dc, ch 3, 2 dc) in ch-3 sp **, dc in next 2 sts; rep from * twice more, then from * to ** once more, join with slip st into top of beginning ch. End Color B. (24 sts, 4 ch sps.)

**ROUND 3:** Join Color C, ch 3 (counts as 1 dc), * dc in each st to ch-3 sp, (2 dc, ch 3, 2 dc) in ch-3 sp; rep from * 3 more times, dc in each st to end of round, join with slip st into top of beginning ch. End Color C. (40 sts, 4 ch sps.)

**ROUND 4:** Join Color A, ch 3 (counts as 1 dc), dc in each st to corner ch-3 sp, * ch 2, work (PC, ch 3, PC) in ch-3 sp, ch 2 **, dc in each st to corner ch-3 sp; rep from * twice more, then from * to ** once more, dc in each st to end of round, join with slip st into top of beginning ch. End Color A. (8 PC, 40 sts, 12 ch sps.)

**ROUND 5:** Join Color D, ch 3 (counts as 1 dc), * dc in each st to ch-2 sp, 2 dc in ch-2 sp, ch 2, work (PC, ch 3, PC) in ch-3 sp, ch 2, 2 dc in ch-2 sp; rep from * 3 more times, dc in each st to end of round, join with slip st into top of beginning ch. End Color D. (8 PC, 56 sts, 12 ch sps.)

A: 15 yds/13.7 m
B: 4 yds/3.7 m
C: 6 yds/5.5 m
D: 16 yds/14.6 m

## Yarn requirement for throws

**NOTE:** *All yarn requirements are estimated using an H-size (5 mm) crochet hook and worsted/10-ply yarn. Measurements and yarn requirements do not include joining and edging.*

### Baltic Sea

|   | BABY | LAP | BED |
|---|---|---|---|
| A | 144 yds/132 m | 252 yds/230 m | 616 yds/563 m |
| B | 216 yds/198 m | 378 yds/346 m | 924 yds/845 m |
| C | 360 yds/329 m | 630 yds/576 m | 1540 yds/1408 m |
| D | 468 yds/428 m | 819 yds/749 m | 2002 yds/1831 m |
| E | 576 yds/527 m | 1008 yds/922 m | 2464 yds/2253 m |

### Baltic Sea 2

|   | BABY | LAP | BED |
|---|---|---|---|
| A | 144 yds/132 m | 252 yds/230 m | 616 yds/563 m |
| B | 216 yds/198 m | 378 yds/346 m | 924 yds/845 m |
| C | 360 yds/329 m | 630 yds/576 m | 1540 yds/1408 m |
| D | 468 yds/428 m | 819 yds/749 m | 2002 yds/1831 m |
| E | 576 yds/527 m | 1008 yds/922 m | 2464 yds/2253 m |

### Baltic Coast

|   | BABY | LAP | BED |
|---|---|---|---|
| A | 540 yds/494 m | 945 yds/864 m | 2310 yds/2112 m |
| B | 144 yds/132 m | 252 yds/230 m | 616 yds/563 m |
| C | 216 yds/198 m | 378 yds/346 m | 924 yds/845 m |
| D | 576 yds/527 m | 1008 yds/922 m | 2464 yds/2253 m |

# Blueberry Patch

- **A:** 17 yds/15.5 m
- **B:** 10 yds/9.1 m
- **C:** 7 yds/6.4 m
- **D:** 8 yds/7.3 m

• **SKILL LEVEL:** *Intermediate*

## Method

**SPECIAL STITCH:**

• Bobble—B: Work 7 tr in same st, leaving last loop of each st on hook (8 loops on hook), yo and draw through all loops on hook.

**FOUNDATION ROW:** Using Color A, 12 ch.

**ROW 1:** Begin with 2nd ch from hook, sc in each ch across, turn. (11 sc.)

**ROW 2:** Ch 3 (counts as 1 dc), dc in next st, [make B in next st, dc in next 2 sts] 3 times, turn. (8 dc, 3 B.)

**ROW 3:** Repeat Row 1.

**ROW 4:** Repeat Row 2.

**ROW 5:** Repeat Row 1.

**ROW 6:** Repeat Row 2.

**ROW 7:** Repeat Row 1. End Color A. Do not turn.

**ROUND 8:** Join Color B, now working in the round, ch 1 and 2 sc in same st, * [sc in side of sc, 2 sc around post of dc] 3 times, sc in side of sc **, sc in next 10 foundation-ch, 2 sc in next foundation-ch; rep from * to ** once more, sc in next 10 sts, join to first sc made. End Color B. (44 sts.)

**ROUND 9:** Join Color C, ch 5 (counts as 1 dc, ch 2), dc in same space, * dc in next 10 sts, (dc, ch 2, dc) in next st; rep from * twice more, dc in next 10 sts, join with slip st into 3rd ch of beginning ch. End Color C. (48 sts, 4 ch sps.)

**ROUND 10:** Join Color D in ch-2 sp, ch 3 (counts as 1 dc), dc, ch 2, 2 dc in same ch-2 sp, * dc in next st, ch 1, skip 1 st, dc in next 8 sts, ch 1, skip 1 st, dc in next st **, (2 dc, ch 2, 2 dc) in ch-2 sp; rep from * twice more, then from * to ** once more, join with slip st into top of beginning ch. End Color D. (56 sts, 12 ch sps.)

**ROUND 11:** Join Color B, ch 1 and sc in same sp, sc in next st, * (sc, hdc, sc) in ch-2 sp, sc in next 3 sts, sc over ch-1 sp into dc of Round 9, sc in next 8 sts, sc over ch-1 sp into dc of Round 9 **, sc in next 3 sts; rep from * twice more, then from * to ** once more, sc in next st, join with slip st into first sc made. End Color B. (76 sts.)

Blueberry Patch

Blueberry Patch 2

## COLOR VARIATION

### Blueberry Patch 2

Follow the written instructions or the chart, using colors as follows:

- **A:** 23 yds/21 m
- **B:** 4 yds/3.7 m
- **C:** 7 yds/6.4 m
- **D:** 8 yds/7.3 m

Winter Blueberry Patch

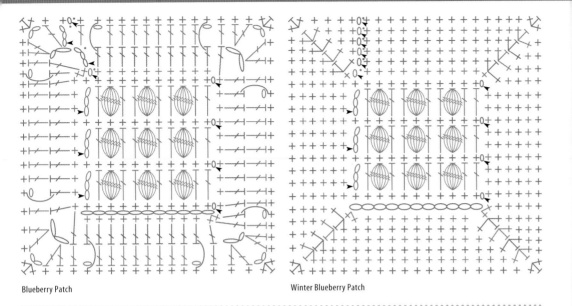

Blueberry Patch

Winter Blueberry Patch

## Yarn requirement for throws

**NOTE:** *All yarn requirements are estimated using an H-size (5 mm) crochet hook and worsted/10-ply yarn. Measurements and yarn requirements do not include joining and edging.*

### Blueberry Patch

|   | BABY | LAP | BED |
|---|------|-----|-----|
| A | 612 yds/560 m | 1071 yds/979 m | 2618 yds/2394 m |
| B | 360 yds/329 m | 630 yds/576 m | 1540 yds/1408 m |
| C | 252 yds/230 m | 441 yds/403 m | 1078 yds/986 m |
| D | 288 yds/263 m | 504 yds/461 m | 1232 yds/1127 m |

### Blueberry Patch 2

|   | BABY | LAP | BED |
|---|------|-----|-----|
| A | 828 yds/757 m | 1449 yds/1325 m | 3542 yds/3239 m |
| B | 144 yds/132 m | 252 yds/230 m | 616 yds/563 m |
| C | 252 yds/230 m | 441 yds/403 m | 1078 yds/986 m |
| D | 288 yds/263 m | 504 yds/461 m | 1232 yds/1127 m |

### Winter Blueberry Patch

|   | BABY | LAP | BED |
|---|------|-----|-----|
| A | 828 yds/757 m | 1449 yds/1325 m | 3542 yds/3239 m |
| B | 324 yds/296 m | 567 yds/518 m | 1386 yds/1267 m |
| C | 144 yds/132 m | 252 yds/230 m | 616 yds/563 m |
| D | 396 yds/362 m | 693 yds/634 m | 1694 yds/1549 m |

## STITCH VARIATION

## Winter Blueberry Patch

● A: 23 yds/21 m
○ B: 9 yds/8.2 m
● C: 4 yds/3.7 m
● D: 11 yds/10 m

• **SKILL LEVEL:** *Intermediate*

## Method

**SPECIAL STITCH:**

• Bobble—B: Work 7 tr in same st, leaving last loop of each st on hook (8 loops on hook), yo and draw through all loops on hook.

**FOUNDATION ROW:** Using Color A, ch 12. (11 sts + 1 turning ch.)

**ROW 1:** Beg with 2nd ch from hook, sc in each ch across, turn. (11 sc.)

**ROW 2 (WS):** Ch 3 (counts as 1 dc), dc in next st, [make B in next st, dc in next 2 sts] 3 times, turn. (8 dc, 3 B.)

**ROW 3:** Ch 1 and work sc in same st, sc in each st across, turn.

**ROW 4:** Repeat Row 2.

**ROW 5:** Repeat Row 3.

**ROW 6:** Repeat Row 2.

**ROW 7:** Repeat Row 3. End Color A.

**ROUND 8:** Join Color B into corner st, now working in the round, ch 1 and sc in same st, * [sc in base of sc, 2 sc around post of dc] 3 times, sc in base of sc **, 2 sc in first foundation ch, sc in next 9 foundation ch,

2 sc in last foundation ch; rep from * to ** once more, sc in next 10 sts, join with slip st into first sc made. End Color B. (44 sts.)

**ROUND 9:** Join Color C, ch 1, * (sc, hdc, sc) in same st, sc in next 10 sts; rep from * 3 more times, join with slip st into first sc made. End Color C. (52 sts.)

**ROUND 10:** Join Color D, ch 1 and sc in same st, * (sc, hdc, sc) in hdc **, sc in each st to hdc; rep from * twice more, then from * to ** once more, sc in each st to end of round, join with slip st into first sc made. End Color D. (60 sts.)

**ROUND 11:** Repeat Round 10 using Color B. (68 sts.)

**ROUND 12:** Repeat Round 10 using Color D. (76 sts.)

**ROUND 13:** Repeat Round 10 using Color A. (84 sts.)

# Target

• **SKILL LEVEL:** *Beginner*

## Method

**FOUNDATION RING:** Using Color A, make a Magic Ring.

**ROUND 1:** Ch 3 (counts as 1 dc), 11 dc into ring, join with slip st into top of beginning ch. End Color A. (12 sts.)

**ROUND 2:** Join Color B, ch 3 (counts as 1 dc), tr, dc in same sp, [dc in next 2 sts, (dc, tr, dc) in next st] 3 times, dc in next 2 sts, join with slip st into top of beginning ch. End Color B. (20 sts.)

**ROUND 3:** Join Color C, ch 1 and sc in same sp, [(sc, hdc, sc) in next st, sc in each st to corner tr, (sc, hdc, sc) in corner tr] 3 times, sc in each st to end of round, join with slip st into first sc made. End Color C. (28 sts.)

- ◐ A: 2 yds/1.8 m
- ◕ B: 3 yds/2.7 m
- ○ C: 6 yds/5.5 m
- ● D: 6 yds/5.5 m
- ◑ E: 9 yds/8.2 m
- ◕ F: 5 yds/4.6 m

**ROUND 4:** Join Color D, ch 3 (counts as 1 dc), [dc in each st to hdc, (2 dc, tr, 2 dc) in hdc] 4 times, dc in each st to end of round, join with slip st into top of beginning ch. End Color D. (44 sts.)

**ROUND 5:** Join Color C ch 1 and sc in same sp, * sc in each st to corner tr, (sc, hdc, sc) in tr; rep from * 3 more times, sc in each st to end of round, join with slip st into first sc made. End Color C. (52 sts)

**ROUND 6:** Join Color E and repeat Round 4. End Color E. (68 sts)

**ROUND 7:** Join Color F and repeat Round 5. End Color F. (76 sts)

Target

Target 2

## COLOR VARIATION

### Target 2

Follow the written instructions or the chart, using colors as follows:

**ROUND 1:** Color A
**ROUNDS 2–3:** Color B
**ROUNDS 4–5:** Color C
**ROUNDS 6–7:** Color D

- ◕ A: 2 yds/1.8 m
- ◕ B: 5 yds/4.6 m
- ◔ C: 10 yds/9.1 m
- ● D: 14 yds/12.8 m

Appliqué Posy

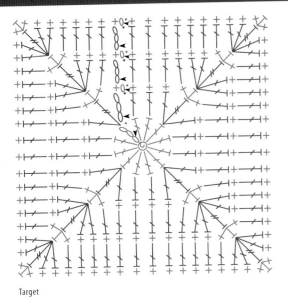

Target

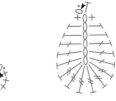

Appliqué Posy

## Yarn requirement for throws

**NOTE:** *All yarn requirements are estimated using an H-size (5 mm) crochet hook and worsted/10-ply yarn. Measurements and yarn requirements do not include joining and edging.*

### Target

| | BABY | LAP | BED |
|---|---|---|---|
| A | 72 yds/66 m | 126 yds/115 m | 308 yds/282 m |
| B | 108 yds/99 m | 189 yds/173 m | 462 yds/422 m |
| C | 216 yds/198 m | 378 yds/346 m | 924 yds/845 m |
| D | 216 yds/198 m | 378 yds/346 m | 924 yds/845 m |
| E | 324 yds/296 m | 567 yds/518 m | 1386 yds/1267 m |
| F | 180 yds/165 m | 315 yds/288 m | 770 yds/704 m |

### Target 2

| | BABY | LAP | BED |
|---|---|---|---|
| A | 72 yds/66 m | 126 yds/115 m | 308 yds/282 m |
| B | 180 yds/165 m | 315 yds/288 m | 770 yds/704 m |
| C | 360 yds/329 m | 630 yds/576 m | 1540 yds/1408 m |
| D | 504 yds/461 m | 882 yds/807 m | 2156 yds/1971 m |

### Appliqué Posy

| | BABY | LAP | BED |
|---|---|---|---|
| A | 1116 yds/1020 m | 1953 yds/1786 m | 4774 yds/4365 m |
| B | 216 yds/198 m | 378 yds/346 m | 924 yds/845 m |
| C | 72 yds/66 m | 126 yds/115 m | 308 yds/282 m |
| D | 36 yds/33 m | 63 yds/58 m | 154 yds/141 m |
| E | 108 yds/99 m | 189 yds/173 m | 462 yds/422 m |
| F | Small amounts for sewing | | |

## STITCH VARIATION

## Appliqué Posy

- **SKILL LEVEL:** *Beginner*

- A: 31 yds/28 m
- B: 6 yds/5.5 m
- C: 2 yds/1.8 m
- D: 1 yd/0.9 m
- E: 3 yds/2.7 m
- F: small amount

## Method

### BLOCK
Follow the written instructions or the chart for Basic Block using Color A.

### APPLIQUÉ LEAVES—MAKE 2
**FOUNDATION ROW:** Using Color B, ch 7.
**ROUND 1:** Working through top loops of ch only, sc in 2nd ch from hook, hdc in next 2 ch, dc in next 2 ch, (dc, 6 tr, dc) in last ch, working through bottom loops of ch only, dc in next 2 ch, hdc in next 2 ch, (sc, hdc) in last ch, join with slip st into first sc made. End Color B. (19 sts.)

### APPLIQUÉ BERRIES—MAKE 2
**FOUNDATION RING:** Using Color C, make a Magic Ring.
**ROUND 1:** Ch 1, 10 sc into ring, join with slip st into first sc made. Leaving a long tail, end Color C. (10 sts.) Thread the long tail through the top of each sc, pull tightly to form berry.

### APPLIQUÉ FLOWER—MAKE 1
**FOUNDATION RING:** Using Color D, make a Magic Ring.
**ROUND 1:** Ch 1, [sc into ring, ch 2] 5 times, join with slip st into first sc made. End Color D. (5 sts, 5 ch sps)
**ROUND 2:** Join Color E in ch-2 sp, * (ch 2, 2 dc, ch2, sl st) into same ch-2 sp **, sl st into next ch-2 sp; rep from * 3 more times, then from * to ** once more. End Color E. (5 petals)

### FINISHING
Use 2 strands of Color F to sew leaves to block. Use 1 strand of Color D to sew center of flower to block. Use long tail of berries to sew into place.

# Aztec Sun

● A: 5 yds/4.6 m
● B: 3 yds/2.7 m
|||| C: 5 yds/4.6 m
● D: 18 yds/16.5 m

• **SKILL LEVEL:** *Intermediate*

## Method

**FOUNDATION RING:** Using Color A, make a Magic Ring.

**ROUND 1:** Ch 3 (counts as 1 dc), 11 dc in ring, join with slip st into top of beginning ch. End Color A. (12 sts.)

**ROUND 2:** Join Color B, ch 3 (counts as 1 dc), dc in same st, 2 dc in each st around, join with slip st into top of beginning ch. End Color B. (24 sts.)

**ROUND 3:** Join Color C, ch 3 (counts as 1 dc), dc in same st, [1 dc in next st, 2 dc in next st] 11 times, dc in next st, join with slip st into top of beginning ch. End Color C. (36 sts.)

**ROUND 4:** Join Color A, ch 1, sc in each st around, join with slip st into first sc made. End Color A. (36 sts.)

**ROUND 5:** Join Color D (or E—see project notes opposite) through back loop, ch 6 (counts as 1 tr, ch 2), tr tbl in same st, * dc tbl in next 2 sts, hdc tbl in next st, sc tbl in next 2 sts, hdc tbl in next st, dc tbl in next 2 sts **, (tr tbl, ch 2, tr tbl) in next st; rep from * twice more, then from * to ** once more, join with slip st into 3rd ch of beginning ch. (40 sts, 4 ch sps.)

**ROUND 6:** Ch 3 (counts as 1 dc), * work (2 dc, ch 2, 2 dc) in corner ch sp **, dc in each st to next corner ch-2 sp; rep from * twice more, then from * to ** once more, dc in each st to end of round, join with slip st into top of beginning ch. (56 sts, 4 ch sps.)

**ROUND 7:** Ch 1 and sc in same sp, sc in each st to corner ch-2 sp, work 3 sc in corner ch-2 sp; rep from * 3 more times, sc in each st to end of round, join with slip st into first sc made. End Color D (or E—see project notes opposite). (68 sts.)

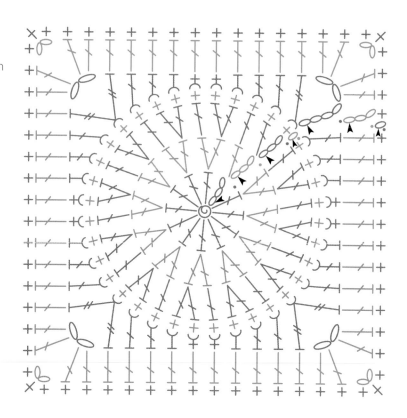

## Yarn requirement for throws

**NOTE:** *All yarn requirements are estimated using an H-size (5 mm) crochet hook and worsted/10-ply yarn. Measurements and yarn requirements do not include joining and edging.*

| Aztec Sun | | | |
|---|---|---|---|
| | BABY | LAP | BED |
| A | 180 yds/165 m | 315 yds/288 m | 770 yds/704 m |
| B | 108 yds/99 m | 189 yds/173 m | 462 yds/422 m |
| C | 180 yds/165 m | 315 yds/288 m | 770 yds/704 m |
| D | 648 yds/593 m | 1134 yds/1037 m | 2772 yds/2535 m |

## Project Notes

- **LAP BLANKET MEASUREMENTS:**
  *55 x 44 in./139.5 x 112 cm
  without edging*
- **JOINING METHOD:** *Mattress stitch*
- **EDGING:** *Ridged edge*

- ● A: 315 yds/288 m
- ● B: 189 yds/173 m
- ○ C: 315 yds/288 m
- ● D: 504 yds/461 m
- ● E: 630 yds/576 m

Following the Method instructions
opposite, make 63 squares:
28 squares edged in turquoise (D)
35 squares edged in navy (E)

Then follow the instructions below:

### JOINING
Using mattress stitch method, join
squares in nine rows of seven
squares, following the photograph
for reference.

### EDGING
**ROUND 1:** Join Color E in a corner
st, ch 1, 3 sc in same st, sc in each
st around and work 3 sc in each
corner st, join with slip st in first
sc made.

**ROUND 2:** Ch 3 (counts as 1 dc), dc
in each st around and work 3 dc in
each corner st, end with slip st in
top of beginning ch. End Color E.

**ROUND 3:** Join Color A, sc tbl in
each st around and work 3 sc tbl in
each corner st, join with slip st into
first sc made. End Color A.

**ROUND 4:** Join Color B and repeat
Round 3. End Color B.

**ROUND 5:** Join Color C and repeat
Round 3. End Color C.

# Puffy Flower

- A: 5 yds/4.6 m
- B: 15 yds/13.7 m
- C: 20 yds/18.3 m

- **SKILL LEVEL:** *Intermediate*

## Method

**SPECIAL STITCH:**

- Puff Stitch—PS: Draw up loop on hook to the height of a hdc, (yo, insert hook into same st and draw loop to height of a hdc) 4 times (9 loops on hook), yo and draw through all loops on hook, ch 1 pulling tight to close stitch.

**FOUNDATION RING:** Using Color A, ch 5 and join with slip st to form a ring.

**ROUND 1:** Ch 1, 8 sc into ring. (8 sc.)

**ROUND 2:** * Work PS in sc, ch 3; rep from * 7 more times, join with slip st into top of first PS made. End Color A. (8 PS, 8 ch sps.)

**ROUND 3:** Join Color B in ch-3 sp, ch 3 (counts as 1 dc), 3 dc, ch 1, 4 dc in same sp, ch 1, * (4 dc, ch 1, 4 dc) in next ch-3 sp, ch 1; rep from * 6 more times, join with slip st into top of beginning ch. End Color B. (64 sts, 16 ch sps.)

**ROUND 4:** With Color C on hook * work sc into PS of Round 2 over ch-1 sp of Round 3, ch 4; rep from * 7 more times, join with slip st into first sc made. (8 sts, 8 ch sps.)

**ROUND 5:** Ch 3 (counts as 1 dc), * 5 dc into next ch-4 sp, dc in sc, 3 dc in next ch-4 sp, tr into ch 1 of Round 3 working over ch-4 sp, 3 dc in same ch-4 sp **, dc in sc; rep from * twice more, then from * to ** once more, join with slip st into top of beginning ch. (56 sts.)

**ROUND 6:** Ch 3 (counts as 1 dc), dc in next 2 sts, * dc into ch 1 sp of Round 3 and next dc, dc in next 6 sts, (dc, tr, dc) in tr **, dc in next 6 sts; rep from * twice more, then from * to ** once more, dc in next 3 sts, join with slip st into top of beginning ch. End Color C. (64 sts.)

**ROUND 7:** Join Color B, ch 1 and sc in same sp, * sc in each dc to corner tr, work (sc, hdc, sc) in corner tr; rep from * 3 more times, sc in next 4 sts, join with slip st into first sc made. End Color B. (72 sts.)

Puffy Flower

Puffy Flower 2

---

**COLOR VARIATION**

## Puffy Flower 2

Follow the written instructions or the chart, using colors as follows:

- A: 5 yds/4.6 m
- B: 15 yds/13.7 m
- C: 20 yds/18.3 m

Puffy Picot Flower

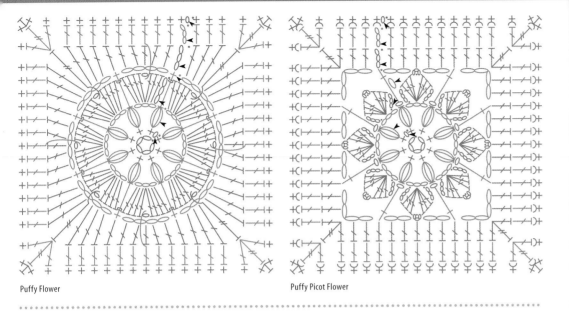

Puffy Flower

Puffy Picot Flower

## Yarn requirement for throws

**NOTE:** *All yarn requirements are estimated using an H-size (5 mm) crochet hook and worsted/10-ply yarn. Measurements and yarn requirements do not include joining and edging.*

| Puffy Flower | | | |
|---|---|---|---|
| | **BABY** | **LAP** | **BED** |
| **A** | 180 yds/165 m | 315 yds/288 m | 770 yds/704 m |
| **B** | 540 yds/494 m | 945 yds/864 m | 2310 yds/2112 m |
| **C** | 720 yds/658 m | 1260 yds/1152 m | 3080 yds/2816 m |

| Puffy Flower 2 | | | |
|---|---|---|---|
| | **BABY** | **LAP** | **BED** |
| **A** | 180 yds/165 m | 315 yds/288 m | 770 yds/704 m |
| **B** | 540 yds/494 m | 945 yds/864 m | 2310 yds/2112 m |
| **C** | 720 yds/658 m | 1260 yds/1152 m | 3080 yds/2816 m |

| Puffy Picot Flower | | | |
|---|---|---|---|
| | **BABY** | **LAP** | **BED** |
| **A** | 180 yds/165 m | 315 yds/288 m | 770 yds/704 m |
| **B** | 576 yds/527 m | 1008 yds/922 m | 2464 yds/2253 m |
| **C** | 720 yds/658 m | 1260 yds/1152 m | 3080 yds/2816 m |

## STITCH VARIATION

## Puffy Picot Flower

- A:  5 yds/4.6 m
- B:  16 yds/14.6 m
- C:  20 yds/18.3 m

• **SKILL LEVEL:** *Intermediate*

## Method

**SPECIAL STITCHES:**

• Puff Stitch—PS: Draw up loop to the height of a hdc, (yo, insert hook into st and draw loop to height of a hdc) 4 times (9 loops on hook), yo and draw through all loops on hook, ch 1 pulling tight to close stitch.

• Picot: Ch 3, slip st into first ch.

**FOUNDATION RING:** Using Color A, ch 5 and join with slip st to form a ring.

**ROUND 1:** Ch 1, 8 sc into ring, join with slip st into first sc made. (8 sc.)

**ROUND 2:** *Work PS in sc, ch 3; rep from * 7 more times, join with slip st into top of first PS made. End Color A. (8 PS, 8 ch sps.)

**ROUND 3:** Join Color B in ch-3 sp, ch 3 (counts as 1 dc), * 3 dc, picot, 3 dc, ch 3, slip st in same sp, ** ch 1, slip st into next ch-3 sp; rep from * 6 more times, then from * to ** once more, ch 1, slip st into beginning slip st. End Color B. (64 sts, 8 picots, 16 ch.)

**ROUND 4:** Join Color C in PS of Round 2, ch 1, * work sc into PS over ch-1 sp of Round 3, ch 4; rep from * 7 more times, join with slip st into first sc made. (8 sts, 8 ch sps.)

**ROUND 5:** Ch 3 (counts as 1 dc), * (3 dc, tr, 3 dc) in next ch-4 sp, dc in sc, 5 dc in next ch-4 sp **, dc in sc; rep from * twice more, then from * to ** once more, join with slip st into top of beginning ch. (56 sts.)

**ROUND 6:** Ch 3 (counts as 1 dc), dc in each st to corner tr, (dc, tr, dc) in tr; rep from * 3 more times, dc in each st to end of round, join with slip st into top of beginning ch. End Color C. (64 sts.)

**ROUND 7:** Join Color B tbl, ch 1 and sc tbl in same st, * sc tbl in each dc to corner tr, work (sc tbl, hdc tbl, sc tbl) in corner tr; rep from * 3 more times, sc tbl to end of round, join with slip st into first sc made. End Color B. (72 sts.)

# Connect Four

● A: 7 yds/6.4 m
◐ B: 16 yds/14.6 m
○ C: 7 yds/6.4 m
◐ D: 7 yds/6.4 m
◑ E: 7 yds/6.4 m

• **SKILL LEVEL:** *Beginner*

## Method

**FIRST SQUARE**

**FOUNDATION RING:** Using Color A, ch 4 and join with slip st to form a ring.

**ROUND 1:** Ch 3 (counts as 1 dc), 2 dc into ring, ch 2, [3 dc into ring, ch 2] twice, 3 dc into ring, join with hdc to top of beginning ch (counts as ch 2). (12 sts, 4 ch sps.)

**ROUND 2:** Ch 3 (counts as 1 dc), 1 dc into same sp, * 1dc in each st across to corner ch-2 sp, (2 dc **, ch 2, 2 dc) into ch-2 sp; rep from * twice more, then from * to ** once more, join with hdc into top of beginning ch (counts as ch 2). End Color A. (28 sts, 4 ch sps.)

**ROUND 3:** Join Color B, ch 1, sc in same space, * sc in each st across to ch-2 sp, (sc, hdc, sc) in ch-2 sp; rep from * 3 more times, join with slip st into first st made. End Color B. (40 sts.)

**SECOND SQUARE:** Follow instructions for First Square using Color C for Rounds 1 and 2 and Color B for Round 3.

**THIRD SQUARE:** Follow instructions for First Square using Color D for Rounds 1 and 2 and Color B for Round 3.

**FOURTH SQUARE:** Follow instructions for First Square using Color E for Rounds 1 and 2 and Color B for Round 3.

**JOIN SQUARES:** Join squares by holding squares with RS facing. Using Color B sew in overcast stitch through back loops.

Connect Four

Connect Four 2

**COLOR VARIATION**

## Connect Four 2

● A: 7 yds/6.4 m
◐ B: 16 yds/14.6 m
○ C: 7 yds/6.4 m
◐ D: 7 yds/6.4 m
◑ E: 7 yds/6.4 m

**FIRST SQUARE:** Follow instructions for First Square using Color A for Rounds 1 and 2 and Color E for Round 3.

**SECOND SQUARE:** Follow instructions for First Square using Color C for Rounds 1 and 2 and Color E for Round 3.

**THIRD SQUARE:** Follow instructions for First Square using Color D for Rounds 1 and 2 and Color E for Round 3.

**FOURTH SQUARE:** Follow instructions for First Square using Color B for Rounds 1 and 2 and Color E for Round 3.

**JOINING:** Join squares in the same way using Color E.

Square of Four

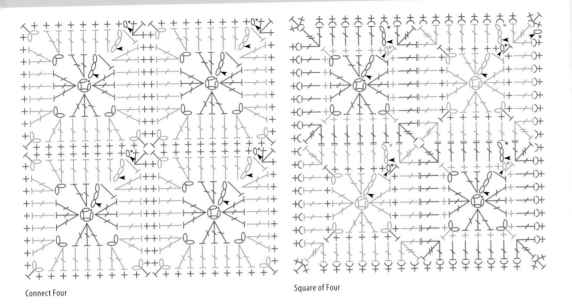

Connect Four

Square of Four

## Yarn requirement for throws

**NOTE:** *All yarn requirements are estimated using an H-size (5 mm) crochet hook and worsted/10-ply yarn. Measurements and yarn requirements do not include joining and edging.*

### Connect Four

|   | BABY | LAP | BED |
|---|------|-----|-----|
| A | 252 yds/230 m | 441 yds/403 m | 1078 yds/986 m |
| B | 576 yds/527 m | 1008 yds/922 m | 2464 yds/2253 m |
| C | 252 yds/230 m | 441 yds/403 m | 1078 yds/986 m |
| D | 252 yds/230 m | 441 yds/403 m | 1078 yds/986 m |
| E | 252 yds/230 m | 441 yds/403 m | 1078 yds/986 m |

### Connect Four 2

|   | BABY | LAP | BED |
|---|------|-----|-----|
| A | 252 yds/230 m | 441 yds/403 m | 1078 yds/986 m |
| B | 576 yds/527 m | 1008 yds/922 m | 2464 yds/2253 m |
| C | 252 yds/230 m | 441 yds/403 m | 1078 yds/986 m |
| D | 252 yds/230 m | 441 yds/403 m | 1078 yds/986 m |
| E | 252 yds/230 m | 441 yds/403 m | 1078 yds/986 m |

### Square of Four

|   | BABY | LAP | BED |
|---|------|-----|-----|
| A | 288 yds/263 m | 504 yds/461 m | 1232 yds/1127 m |
| B | 612 yds/560 m | 1071 yds/979 m | 2618 yds/2394 m |
| C | 288 yds/263 m | 504 yds/461 m | 1232 yds/1127 m |
| D | 288 yds/263 m | 504 yds/461 m | 1232 yds/1127 m |
| E | 288 yds/263 m | 504 yds/461 m | 1232 yds/1127 m |

## STITCH VARIATION

## Square of Four

- **SKILL LEVEL:** *Beginner*

## Method

**FIRST SQUARE**

**FOUNDATION RING:** Using Color A, ch 4 and join with slip st to form a ring.

**ROUND 1:** Ch 3 (counts as 1 dc), 2 dc into ring, ch 2, [3 dc into ring, ch 2] twice, 3 dc into ring, join with hdc to top of beginning ch (counts as ch 2). End Color A. (12 sts, 4 ch sps.)

**ROUND 2:** Join Color B, ch 1, sc in same space, * sc in each st across to corner ch-2 sp, work sc, hdc **, sc in corner ch-2 sp; rep from * twice more, then from * to ** once more, join with slip st into first sc made. End Color B. (24 sts.)

**ROUND 3:** Join Color A, ch 3 (counts as 1 dc), dc in next 4 sts, * (dc, tr, dc) in hdc **, sc in next 5 sts; rep from * twice more, then from * to ** once more, join with slip st into top of beginning ch. End Color A. (32 sts.)

- A: 8 yds/7.3 m
- B: 17 yds/15.5 m
- C: 8 yds/7.3 m
- D: 8 yds/7.3 m
- E: 8 yds/7.3 m

**SECOND SQUARE:** Follow instructions for First Square using Color C for Rounds 1 and 3 and Color B for Round 2.

**THIRD SQUARE:** Follow instructions for First Square using Color D for Rounds 1 and 3 and Color B for Round 2.

**FOURTH SQUARE:** Follow instructions for First Square using Color E for Rounds 1 and 3 and Color B for Round 2.

**JOIN SQUARES:** Join squares by using the Woven Stitch method.

**EDGING:** Join Color B in any corner tr, 1ch sc, hdc, sc in same, sc in each st to corner tr, (sc, hdc, sc) in tr, rep from * twice, sc in each st to start of round, join to first sc made. End Color B. (76 sts.)

# Magic Carpet

• **SKILL LEVEL:** *Beginner*

## Method

**FOUNDATION RING:** Using Color A, make a Magic Ring.

**ROUND 1:** Ch 1, 12 sc into ring, join into first st made. End Color A. (12 sts.)

**ROUND 2:** Join Color B, ch 1, *(sc, hdc, sc) in next st, sc into next 2 sts; rep from * 3 more times, join with slip st into first sc made. End Color B. (20 sts.)

**ROUND 3:** Join Color C in corner hdc, ch 1, * (sc, hdc, sc) in hdc, sc in each st to next corner hdc; rep from * 3 more times, join with slip st into first sc made. End Color C. (28 sts.)

**ROUND 4:** Using Color D, rep Round 3. (36 sts.)

**ROUND 5:** Using Color E, rep Round 3. (44 sts.)

**ROUND 6:** Using Color F, rep Round 3. (52 sts.)

**ROUND 7:** Using Color G, rep Round 3. (60 sts.)

**ROUND 8:** Using Color H, rep Round 3. (68 sts.)

**ROUND 9:** Using Color I, rep Round 3. (76 sts.)

**ROUND 10:** Using Color B, rep Round 3. (84 sts.)

**ROUND 11:** Using Color A, rep Round 3. (92 sts.)

A: 9 yds/8.2 m
B: 8 yds/7.3 m
C: 3 yds/2.7 m
D: 3 yds/2.7 m
E: 4 yds/3.7 m
F: 4 yds/3.7 m
G: 5 yds/4.6 m
H: 5 yds/4.6 m
I: 5 yds/4.6 m

Magic Carpet

Magic Carpet 2

**COLOR VARIATION**

## Magic Carpet 2

Follow the written instructions or the chart, using colors as follows:

**FOUNDATION RING:** Color A
**ROUND 1:** Color A
**ROUND 2:** Color B
**ROUND 3:** Color C
**ROUND 4:** Color D
**ROUND 5:** Color E
**ROUND 6:** Color F
**ROUND 7:** Color G
**ROUND 8:** Color H
**ROUND 9:** Color I
**ROUND 10:** Color A
**ROUND 11:** Color B

A: 9 yds/8.2 m
B: 8 yds/7.3 m
C: 3 yds/2.7 m
D: 3 yds/2.7 m
E: 4 yds/3.7 m
F: 4 yds/3.7 m
G: 5 yds/4.6 m
H: 5 yds/4.6 m
I: 5 yds/4.6 m

Flying Carpet

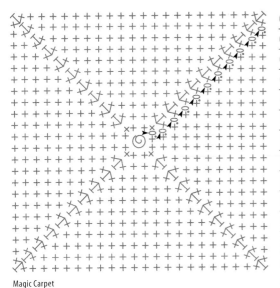

Magic Carpet

Flying Carpet

## STITCH VARIATION

## Flying Carpet

- **SKILL LEVEL:** *Beginner*

## Method

**FOUNDATION RING:** Using Color A, make a Magic Ring.

**ROUND 1:** Ch 1, 8 sc into ring, join with slip st into first sc made. (8 sts.)

**ROUND 2:** Ch 1, * (sc, ch 2, sc) in next st, sc in next st; rep from * 3 more times, join with slip st into first st made. End Color A. (12 sts, 4 ch sps.)

**ROUND 3:** Join Color B in corner ch sp, ch 1, (sc, ch 2, sc) in same space, * [ch 1, skip 1 st, sc in next st] to corner ch-2 sp, ch 1 **, skip 1 st, (sc, ch 2, sc) in corner ch-2; rep from * twice more, then from * to ** once more, join with slip st into first st made. End Color B. (12 sts, 12 ch sps.)

**ROUND 4:** Using Color C, rep Round 3. (16 sts, 16 ch sps.)

- A: 9 yds/8.2 m
- B: 7 yds/6.4 m
- C: 8 yds/7.3 m
- D: 16 yds/2.7 m
- E: 10 yds/3.7 m

**ROUND 5:** Using Color D, rep Round 3. (20 sts, 20 ch sps.)

**ROUND 6:** Using Color E, rep Round 3. (24 sts, 24 ch sps.)

**ROUND 7:** Using Color A, rep Round 3. (28 sts, 28 ch sps.)

**ROUND 8:** Using Color C, rep Round 3. (32 sts, 32 ch sps.)

**ROUND 9:** Using Color B, rep Round 3. (36 sts, 36 ch sps.)

**ROUND 10:** Using Color E, rep Round 3. (40 sts, 40 ch sps.)

**ROUND 11:** Using Color D, rep Round 3. (44 sts, 44 ch sps.)

**ROUND 12:** Using Color C, rep Round 3. (48 sts, 48 ch sps.)

## Yarn requirement for throws

**NOTE:** *All yarn requirements are estimated using an H-size (5 mm) crochet hook and worsted/10-ply yarn. Measurements and yarn requirements do not include joining and edging.*

### Magic Carpet

|   | BABY | LAP | BED |
|---|------|-----|-----|
| A | 324 yds/296 m | 567 yds/518 m | 1386 yds/1267 m |
| B | 288 yds/263 m | 504 yds/461 m | 1232 yds/1127 m |
| C | 108 yds/99 m | 189 yds/173 m | 462 yds/422 m |
| D | 108 yds/99 m | 189 yds/173 m | 462 yds/422 m |
| E | 144 yds/132 m | 252 yds/230 m | 616 yds/563 m |
| F | 144 yds/132 m | 252 yds/230 m | 616 yds/563 m |
| G | 180 yds/165 m | 315 yds/288 m | 770 yds/704 m |
| H | 180 yds/165 m | 315 yds/288 m | 770 yds/704 m |
| I | 180 yds/165 m | 315 yds/288 m | 770 yds/704 m |

### Magic Carpet 2

|   | BABY | LAP | BED |
|---|------|-----|-----|
| A | 324 yds/296 m | 567 yds/518 m | 1386 yds/1267 m |
| B | 288 yds/263 m | 504 yds/461 m | 1232 yds/1127 m |
| C | 108 yds/99 m | 189 yds/173 m | 462 yds/422 m |
| D | 108 yds/99 m | 189 yds/173 m | 462 yds/422 m |
| E | 144 yds/132 m | 252 yds/230 m | 616 yds/563 m |
| F | 144 yds/132 m | 252 yds/230 m | 616 yds/563 m |
| G | 180 yds/165 m | 315 yds/288 m | 770 yds/704 m |
| H | 180 yds/165 m | 315 yds/288 m | 770 yds/704 m |
| I | 180 yds/165 m | 315 yds/288 m | 770 yds/704 m |

### Flying Carpet

|   | BABY | LAP | BED |
|---|------|-----|-----|
| A | 324 yds/296 m | 567 yds/518 m | 1386 yds/1267 m |
| B | 252 yds/230 m | 441 yds/403 m | 1078 yds/986 m |
| C | 288 yds/263 m | 504 yds/461 m | 1232 yds/1127 m |
| D | 576 yds/527 m | 1008 yds/922 m | 2464 yds/2253 m |
| E | 360 yds/329 m | 630 yds/576 m | 1540 yds/1408 m |

# Octagon-framed Flower

• **SKILL LEVEL:** *Intermediate*

## Method

**SPECIAL STITCH**

• Cluster—Cl: Work tr in next 3 stitches, leaving last 2 loops of each stitch on hook (7 loops on hook), yo, pull through all loops on hook, ch 1 to close the Cluster. The ch-1 counts as the top of the stitch.

**FOUNDATION RING:** Using Color A, ch 5, join to form a ring.

**ROUND 1:** Ch 1, 16 sc into ring, join with slip st into first sc made. (16 sc.)

**ROUND 2:** Join Color B, ch 3 (counts as 1 dc), 2 dc in same sp, * ch 3, skip 1 st, 3 dc in next st; rep from * 6 more times, ch 3, join with slip st into top of beginning ch. (24 sts, 8 ch sps.)

**ROUND 3:** Ch 3, *Cl over next 3 sts, ch 3, slip st in ch-3 sp **, ch 3; rep from * 6 more times, then from * to ** once more. End Color B. (8 Cl, 16 ch sps.)

**ROUND 4:** Join Color C in ch-3 sp of Round 2, ch 4 (counts as 1 tr), 2 dc in same st, * sc in top of Cl, (2 dc, tr, 2 dc) in next ch-3 sp of Round 2; rep from * 6 more times, sc in top of next Cl, 2 dc in next ch-3 sp of Round 2, join with slip st into top of beginning ch. End Color C. (48 sts.)

**ROUND 5:** Join Color D in corner tr, ch 1, 3 sc in same sp, * sc in each st to next tr, 3 sc in next tr; rep from * 6 more times, sc in each st to end of round, join with slip st into first sc made. End Color D. (64 sts.)

**ROUND 6:** Join Color E in 2nd sc of corner 3 sc, ch 1, sc in same st, sc in next st, * hdc in next st, dc in next st, tr in next st, (tr, ch 3, tr) in next st, tr in next st, dc in next st, hdc in next st **, sc in next 9 sts; rep from * twice more, then from * to ** once more, sc in next 7 sts, join with slip st into first sc made. End Color E. (68 sts, 4 ch sps.)

**ROUND 7:** Join Color F in side of square, ch 1, * sc in each st to corner ch-3 sp, (2 sc, hdc, 2 sc) in ch-3 sp; rep from * 3 more times, sc in each st to end of round, join with slip st into first sc made. End Color F. (88 sts.)

A:  2 yds/1.8 m
B:  9 yds/8.2 m
C:  8 yds/7.3 m
D:  5 yds/4.6 m
E:  7 yds/6.4 m
F:  6 yds/5.5 m

Octagon-framed Flower

Octagon-framed Flower 2

## COLOR VARIATION

### Octagon-framed Flower 2

Follow the written instructions or the chart, using colors as follows:

A:  2 yds/1.8 m
B:  9 yds/8.2 m
C:  8 yds/7.3 m
D:  5 yds/4.6 m
E:  7 yds/6.4 m
F:  6 yds/5.5 m

Octagon Flower

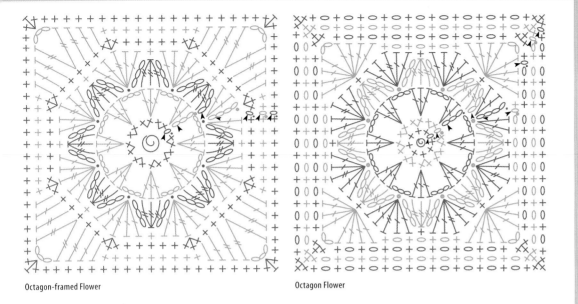

Octagon-framed Flower

Octagon Flower

---

## STITCH VARIATION

## Octagon Flower

• **SKILL LEVEL:** *Intermediate*

## Method

**SPECIAL STITCH**
• Cluster—Cl: Made of 3 tr, ch 1.
**FOUNDATION RING:** Using Color A, make a Magic Ring.
**ROUND 1:** Ch 1, 8 sc into ring, join with slip st into first sc made. (8 sc.)
**ROUND 2:** Ch 1, 2 sc in each st around, join with slip st into first sc made. End Color A. (16 sc.)
**ROUND 3:** Join Color B, ch 3 (counts as 1 dc), 2 dc in same sp, * ch 3, skip 1 st, 3 dc in next st; rep from * 6 more times, ch 3, join with slip st into top of beginning ch. (24 sts, 8 ch sps.)
**ROUND 4:** Ch 3, *Cl over next 3 sts, ch 3, slip st in ch-3 sp **, ch 3: rep from * 7 more times, then from * to ** once more. End Color C. (8 Cl, 16 ch sps.)
**ROUND 5:** Join Color C in ch-3 sp of Round 3, ch 4 (counts as 1 tr), 2 dc in same sp, * sc in top of Cl, (2 dc, tr, 2 dc) in next ch-3 sp of Round 3; rep from * 6 more times, sc in top of next Cl, 2 dc in next ch-3 sp of Round 3, join with slip st into top of beginning ch. End Color C. (48 sts.)

**ROUND 6:** Join Color A, ch 1, sc in same sp, * skip 2 sts, (4 dc, ch 2, 4 dc) in next st, skip 2 sts, [sc in next st, ch 1, skip 1 st] 3 times **, sc in next st; rep from * 3 more times, then from * to ** once more, join with slip st into first sc made. End Color A. (48 sts, 16 ch sps.)
**ROUND 7:** Join Color D in st before corner ch-2 sp, sc in same sp, * 3 sc in corner ch-2 sp, [sc in next st, ch 1, skip 1 st] 7 times **, sc in next st; rep from * twice more, then from * to ** once more, join with slip st into first sc made. End Color D. (44 sts, 28 ch sps.)
**ROUND 8:** Join Color E in 2nd st of corner 3 sc, ch 1, 3 sc in same st, * [ch 1, skip 1 st, sc in next st] 8 times, ch 1, skip 1 st **, 3 sc in next st; rep from * twice more, then from * to ** once more, ch 1, join with slip st into first sc made. End Color E. (44 sts, 36 ch sps.)
**ROUND 9:** Join Color F in 2nd st of corner 3 sc, ch 1, 3 sc in same st, [sc in next st, ch 1, skip 1 st] 9 times, sc in next st **, 3 sc in next st; rep from * twice more, then from * to ** once more, join with slip st into first sc made. End Color F. (52 sts, 36 ch sps.)

○ A: 10 yds/9.1 m
● B: 9 yds/8.2 m
● C: 8 yds/7.3 m
○ D: 5 yds/4.6 m
◐ E: 5 yds/4.6 m
◑ F: 5 yds/4.6 m

## Yarn requirement for throws

**NOTE:** *All yarn requirements are estimated using an H-size (5 mm) crochet hook and worsted/10-ply yarn. Measurements and yarn requirements do not include joining and edging.*

### Octagon-framed Flower

| | BABY | LAP | BED |
|---|---|---|---|
| **A** | 72 yds/66 m | 126 yds/115 m | 306 yds/280 m |
| **B** | 324 yds/296 m | 567 yds/518 m | 1386 yds/1267 m |
| **C** | 288 yds/263 m | 504 yds/461 m | 1232 yds/1127 m |
| **D** | 180 yds/165 m | 315 yds/288 m | 770 yds/704 m |
| **E** | 252 yds/230 m | 441 yds/403 m | 1078 yds/986 m |
| **F** | 216 yds/198 m | 378 yds/346 m | 924 yds/845 m |

### Octagon-framed Flower 2

| | BABY | LAP | BED |
|---|---|---|---|
| **A** | 72 yds/66 m | 126 yds/115 m | 306 yds/280 m |
| **B** | 324 yds/296 m | 567 yds/518 m | 1386 yds/1267 m |
| **C** | 288 yds/263 m | 504 yds/461 m | 1232 yds/1127 m |
| **D** | 180 yds/165 m | 315 yds/288 m | 770 yds/704 m |
| **E** | 252 yds/230 m | 441 yds/403 m | 1078 yds/986 m |
| **F** | 216 yds/198 m | 378 yds/346 m | 924 yds/845 m |

### Octagon Flower

| | BABY | LAP | BED |
|---|---|---|---|
| **A** | 360 yds/329 m | 630 yds/576 m | 1540 yds/1408 m |
| **B** | 324 yds/296 m | 567 yds/518 m | 1386 yds/1267 m |
| **C** | 288 yds/263 m | 504 yds/461 m | 1232 yds/1127 m |
| **D** | 180 yds/165 m | 315 yds/288 m | 770 yds/704 m |
| **E** | 180 yds/165 m | 315 yds/288 m | 770 yds/704 m |
| **F** | 180 yds/165 m | 315 yds/288 m | 770 yds/704 m |

# Diagonal Bobbles

- ● A: 2 yds/1.8 m
- ● B: 3 yds/2.7 m
- ● C: 3 yds/2.7 m
- ● D: 4 yds/3.7 m
- ● E: 6 yds/5.5 m
- F: 4 yds/3.7 m
- ● G: 5 yds/4.6 m

• **SKILL LEVEL:** *Beginner*

## Method

**SPECIAL STITCHES:**
• Bobble—B: Made of 5 tr.
• Dec3tog: [Insert hook into next st, yo and draw through a loop] 3 times (4 loops on hook), yo and draw though all loops on hook. (2 sts decreased)

**FOUNDATION ROW:** Using Color A, ch 2.

**ROW 1:** Work 3 sc in 2nd ch from hook, turn. (3 sts.)

**ROW 2:** Ch 1, 2 sc in first st, sc in each st to last st, 2 sc in last st, turn. (5 sts.)

**ROW 3:** Repeat Row 2. End Color A. (7 sts.)

**ROW 4:** Join Color B, repeat Row 2. (9 sts.)

**ROW 5:** Ch 1, sc in each st across. (9 sts.)

**ROW 6:** Repeat Row 2. End Color B. (11 sts.)

**ROW 7:** Join Color C, repeat Row 2. (13 sts.)

**ROW 8:** Repeat Row 2. (15 sts.)

**ROW 9:** Repeat Row 5. End Color C. (15 sts.)

**ROW 10:** Join Color D, repeat Row 2. (17 sts.)

**ROWS 11–12:** Repeat Row 2. End Color D. (21 sts.)

**ROW 13:** Join Color E, repeat Row 5. (21 sts.)

**ROWS 14–15:** Repeat Row 2. End Color E. (25 sts.)

**ROW 16:** Join Color F, repeat Row 2. End Color F. (27 sts.)

**ROW 17:** Join Color G, 2 sc in first st, [make B in next st, sc in next 2 sts] 8 times, make B in next st, 2 sc in last st, turn. End Color G. (29 sts.)

**ROW 18:** Join Color F, ch 1, skip 1 st, sc in each st to last 2 sts, skip 1 st, sc in last st. End Color F. (27 sts.)

**ROW 19:** Join Color E and repeat Row 18. (25 sts.)

**ROW 20:** Repeat Row 18. (23 sts.)

**ROW 21:** Repeat Row 5. End Color E. (23 sts.)

**ROW 22:** Join Color D, repeat Row 18. (21 sts.)

**ROWS 23–24:** Repeat Row 18. End Color D. (17 sts.)

**ROW 25:** Join Color C, repeat Row 5. (17 sts.)

**ROWS 26–27:** Repeat Row 18. End Color C. (13 sts.)

**ROW 28:** Join Color B, repeat Row 18. (11 sts.)

**ROW 29:** Repeat Row 5. (11 sts.)

**ROW 30:** Repeat Row 18. End Color B. (9 sts.)

**ROW 31:** Join Color A, repeat Row 18. (7 sts.)

**ROWS 32–33:** Repeat Row 18. (3 sts.)

**ROW 34:** Dec3tog. End Color A. (1 st.)

Diagonal Bobbles

Diagonal Bobbles 2

## COLOR VARIATION

### Diagonal Bobbles 2

- ● A: 8 yds/7.3 m
- B: 4 yds/3.7 m
- ● C: 5 yds/4.6 m
- ● D: 8 yds/7.3 m

Follow the written instructions or the chart, using colors as follows:

**ROWS 1–14:** Color A
**ROWS 15–16:** Color B
**ROW 17:** Color C
**ROWS 18–19:** Color B
**ROWS 20–34:** Color D

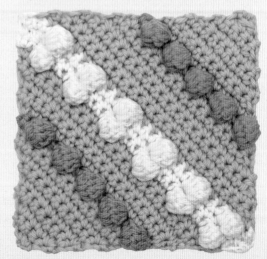

Multi Diagonal Bobbles

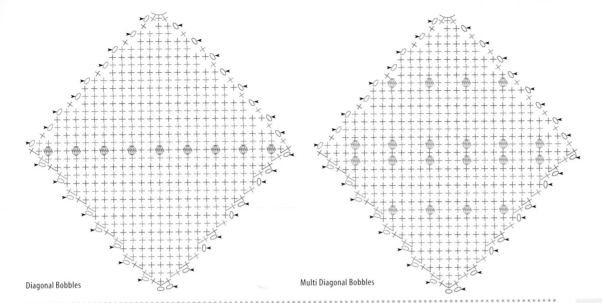

Diagonal Bobbles

Multi Diagonal Bobbles

## STITCH VARIATION

## Multi Diagonal Bobbles

- **SKILL LEVEL:** *Beginner*

- A: 11 yds/10 m
- B: 3 yds/2.7 m
- C: 10 yds/9.1 m
- D: 3 yds/2.7 m

## Method

**SPECIAL STITCHES:**

• Bobble—B: Made of 5 tr.

• Dec3tog: [Insert hook into next st, yo and draw through a loop] 3 times (4 loops on hook), yo and draw though all loops on hook. (2 sts decreased.)

**FOUNDATION ROW:** Using Color A, ch 2.

**ROW 1:** Work 3 sc in 2nd ch from hook, turn. (3 sts.)

**ROW 2:** Ch 1, 2 sc in first st, sc in each st to last st, 2 sc in last st, turn. (5 sts.)

**ROWS 3–4:** Repeat Row 2. (2 sts increased on each row—9 sts.)

**ROW 5:** Ch 1, sc in each st across. (9 sts.)

**ROWS 6–8:** Repeat Row 2. (2 sts increased on each row—15 sts.)

**ROW 9:** Repeat Row 5. End Color A. (15 sts.)

**ROW 10:** Join Color B, ch 1, 2 sc in first st, [make B in next st, sc in next 3 sts] 3 times, make B in next st, 2 sc in last st, turn. End Color B. (17 sts.)

**ROW 11:** Join Color A, repeat Row 2. (19 sts.)

**ROW 12:** Repeat Row 2. (21 sts.)

**ROW 13:** Repeat Row 5. (21 sts.)

**ROWS 14–15:** Repeat Row 2. End Color A. (2 sts increased on each row—25 sts.)

**ROW 16:** Join Color C, ch 1, 2 sc in first st, sc in next st, [make B in next st, sc in next 3 sts] 5 times, make B in next st, 2 sc in last st, turn. (27 sts.)

**ROW 17:** Repeat Row 2. (29 sts.)

**ROW 18:** Ch 1, skip 1 st, sc in next 3 sts, [make B in next st, sc in next 3 sts] 5 times, make B in next st, sc in next 2 sts, skip 1 st, sc in last st. End Color C. (27 sts.)

**ROW 19:** Join Color A, ch 1, skip 1 st, sc in each st to last 2 sts, skip 1 st, sc in last st. (25 sts.)

**ROW 20:** Repeat Row 19. (23 sts.)

**ROW 21:** Repeat Row 5. (23 sts.)

**ROWS 22–24:** Repeat Row 19. (2 sts decreased each row—17 sts.)

**ROW 25:** Repeat Row 5. End Color A. (17 sts.)

**ROW 26:** Join Color D, ch 1, skip 1 st, sc in next st, [make B in next st, sc in next 3 sts] 3 times, make B in next st, skip 1 st, sc in last st. End Color D. (15 sts.)

**ROW 27:** Join Color A, repeat Row 19. (13 sts.)

**ROW 28:** Repeat Row 19. (11 sts.)

**ROW 29:** Repeat Row 5. (11 sts.)

**ROWS 30–33:** Repeat Row 19. (2 sts decreased each row—3 sts.)

**ROW 34:** Dec3tog. End Color A. (1 st.)

## Yarn requirement for throws

**NOTE:** *All yarn requirements are estimated using an H-size (5 mm) crochet hook and worsted/10-ply yarn. Measurements and yarn requirements do not include joining and edging.*

### Diagonal Bobbles

|   | BABY | LAP | BED |
|---|------|-----|-----|
| A | 72 yds/66 m | 126 yds/115 m | 308 yds/282 m |
| B | 108 yds/99 m | 189 yds/173 m | 462 yds/422 m |
| C | 108 yds/99 m | 189 yds/173 m | 462 yds/422 m |
| D | 144 yds/132 m | 252 yds/230 m | 616 yds/563 m |
| E | 216 yds/198 m | 378 yds/346 m | 924 yds/845 m |
| F | 144 yds/132 m | 252 yds/230 m | 616 yds/563 m |
| G | 180 yds/165 m | 315 yds/288 m | 770 yds/704 m |

### Diagonal Bobbles 2

|   | BABY | LAP | BED |
|---|------|-----|-----|
| A | 288 yds/263 m | 504 yds/461 m | 1232 yds/1127 m |
| B | 144 yds/132 m | 252 yds/230 m | 616 yds/563 m |
| C | 180 yds/165 m | 315 yds/288 m | 770 yds/704 m |
| D | 288 yds/263 m | 504 yds/461 m | 1232 yds/1127 m |

### Multi Diagonal Bobbles

|   | BABY | LAP | BED |
|---|------|-----|-----|
| A | 396 yds/362 m | 693 yds/634 m | 1694 yds/1549 m |
| B | 108 yds/99 m | 189 yds/173 m | 462 yds/422 m |
| C | 360 yds/329 m | 630 yds/576 m | 1540 yds/1408 m |
| D | 108 yds/99 m | 189 yds/173 m | 462 yds/422 m |

# Savannah Sunrise

| | | |
|---|---|---|
| ● | A: | 7 yds/6.4 m |
| ○ | B: | 8 yds/7.3 m |
| ● | C: | 8 yds/7.3 m |
| ○ | D: | 4 yds/3.7 m |
| ● | E: | 5 yds/4.6 m |

• **SKILL LEVEL:** *Beginner*

## Method

**FOUNDATION RING:** Using Color A, make a Magic Ring.

**ROW 1 (WS):** Ch 3 (counts as 1 dc), dc, tr, 2 dc in ring, turn. (5 sts.)

**ROW 2 (RS):** Ch 3 (counts as 1 dc), dc in next st, (2 dc, tr, 2 dc) in tr, dc in next 2 sts, turn. End Color A. (9 sts.)

**ROW 3:** Join Color B, ch 3 (counts as 1 dc), dc in each st to tr, (2 dc, tr, 2 dc) in tr, dc in each st to end of row, turn. (13 sts.)

**ROW 4:** Rep Row 3. End Color B. (17 sts.)

**ROW 5:** Join Color C, rep Row 3. End Color C. (21 sts.)

**ROW 6:** Join Color D, ch 1 and sc in same place, sc in each st to tr, 3 sc in tr, sc in each st to end of row, turn. End Color D. (23 sts.)

**ROW 7:** Join Color E and rep Row 6. End Color E. (25 sts.)

**ROW 8:** Join Color A, ch 3 (counts as 1 dc), dc in next 11 sts, (2 dc, tr, 2 dc) in next st, dc in each st to end, turn. End Color A. (29 sts.)

**ROW 9:** Join Color B and rep Row 3. End Color B. (33 sts.)

**ROW 10:** Join Color C and rep Row 3. End Color C. (37 sts.)

**ROW 11:** Join Color D and rep Row 6. End Color D. (39 sts.)

**ROW 12:** Join Color E and rep Row 6. End Color E. (41 sts.)

Savannah Sunrise

## COLOR VARIATION

### Savannah Sunrise 2

Follow the written instructions or the chart, using colors as follows:

| | | |
|---|---|---|
| ● | A: | 7 yds/6.4 m |
| ● | B: | 8 yds/7.3 m |
| ○ | C: | 8 yds/7.3 m |
| ● | D: | 4 yds/3.7 m |
| ○ | E: | 5 yds/4.6 m |

Savannah Sunrise 2

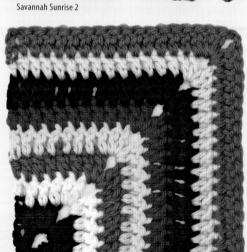

Savannah Sunset

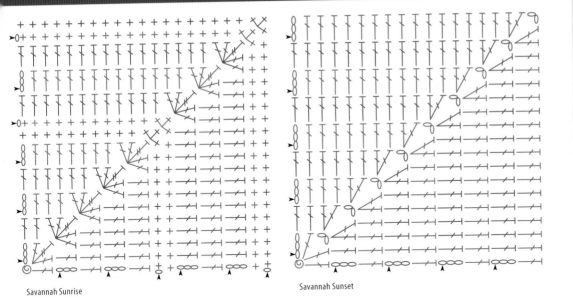

Savannah Sunrise          Savannah Sunset

## Yarn requirement for throws

**NOTE:** *All yarn requirements are estimated using an H-size (5 mm) crochet hook and worsted/10-ply yarn. Measurements and yarn requirements do not include joining and edging.*

**Savannah Sunrise**

|   | BABY | LAP | BED |
|---|------|-----|-----|
| A | 234 yds/214 m | 410 yds/375 m | 1001 yds/915 m |
| B | 288 yds/263 m | 504 yds/461 m | 1232 yds/1127 m |
| C | 288 yds/263 m | 504 yds/461 m | 1232 yds/1127 m |
| D | 144 yds/132 m | 252 yds/230 m | 616 yds/563 m |
| E | 180 yds/165 m | 315 yds/288 m | 770 yds/704 m |

**Savannah Sunrise 2**

|   | BABY | LAP | BED |
|---|------|-----|-----|
| A | 234 yds/214 m | 410 yds/375 m | 1001 yds/915 m |
| B | 288 yds/263 m | 504 yds/461 m | 1232 yds/1127 m |
| C | 288 yds/263 m | 504 yds/461 m | 1232 yds/1127 m |
| D | 144 yds/132 m | 252 yds/230 m | 616 yds/563 m |
| E | 180 yds/165 m | 315 yds/288 m | 770 yds/704 m |

**Savannah Sunset**

|   | BABY | LAP | BED |
|---|------|-----|-----|
| A | 216 yds/198 m | 378 yds/346 m | 924 yds/845 m |
| B | 72 yds/66 m | 126 yds/115 m | 308 yds/282 m |
| C | 216 yds/197 m | 378 yds/346 m | 924 yds/845 m |
| D | 252 yds/230 m | 441 yds/403 m | 1078 yds/986 m |
| E | 252 yds/230 m | 441 yds/403 m | 1078 yds/986 m |

## STITCH VARIATION

## Savannah Sunset

- **SKILL LEVEL:** *Beginner*

## Method

**FOUNDATION RING:** Using Color A, make a Magic Ring.

**ROW 1 (WS):** Ch 3 (counts as 1 dc), dc, ch 2, 2 dc in ring, turn. (4 sts.)

**ROW 2 (RS):** Ch 3 (counts as 1 dc), dc in next st, (2 dc, ch 2, 2 dc) in ch-2 sp, dc in next 2 sts, turn. End Color A. (8 sts.)

**ROW 3:** Join Color B, ch 3 (counts as 1 dc), dc in each st to ch-2 sp, (2 dc, ch 2, 2 dc) in ch-2 sp, dc in each st to end of row, turn. End Color B. (12 sts.)

**ROW 4:** Join Color C, rep Row 3. End Color C. (16 sts.)

- ● A: 6 yds/5.5 m
- ○ B: 2 yds/1.8 m
- ◑ C: 6 yds/5.5 m
- ◔ D: 7 yds/6.4 m
- ◕ E: 7 yds/6.4 m

**ROW 5:** Join Color D, rep Row 3. End Color D. (20 sts.)

**ROW 6:** Join Color E, rep Row 3. End Color E. (24 sts.)

**ROW 7:** Join Color A and rep Row 3. End Color A. (28 sts.)

**ROW 8:** Join Color D, rep Row 3. End Color D. (32 sts.)

**ROW 9:** Join Color C and rep Row 3. End Color C. (36 sts.)

# Candy

• **SKILL LEVEL:** *Intermediate*

A: 10 yds/9.1 m
B: 5 yds/4.6 m
C: 13 yds/11.9 m
D: 7 yds/6.4 m

## Method

**SPECIAL STITCHES:**

• Beginning Cluster—Beg C: Made of ch 2, 3 dc, ch 1.

• Cluster—Cl: Made of 4 dc, ch 1.

• Puff Stitch—PS: Yo, insert hook into the ch sp, [yo, draw up a loop] 4 times, yo, draw through all loops on hook, ch 1 to close stitch.

**FOUNDATION RING:** Using Color A, ch 5 and join with slip st to form a ring.

**ROUND 1:** Beg C, * ch 3, Cl; rep from * 4 more times, ch 3, join with slip st into top of first Cl. End Color A. (6 Clusters, 6 ch sps.)

**ROUND 2:** Join Color B, ch 3 (counts as 1 dc), 1 dc into same space, * 4 dc in ch-3 sp **, 2 dc in top of Cl; rep from * 4 more times, then from * to ** once more, join with slip st into top of beginning ch. End Color B. (36 sts.)

**ROUND 3:** Join Color C, ch 3 (counts as 1 dc), * 2 dc in next st, dc in next 2 sts; rep from * 10 more times, 2 dc in next st, dc in next st, join with slip st into top of beginning ch. End Color C. (48 sts.)

**ROUND 4:** Join Color D, ch 1, sc in same space, sc in next st, * hdc in next 2 sts, dc in next 2 sts, (tr, ch 2, tr) in next st, dc in next 2 sts, hdc in next 2 sts **, sc in next 3 sts; rep from * twice more, then from * to ** once more, sc in next st, join with slip st into first sc made. End Color D. (52 sts, 4 ch sps.)

**ROUND 5:** Join Color A, ch 1, sc in same space, * sc in each st to ch-2 sp, (ch 2, PS, ch 2) in ch-2 sp; rep from * 3 more times, sc in each st to end of round, join with slip st into first sc made. End Color A. (52 sts, 4 [ch-2, PS, ch-2] corners.)

**ROUND 6:** Join Color C, ch 1, sc in same space, * sc in each st to ch-2 sp, 2 sc in ch-2 sp, sc in PS, 2 sc in ch-2 sp; rep from * 3 more times, sc in each st to end of round, join with slip st into first sc made. End Color C. (72 sts.)

Candy

Candy 2

## COLOR VARIATION

## Candy 2

Follow the written instructions or the chart, using colors as follows:

A: 10 yds/9.1 m
B: 5 yds/4.6 m
C: 7 yds/6.4 m
D: 7 yds/6.4 m
E: 6 yds/5.5 m

**FOUNDATION RING AND ROUND 1:** Color A
**ROUND 2:** Color B
**ROUND 3:** Color C

**ROUND 4:** Color D
**ROUND 5:** Color A
**ROUND 6:** Color E

Candy Frills

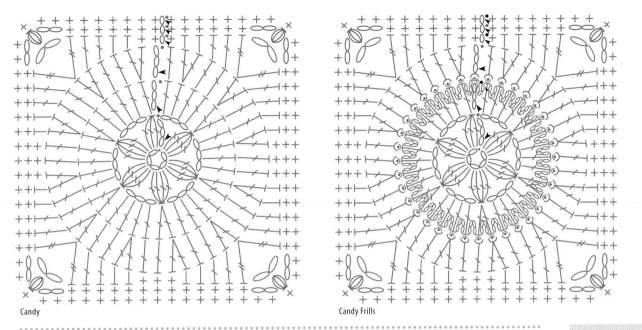

Candy

Candy Frills

---

## STITCH VARIATION

# Candy Frills

- **SKILL LEVEL:** *Advanced*

## Method

**SPECIAL STITCHES:**
- Beginning Cluster—Beg C: Made of ch 2, 3 dc, ch 1.
- Cluster—Cl: Made of 4 dc, ch 1.
- Puff Stitch—PS: Yo, insert hook into the ch sp, [yo, draw up a loop] 4 times, yo, draw through all loops on hook, ch 1 to close stitch.

**FOUNDATION RING:** Using Color A, ch 5 and join with slip st to form a ring.

**ROUND 1:** Beg C, * ch 3, Cl; rep from * 5 more times, ch 3 and join with slip st into top of first Cl. End Color A. (6 Clusters, 6 ch sps.)

**ROUND 2:** Join Color B, ch 3 (counts as 1 dc), 1 dc into same space, * 4 dc in ch-3 sp **, 2 dc in top of Cl; rep from * 4 more times, then from * to ** once more, join with slip st into Back Loop of top of beginning ch. (36 sts.)

**ROUND 3:** Working through Back Loops only, ch 3 (counts as 1 dc), * 2 dc tbl in next st, dc tbl in next 2 sts; rep from * 10 more times, 2 dc tbl in next st, dc tbl in next st, join with slip st in top of beginning ch. End Color C. (48 sts.)

**ROUND 4:** Join Color C, ch 1, sc in same space, sc in next st, * hdc in next 2 sts, dc in next 2 sts, (tr, ch 2, tr) in next st, dc in next 2 sts, hdc in next 2 sts **, sc in next 3 sts; rep from * twice more, then from * to ** once more, sc in next st, join with slip st into first sc made. End Color C. (52 sts, 4 ch sps.)

**ROUND 5:** Join Color D, ch 1, sc in same space, * sc in each st to ch-2 sp, (ch 2, PS, ch 2) in ch-2 sp; rep from * 3 more times, sc in each st to end of round, join with slip st into first sc made. End Color D. (54 sts, 4 [ch 2, PS, ch 2] corners.)

**ROUND 6:** Join Color A, ch 1, sc in same space, * sc in each st to ch-2 sp, 2 sc in ch sp, sc in PS, 2 sc in ch-2 sp; rep from * 3 more times, sc in each st to end of round, join with slip st into first sc made. End Color A. (72 sts.)

**SURFACE CROCHET:** Join Color E with slip st through Front Loop only of any st on Round 2, [ch 4, slip st into Front Loop of next stitch] 35 times, ch 4, join with slip st into first slip st made. End Color E. (36 ch sps, 36 slip sts.)

- A: 10 yds/9.1 m
- B: 12 yds/11 m
- C: 7 yds/6.4 m
- D: 6 yds/5.5 m
- E: 6 yds/5.5 m

## Yarn requirement for throws

**NOTE:** *All yarn requirements are estimated using an H-size (5 mm) crochet hook and worsted/10-ply yarn. Measurements and yarn requirements do not include joining and edging.*

### Candy

| | BABY | LAP | BED |
|---|---|---|---|
| A | 360 yds/329 m | 630 yds/576 m | 1540 yds/1408 m |
| B | 180 yds/165 m | 315 yds/288 m | 770 yds/704 m |
| C | 468 yds/428 m | 819 yds/749 m | 2002 yds/1831 m |
| D | 252 yds/230 m | 441 yds/403 m | 1076 yds/984 m |

### Candy 2

| | BABY | LAP | BED |
|---|---|---|---|
| A | 360 yds/329 m | 630 yds/576 m | 1540 yds/1408 m |
| B | 180 yds/165 m | 315 yds/288 m | 770 yds/704 m |
| C | 252 yds/230 m | 441 yds/403 m | 1076 yds/984 m |
| D | 252 yds/230 m | 441 yds/403 m | 1076 yds/984 m |
| E | 216 yds/198 m | 378 yds/346 m | 924 yds/845 m |

### Candy Frills

| | BABY | LAP | BED |
|---|---|---|---|
| A | 360 yds/329 m | 630 yds/576 m | 1540 yds/1408 m |
| B | 432 yds/395 m | 756 yds/691 m | 1848 yds/1690 m |
| C | 252 yds/230 m | 441 yds/403 m | 1078 yds/986 m |
| D | 216 yds/198 m | 378 yds/346 m | 924 yds/845 m |
| E | 216 yds/198 m | 378 yds/346 m | 924 yds/845 m |

# Lace Ripple

● A: 4 yds/3.7 m
● B: 4 yds/3.7 m
● C: 4 yds/3.7 m
|||| D: 12 yds/11 m

• **SKILL LEVEL:** *Intermediate*

## Method

**FOUNDATION ROW:** Using Color A, ch a multiple of 13 + 11 + 1 turning ch.

**ROW 1:** Beg with 2nd ch from hook, sc in next 5 chs, * 3 sc in next ch, sc in next 5 ch, skip 2 ch, sc in next 5 ch; rep from * to last 6 ch, 3 sc in next ch, sc in next 5 ch, turn. End Color A.

**ROW 2:** Join Color B, ch 1, skip first sc, sc in next 5 sts, * 3 sc in next st, sc in next 5 sts, skip 2 sts, sc in next 5 sts; rep from * to last 7 sts, 3 sc in next st, sc in next 4 sts, skip 1 st, sc in last st, turn. End Color B.

**ROW 3:** Join Color C, repeat Row 2. End Color C.

**ROW 4:** Join Color D, slip st into next st, ch 4 (counts as 1 dc, ch 1) in next st, skip 1 st, dc in next st, ch 1, skip 1 st, dc in next st, * (dc, ch 2, dc) in next st, dc in next st, [ch 1, skip 1 st, dc in next st] twice, skip 2 sts, dc in next st, [ch 1, skip 1 st, dc in next st] twice; rep from * to last 7 sts, (dc, ch 2, dc) in next st, dc in next st, ch 1, skip 1 st, dc in next st, ch 1, skip 2 sts, dc in last st, turn.

**ROW 5:** Slip st into ch-sp, ch 4 (counts as 1 dc, ch 1), skip 1 st, dc in ch-1 sp, ch 1, skip 1 st, dc in next st, * (dc, ch 2, dc) in next ch-2 sp, dc in next st, [ch 1, skip 1 st, dc in next ch-1 sp] twice, skip 2 sts, dc in next ch-1 sp, [ch 1, skip 1 st, dc in next ch-1 sp] twice; rep from * to last ch-2 sp, (dc, ch 2, dc) in next ch-2 sp, dc in next st, ch 1, skip 1 st, dc in ch-1 sp, ch 1, skip 1 st, dc in 3rd ch of beginning ch from previous row, turn.

**ROW 6:** Repeat Row 5. End Color D.

**ROW 7:** Join Color A, ch 1, skip 1 st, sc in next ch-1 sp, sc in next st, sc in next ch-1 sp, sc in next 2 sts, * 3 sc in ch-2 sp, sc in next 2 sts, sc in ch-1 sp, sc in next st, sc in next ch-1 sp, skip 2 sts, sc in next ch-1 sp, sc in next st, sc in ch-1 sp, sc in next 2 sts; rep from * to last ch-2 sp, 3 sc in ch-2 sp, sc in next 2 sts, sc in ch-1 sp, sc in next st, sc in 3rd ch of beginning ch from previous row, turn. End Color A.

**ROW 8:** Join Color B, repeat Row 2. End Color B.

**ROW 9:** Join Color C, repeat Row 2. End Color C.

**ROWS 10–12:** Join Color D, repeat Rows 4–6. End Color D.

Continue repeating Rows 7–12.

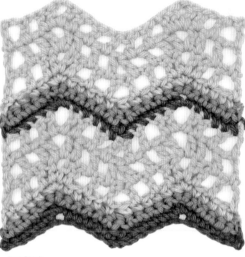

Lace Ripple

Lace Ripple 2

---

**COLOR VARIATION**

## Lace Ripple 2

Follow the written instructions or the chart, using colors as follows:

● A: 4 yds/3.7 m
● B: 4 yds/3.7 m
● C: 4 yds/3.7 m
● D: 12 yds/11 m

Lace Waves

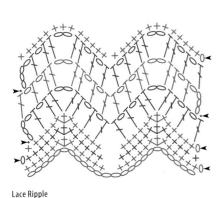

Lace Ripple

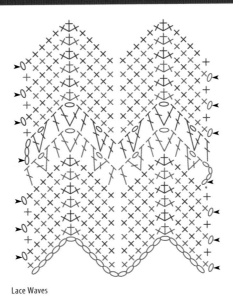

Lace Waves

## Yarn requirement for throws

**NOTE:** *All yarn requirements are estimated using an H-size (5 mm) crochet hook and worsted/10-ply yarn. Measurements and yarn requirements do not include joining and edging.*

| Lace Ripple | | | |
|---|---|---|---|
| | **BABY** | **LAP** | **BED** |
| A | 144 yds/132 m | 252 yds/230 m | 616 yds/563 m |
| B | 144 yds/132 m | 252 yds/230 m | 616 yds/563 m |
| C | 144 yds/132 m | 252 yds/230 m | 616 yds/563 m |
| D | 432 yds/395 m | 756 yds/691 m | 1848 yds/1690 m |

**Baby:** Ch 129—9 repeats.
**Lap:** Ch 207—15 repeats.
**Bed:** Ch 506—38 repeats..

| Lace Ripple 2 | | | |
|---|---|---|---|
| | **BABY** | **LAP** | **BED** |
| A | 144 yds/132 m | 252 yds/230 m | 616 yds/563 m |
| B | 144 yds/132 m | 252 yds/230 m | 616 yds/563 m |
| C | 144 yds/132 m | 252 yds/230 m | 616 yds/563 m |
| D | 432 yds/395 m | 756 yds/691 m | 1848 yds/1690 m |

| Lace Waves | | | |
|---|---|---|---|
| | **BABY** | **LAP** | **BED** |
| A | 288 yds/263 m | 504 yds/461 m | 1232 yds/1127 m |
| B | 288 yds/263 m | 504 yds/461 m | 1232 yds/1127 m |
| C | 288 yds/263 m | 504 yds/461 m | 1232 yds/1127 m |
| D | 216 yds/198 m | 378 yds/346 m | 924 yds/845 m |

**Baby:** Ch 129—9 repeats.
**Lap:** Ch 207—15 repeats.
**Bed:** Ch 506—38 repeats.

## STITCH VARIATION

## Lace Waves

• **SKILL LEVEL:** *Intermediate*

## Method

**SPECIAL STITCH:**

• V-Stitch—V-St: Work 1 dc, ch 1, 1 dc in same st.

**FOUNDATION ROW:** Using Color A, ch a multiple of 13 + 11 + 1 turning ch.

**ROW 1:** Sc in 2nd ch from hook, sc in next 4 ch, * 3 sc in next ch, sc in next 5 ch, skip 2 ch, sc in next 5 ch; rep from * to last 6 ch, 3 sc in next ch, sc in next 5 ch, turn.

**ROW 2:** Ch 1, skip first sc, sc in next 5 sts, * 3 sc in next st, sc in next 5 sts, skip 2 sts, sc in next 5 sts; rep from * to last 7 sts, 3 sc in next st, sc in next 4 sts, skip 1 st, sc in last st, turn. End Color A.

**ROWS 3–4:** Join Color B and repeat Row 2.

**ROWS 5–6:** Join Color C and repeat Row 2.

**ROW 7:** Join Color D, skip 1 st, ch 4 (counts as 1 dc, ch 1) in next st, * skip 1 st, V-st in next st, skip 1 st, dc in next st, V-st in next st, dc in next st, skip 1 st, V-st in next st **, skip 1 st, dc in next st, skip 2 sts, dc in next st; rep from * to last 11 sts, rep from * to ** once more, skip 2 sts, dc in last st, turn.

**ROW 8:** Ch 3 (counts as 1 dc), skip 1 st, V-st in next ch-1 sp, skip 2 sts, dc in next st, * V-st in next ch-1 sp, dc in next st, skip 2 sts, V-st in next ch-1 sp **, dc in next st, skip 2 sts, dc in next st; rep from * to last 8 sts and 4 ch-1 sps, rep from * to ** once more, skip 1 st and ch-1 sp, dc in last st, turn. End Color D.

**ROW 9:** Join Color A, ch 1, skip 1 st, sc in next st, * sc in ch-1 sp, sc in next 3 dc, 3 sc in ch-1 sp, sc in next 3 sts, sc in ch-1 sp **, sc in next st, skip 2 sts, sc in next st; rep from * to last 8 sts and 3 ch-1 sps, then rep from * to ** once more, skip 1 st, sc in last st.

**ROW 10:** Repeat Row 2. End Color A.

**ROWS 11–12:** Join Color B and repeat Row 2. End Color B.

**ROWS 13–14:** Join Color C and repeat Row 2. End Color C.

- ● A:  8 yds/7.3 m
- ◐ B:  8 yds/7.3 m
- ◔ C:  8 yds/7.3 m
- ○ D:  6 yds/5.5 m

# Woodland Web

● A: 5 yds/4.6 m
◐ B: 20 yds/18.3 m

• **SKILL LEVEL:** *Beginner*

## Method

**FOUNDATION RING:** Using Color A, make a Magic Ring.

**ROUND 1:** Ch 1, 8 sc into ring, join with slip st into first sc made. (8 sts.)

**ROUND 2:** Ch 1, sc in same st, [ch 3, sc in next st] 7 times, ch 3, join with slip st into first sc made. (8 sts, 8 ch sps.)

**ROUND 3:** Ch 1, sc in same st, [ch 4, sc in next st] 7 times, ch 4, join with slip st into first sc made. (8 sts, 8 ch sps.)

**ROUND 4:** Ch 1, sc in same st, [ch 5, sc in next st] 7 times, ch 5, join with slip st into first sc made. End Color A. (8 sts, 8 ch sps.)

**ROUND 5:** Join Color B, ch 1 and sc in same st, * ch 4, (dc, ch 2, dc) in next sc, ch 4 **, sc in next sc; rep from * twice more, then from * to ** once more, join with slip st into first sc made. (12 sts, 12 ch sps.)

**ROUND 6:** Ch 1 and sc in same st, * ch 4, dc in next st, (2 dc, tr, 2 dc) in ch-2 sp, dc in next st, ch 4 **, sc in next st; rep from * twice more, then from * to ** once more, join with slip st into first sc made. (32 sts, 8 ch sps.)

**ROUND 7:** Ch 1 and sc in same st, * ch 4, dc in next 3 sts, (2 dc, tr, 2 dc) in tr, dc in next 3 sts, ch 4 **, sc in next sc; rep from * twice more, then from * to ** once more, join into first sc made. (48 sts, 8 ch sps.)

**ROUND 8:** Ch 6 (counts as hdc, ch 4), * sc in next 5 sts, (sc, hdc, sc) in tr, sc in next 5 sts, ch 4 **, hdc in sc, ch 4; rep from * twice more, then from * to ** once more, join with slip st into 2nd ch of beginning ch. End Color B. (56 sts, 8 ch sps.)

Woodland Web

Woodland Web 2

---

**COLOR VARIATION**

## Woodland Web 2

○ A: 5 yds/4.6 m
◑ B: 20 yds/18.3 m

Follow the written instructions or the chart, using colors as follows:

Woodland Rose

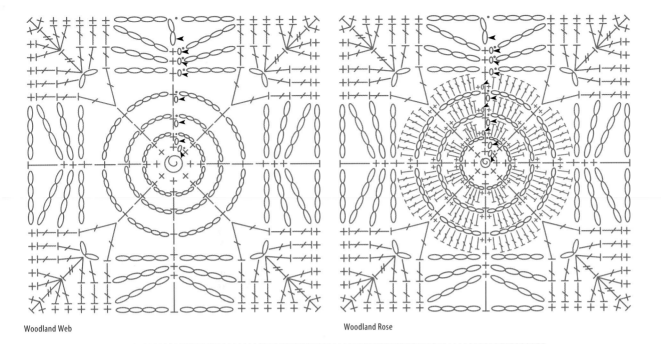

Woodland Web                          Woodland Rose

---

## STITCH VARIATION

## Woodland Rose

● A: 25 yds/22.9 m
○ B: 5 yds/4.6 m
● C: 18 yds/16.5 m

• SKILL LEVEL: *Advanced*

## Method

**FOUNDATION RING:** Using Color A, make a Magic Ring.

**ROUND 1:** Ch 1, 8 sc into ring, join with slip st into first sc made. (8 sts.)

**ROUND 2:** Ch 1, sc in same st, [ch 3, sc in next st] 7 times, ch 3, join with slip st into first sc made. (8 sts, 8 ch sp.)

**ROUND 3:** Ch 1, sc in same st, [ch 4, sc in next st] 7 times, ch 4, join with slip st into first sc made. (8 sts, 8 ch sps.)

**ROUND 4:** Ch 1, sc in same st, [ch 5, sc in next st] 7 times, ch 5, join with slip st into first sc made. (8 sts, 8 ch sps.)

**ROUND 5:** Ch 1, sc in same st, * ch 4, (dc, ch 2, dc) in next sc, ch 4 **, sc in next sc; rep from * twice more, then from * to ** once more, join with slip st into first sc made. (12 sts, 12 ch sps.)

**ROUND 6:** Ch 1, sc in same st, ch 4, dc in next st, * (2 dc, tr, 2 dc) in ch-2 sp, dc in next st, ch 4 **, sc in next st, ch 4, dc in next st; rep from * twice more, then from * to ** once more, join with slip st into first sc made. (32 sts, 8 ch sps.)

**ROUND 7:** Ch 1, sc in same st, ch 4, dc in next 3 sts, * (2 dc, tr, 2 dc) in tr, dc in next 3 sts, ch 4 **, sc in next sc, ch 4, dc in next 3 sts; rep from * twice more, then from * to ** once more, join with slip st into first sc made. (48 sts, 8 ch sps.)

**ROUND 8:** Ch 6 (counts as hdc, ch 4), * sc in next 5 sts, (sc, hdc, sc) in tr, sc in next 5 sts, ch 4 **, hdc in sc, ch 4; rep from * twice more, then from * to ** once more, join with slip st into 2nd ch of beginning ch. End Color A. (56 sts, 8 ch sps.)

### SURFACE CROCHET:

**ROUND 1:** Join Color B into ch-3 sp of Round 2, ch 1, in each ch-3 sp work (sc, hdc, 2 dc, hdc, sc), join with slip st into first sc made. End Color B. (8 petals.)

**ROUND 2:** Join Color C into ch-4 sp of Round 3, ch 1, in each ch-4 sp work (sc, hdc, 4 dc, hdc, sc), join with slip st into first sc made. End Color C. (8 petals.)

**ROUND 3:** Join Color C into ch-5 sp of Round 4, ch 1, in each ch-5 sp work (sc, hdc, 6 dc, hdc sc), join with slip st into first sc made. End Color C. (8 petals.)

## Yarn requirement for throws

**NOTE:** *All yarn requirements are estimated using an H-size (5 mm) crochet hook and worsted/10-ply yarn. Measurements and yarn requirements do not include joining and edging.*

### Woodland Web

|   | BABY | LAP | BED |
|---|------|-----|-----|
| A | 180 yds/165 m | 315 yds/288 m | 770 yds/704 m |
| B | 720 yds/658 m | 1260 yds/1152 m | 3080 yds/2816 m |

### Woodland Web 2

|   | BABY | LAP | BED |
|---|------|-----|-----|
| A | 180 yds/165 m | 315 yds/288 m | 770 yds/704 m |
| B | 720 yds/658 m | 1260 yds/1152 m | 3080 yds/2816 m |

### Woodland Rose

|   | BABY | LAP | BED |
|---|------|-----|-----|
| A | 900 yds/823 m | 1575 yds/1440 m | 3850 yds/3520 m |
| B | 180 yds/165 m | 315 yds/288 m | 770 yds/704 m |
| C | 648 yds/593 m | 1134 yds/1037 m | 2772 yds/2535 m |

# Bold Block

● A: 13 yds/11.9 m
○ B: 13 yds/11.9 m
● C: 15 yds/13.7 m

• **SKILL LEVEL:** *Beginner*

## Method

**SPECIAL STITCH:**

• Cluster—Cl: Work 3 dc in same space, leaving last loop of each stitch on hook (4 loops on hook), yo, pull through all loops on hook.

**FOUNDATION RING:** Using Color A, make a Magic Ring.

**ROUND 1:** Ch 4 (counts as 1 tr), * 5 dc into ring **, tr into ring; rep from * twice more, then from * to ** once more, join with slip st into top of beginning ch. End Color A. (24 sts.)

**ROUND 2:** Join Color B, ch 5 (counts as 1 dc, ch 2), dc in same place, * [ch 1, skip 1 st, Cl in next st] twice, ch 1, skip 1 st **, (dc, ch 2, dc) in next st; rep from * twice more, then from * to ** once more, join with slip st into 3rd ch of beginning ch. End Color B. (8 Cl, 8 dc, 16 ch sps.)

**ROUND 3:** Join Color A in corner ch-2 sp, ch 1, * (sc, hdc, sc) in ch-2 sp, [sc in next st, sc over ch-1 sp into st on Round 1] 3 times, sc in next st; rep from * 3 more times, join with slip st into first sc made. End Color A. (40 sts.)

**ROUND 4:** Join Color C in corner hdc, ch 1, * (sc, hdc, sc) in hdc, sc in each st to next hdc; rep from * 3 more times, join with slip st into first sc made. End Color C. (48 sts.)

**ROUND 5:** Join Color B in corner hdc, ch 5 (counts as 1 dc, ch 2), dc in same place, * [ch 1, skip 1 st, Cl in next st] 5 times, ch 1, skip 1 st **, (dc, ch 2, dc) in corner hdc; rep from * twice more, then from * to ** once more, join with slip st into 3rd ch of beginning ch. End Color B. (20 Cl, 8 dc, 28 ch sps.)

**ROUND 6:** Join Color C in corner ch-2 sp, ch 1, * (sc, hdc, sc) in ch-2 sp, [sc in next st, sc over ch-1 sp into st on Round 4] 6 times, sc in next st; rep from * 3 more times, join with slip st into first sc made. End Color C. (64 sts.)

**ROUND 7:** Join Color A in corner hdc, ch 1, * (sc, hdc, sc) in corner hdc, sc in each st across to next corner hdc; rep from * 3 more times, join with slip st into first sc made. End Color B. (72 sts.)

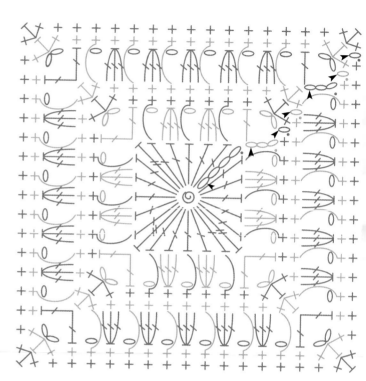

## Yarn requirement for throws

**NOTE:** *All yarn requirements are estimated using an H-size (5 mm) crochet hook and worsted/10-ply yarn. Measurements and yarn requirements do not include joining and edging.*

| Bold Block | | | |
|---|---|---|---|
| | **BABY** | **LAP** | **BED** |
| **A** | 468 yds/428 m | 819 yds/749 m | 2002 yds/1831 m |
| **B** | 468 yds/428 m | 819 yds/749 m | 2002 yds/1831 m |
| **C** | 540 yds/494 m | 945 yds/864 m | 2310 yds/2112 m |

## Project Notes

**YOU WILL NEED:**
- ½ yd (46 cm) cotton fabric for lining
- 2 handles

- ● A: 156 yds/143 m
- ○ B: 156 yds/143 m
- ● C: 180 yds/165 m

Make 12 squares.

Join the squares together following the layout below and using Color B. Holding the squares so right sides are facing, join by single crochet through the back loops of each stitch.

Cut two pieces of fabric to fit, using the crochet bag as a template and allowing for a seam. Sew the pieces together along three sides. Fold back and press the seam allowance and stitch to the opening of the bag.

Hold the handles in place, fold the top of the square over, and hand stitch into place.

Stuff with yarns and hooks!

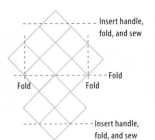

Insert handle, fold, and sew

Fold

Fold  Fold

Insert handle, fold, and sew

Swirly

Circles

Little Square

# Swirly

- ● A: 7 yds/6.4 m
- ● B: 5 yds/4.6 m

- **SKILL LEVEL:** *Advanced*
- **MEASUREMENT:** *3 in./7.5 cm block*

## Method

**FOUNDATION RING:** Using Color A, make a Magic Ring.

**ROUND 1:** Ch 1, 2 sc, 2 hdc, 2 dc into ring, do not join. (6 sts.)

**ROUND 2:** Work 2 dc tbl in next 6 sts, do not join. (12 sts.)

**ROUND 3:** [2 dc tbl into next st, dc tbl in next 2 sts] 4 times, do not join; the round ends before the last st of Round 2, leaving 3 sts unworked. (14 sts + 3 sts from Round 2.)

**ROUND 4:** * (Dc tbl, ch 2, dc tbl) in next st, hdc tbl in next st, sc tbl in next st **, hdc tbl in next st; rep from * twice more, then from * to ** once more, skip 1 st, slip st tbl into next st. End Color A. (20 sts, 4 ch sps.)

**SURFACE CROCHET:** With Color B on hook, start at center of square, work 1 sc in first Front Loop, 2 sc in each Front Loop to last st, work slip st into last Front Loop. End Color E. (59 sts.)

# Circles

- ● A: 1 yd/0.9 m
- ● B: 1 yd/0.9 m
- ● C: 2 yds/1.8 m
- ● D: 2 yds/1.8 m
- ● E: 4 yds/3.7 m

- **SKILL LEVEL:** *Beginner*
- **MEASUREMENT:** *3 in./7.5 cm block*

## Method

**FOUNDATION RING:** Using Color A, make a Magic Ring.

**ROUND 1:** Ch 1, 6 sc into ring, join with slip st into first sc made. End Color A. (6 sts.)

**ROUND 2:** Join Color B, ch 1, 2 sc in each st around, join with slip st into first sc made. End Color B. (12 sts.)

**ROUND 3:** Join Color C, ch 1, sc in same st, * 2 sc in next st, sc in next st; rep from * 4 more times, 2 sc in next st, join with slip st into first sc made. End Color C. (18 sts.)

**ROUND 4:** Join Color D, ch 1, 2 sc in same st, * sc in next 2 sts, 2 sc in next st; rep from * 4 more times, sc in next 2 sts, join with slip st into first sc made. End Color D. (24 sts.)

**ROUND 5:** Join Color E, ch 1, sc in same st, sc in next 2 sts, * hdc in next st, (dc, tr, dc) in next st, hdc in next st **, sc in next 3 sts; rep from * twice more, then from * to ** once more, join with slip st into first sc made. End Color E. (32 sts.)

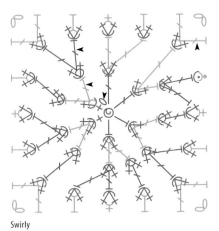

Swirly

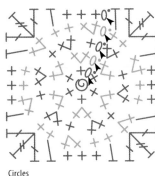

Circles

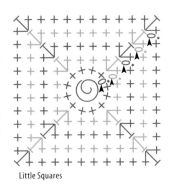

Little Squares

## Yarn requirement for throws

**NOTE:** *All yarn requirements are estimated using an H-size (5 mm) crochet hook and worsted/10-ply yarn. Measurements and yarn requirements do not include joining and edging.*

| Swirly | | | |
|---|---|---|---|
| | BABY | LAP | BED |
| A | 1008 yds/922 m | 1764 yds/1613 m | 4312 yds/3943 m |
| B | 720 yds/658 m | 1260 yds/1152 m | 3080 yds/2816 m |

**Baby:** 144 squares. Join into 12 rows of 12 squares.
**Lap:** 252 squares. Join into 18 rows of 14 squares.
**Bed:** 616 squares. Join into 28 rows of 22 squares.

| Circles | | | |
|---|---|---|---|
| | BABY | LAP | BED |
| A | 144 yds/132 m | 252 yds/230 m | 616 yds/563 m |
| B | 144 yds/132 m | 252 yds/230 m | 616 yds/563 m |
| C | 288 yds/263 m | 504 yds/461 m | 1232 yds/1127 m |
| D | 288 yds/263 m | 504 yds/461 m | 1232 yds/1127 m |
| E | 576 yds/527 m | 1008 yds/922 m | 2464 yds/2253 m |

**Baby:** 144 squares. Join into 12 rows of 12 squares
**Lap:** 252 squares. Join into 18 rows of 14 squares.
**Bed:** 616 squares. Join into 28 rows of 22 squares.

| Little Squares | | | |
|---|---|---|---|
| | BABY | LAP | BED |
| A | 288 yds/263 m | 504 yds/461 m | 1232 yds/1127 m |
| B | 288 yds/263 m | 504 yds/461 m | 1232 yds/1127 m |
| C | 432 yds/395 m | 756 yds/691 m | 1848 yds/1690 m |
| D | 432 yds/395 m | 756 yds/691 m | 1848 yds/1690 m |
| E | 576 yds/527 m | 1008 yds/922 m | 2464 yds/2253 m |

**Baby:** 144 squares. Join 12 rows of 12 squares.
**Lap:** 252 squares. Join 18 rows of 14 squares.
**Beds:** 616 squares. Join 28 rows of 22 squares

# Little Squares

- **SKILL LEVEL:** *Beginner*
- **MEASUREMENT:** *3 in./7.5 cm block*

● A: 2 yds/1.8 m
◐ B: 2 yds/1.8 m
◑ C: 3 yds/2.7 m
● D: 3 yds/2.7 m
● E: 4 yds/3.7 m

## Method

**FOUNDATION RING:** Using Color A, make a Magic Ring.
**ROUND 1:** Ch 1, 12 sc into ring, join with slip st into first sc made. End Color A. (12 sts.)
**ROUND 2:** Join Color B, ch 1, *(sc, hdc, sc) in same st, sc into next 2 sts; rep from * 3 more times, join with slip st into first sc made. End Color B. (20 sts.)

**ROUND 3:** Join Color C in corner hdc, ch 1, * (sc, hdc, sc) in hdc, sc in each st to next corner hdc; rep from * 3 more times, join with slip st into first sc made. End Color C. (28 sts.)
**ROUND 4:** Using Color D, rep Round 3. (36 sts.)
**ROUND 5:** Using Color E, rep Round 3. (44 sts.)

# Ferris Wheel

| | |
|---|---|
| A: | 8 yds/7.3 m |
| B: | 18 yds/16.5 m |
| C: | 11 yds/10 m |
| D: | 18 yds/16.5 m |
| E: | 9 yds/8.2 m |
| F: | 43 yds/39.3 m |

- **SKILL LEVEL:** *Beginner*
- **MEASUREMENT:** *12 in./30.5 cm block*

## Method

**SPECIAL STITCH:**

- V-Stitch—V-st: (Dc, ch 1, dc) in place indicated.

**FOUNDATION RING:** Using Color A, make a Magic Ring.

**ROUND 1:** Ch 3, 15 dc into ring, join with slip st into top of beginning ch. End Color A. (16 sts.)

**ROUND 2:** Join Color B, ch 5 (counts as 1 dc, ch 2), [dc in next st, ch 2] 15 times, join with slip st into 3rd ch of beginning ch. End Color B. (16 sts, 16 ch sps.)

**ROUND 3:** Join Color C in ch-2 sp, ch 3 (counts as 1 dc), 2 dc in same ch-2 sp, [3 dc in next ch-2 sp] 15 times, join with slip st into top of beginning ch. End Color C. (48 sts.)

**ROUND 4:** Join Color D between 2 dc groups, ch 4 (counts as 1 dc, ch 1) dc in same sp, ch 1, [V-st between next 2 dc groups, ch 1] 15 times, join with slip st into 3rd ch of beginning ch. End Color D. (32 sts, 32 ch sps.)

**ROUND 5:** Join Color E in ch-1 of V-st, ch 3 (counts as 1 dc), 2 dc in same sp, [2 dc in next ch-1 sp, 3 dc in next ch-1 sp] 15 times, 2 dc in next ch-1 sp, join with slip st into top of beginning ch. End Color E. (80 sts.)

**ROUND 6:** Join Color A between a group of 3 dc and a group of 2 dc, ch 5 (counts as 1 dc, ch 2), [dc between next 2 dc groups, ch 2] 31 times, join with slip st into 3rd ch of beginning ch. End Color A. (32 sts, 32 ch sps.)

**ROUND 7:** Join Color B in ch-2 sp, ch 3 (counts as 1 dc), 3 dc in same ch-2 sp, [4 dc in next ch-2 sp] 31 times, join with slip st into top of beginning ch. End Color B. (128 sts.)

**ROUND 8:** Join Color C between 2 dc groups, ch 1 and sc in same sp, [ch 3, sc between next 2 dc groups] 31 times, ch 3, join with slip st into first sc made. End Color C. (32 sts, 32 ch sps.)

**ROUND 9:** Join Color D in ch-3 sp, ch 3 (counts as 1 dc), 2 dc in same ch-3 sp, [ch 1, 3 dc in next ch-3 sp] 31 times, ch 1, join with slip st into top of beginning ch. End Color D. (96 sts, 32 ch sps.)

**ROUND 10:** Join Color F in ch-1 sp, ch 1 and sc in same sp, [ch 3, sc in next ch-1 sp] 31 times, ch 3, join with slip st into first sc made. (32 sts, 32 ch sps.)

**ROUND 11:** Sl st into ch-3 sp, ch 1, * [4 sc in ch-3 sp] twice, * 4 hdc in next ch-3 sp, 4 dc in next ch-3 sp, (2 tr, ch 2, 2 tr) in next ch-3 sp, 4 dc in next ch-3 sp, 4 hdc in next ch-3 sp **, [4 sc in next ch-3 sp] 3 times; rep from * twice more, then

from * to ** once more, 4 sc in next ch-3 sp, join with slip st into first sc made. (128 sts, 4 ch sps.)

**ROUND 12:** Ch 1 and sc in same st, sc in next 7 sts, * hdc in next 4 sts, dc in next 4 sts, tr in next 2 sts, (2 tr, ch 2, 2 tr) in ch-2 sp, tr in next 2 sts, dc in next 4 sts, hdc in next 4 sts **, sc in next 12 sts; rep from * twice more, then from * to ** once more, sc in next 4 sts, join with slip st into first sc made. (144 sts, 4 ch sps.)

**ROUND 13:** Ch 1 and sc in same st, * sc in each st across to corner ch-2 sp, (sc, hdc, sc) in ch-2 sp; rep from * 3 more times, sc in each st to end of round, join with slip st into first sc made. End Color F. (156 sts.)

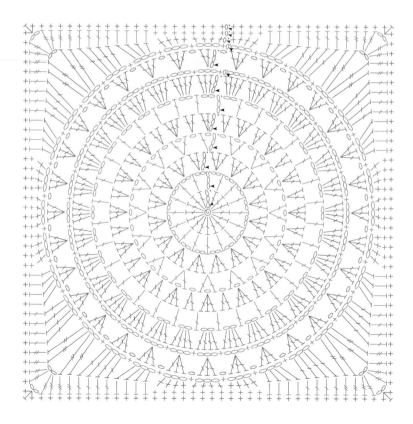

## Yarn requirement for throws

**NOTE:** *All yarn requirements are estimated using an H-size (5 mm) crochet hook and worsted/10-ply yarn. Measurements and yarn requirements do not include joining and edging.*

### Ferris Wheel

|   | BABY | LAP | BED |
|---|------|-----|-----|
| **A** | 72 yds/66 m | 160 yds/146 m | 280 yds/256 m |
| **B** | 162 yds/148 m | 360 yds/329 m | 630 yds/576 m |
| **C** | 99 yds/91 m | 220 yds/201 m | 385 yds/352 m |
| **D** | 162 yds/148 m | 360 yds/329 m | 630 yds/576 m |
| **E** | 81 yds/74 m | 180 yds/165 m | 315 yds/288 m |
| **F** | 387 yds/354 m | 860 yds/786 m | 1505 yds/1376 m |

**Baby (36 x 36 in./91.5 x 91.5 cm):** Make 9 squares and join 3 rows of 3 squares.

**Lap (48 x 60 in./122 x 152.5 cm):** Make 20 squares and join 5 rows of 4 squares.

**Bed (60 x 84 in./152.5 x 213.5 cm):** Make 35 squares and join 7 rows of 5 squares.

# Square Foot Garden

A: 5 yds/4.6 m
B: 6 yds/5.5 m
C: 25 yds/22.9 m
D: 21 yds/19.2 m
E: 8 yds/7.3 m
F: 7 yds/6.4 m
G: 7 yds/6.4 m
H: 13 yds/11.9 m
I: 14 yds/12.8 m

- **SKILL LEVEL:** *Intermediate*
- **MEASUREMENT:** *12 in./30.5 cm block*

## Method

**SPECIAL STITCH:**

- 3 st Cluster—3-Cl: Work dc in each of next 3 sts leaving last loop of each st on hook (4 loops on hook), yo and draw through all loops on hook, ch 1 pulling tight to close group.

**FOUNDATION RING:** Using Color A, make a Magic Ring.

**ROUND 1:** Ch 3 (counts as 1 dc), 2 dc into ring, [ch 3, 3 dc into ring] 3 times, join using ch 1, hdc into top of beginning ch. (12 sts, 4 ch sps.)

**ROUND 2:** [ch 2, 3-Cl over next 3 sts, ch 2, slip st into ch-3 sp] 4 times. End Color A. (4 Cl, 8 ch sps.)

**ROUND 3:** Join Color B in top of 3-Cl, ch 1 and sc in same st, [(3 dc, ch 3, 3 dc) in ch-3 sp of Round 1, sc in 3-Cl] 3 times, (3 dc, ch 3, 3 dc) in ch-3 sp of Round 1, join with slip st into first sc made. End Color B. (28 sts, 4 ch sps.)

**ROUND 4:** Join Color C, ch 1 and sc in same st, [sc in each st to ch-3 sp, (3 dc, ch 3, 3 dc) in ch-3 sp] 4 times, sc in next 3 sts, join with slip st into first sc made. End Color C. (52 sts, 4 ch sps.)

**ROUND 5:** Join Color D, ch 3 (counts as 1 dc), dc in next 3 sts, * hdc in next 3 sts, (sc, hdc, sc) in ch-3 sp, hdc in next 3 sts **, dc in next 7 sts; rep from * twice more, then from * to ** once more, dc in next 3 sts, join with slip st into top of beginning ch. End Color D. (64 sts.)

**ROUND 6:** Join Color E, ch 4 (counts as 1 dc, ch 1), [skip 1 st, dc in next st, ch 1] twice, dc in next 2 sts, * (dc, ch 2, dc) in ch-3 sp, dc in next 2 sts **, [ch 1, skip 1 st, dc in next st] 6 times, dc in next st; rep from * twice more, then from * to ** once more, [ch 1, skip 1 st, dc in next st] twice, ch 1, join with slip st into 3rd ch of beginning ch. End Color E. (44 sts, 28 ch sps.)

**ROUND 7:** Join Color F, ch 1 and sc in same st, [sc over ch-1 sp into st of Round 5, sc in next dc] 3 times, sc in next 2 sts, * (sc, hdc, sc) in ch-2 sp, sc in next 3 sts **, [sc over ch-1 sp into st of Round 5, sc in next dc] 6 times, sc in next 2 sts; rep from * twice more, then from * to ** once more, [sc over ch-1 sp into st of Round 5, sc in next dc] twice, sc over ch-1 sp into st of Round 5, join with slip st into first sc made. End Color F. (80 sts.)

**ROUND 8:** Join Color G, ch 4 (counts as 1 dc, ch 1), [skip 1 st, dc in next st, ch 1] 4 times, * (dc, ch 2, dc) in next st **, [ch 1, skip 1 st, dc in next st] 9 times, ch 1; rep from * twice more, then from * to ** once more, [ch 1, skip 1 st, dc in next st] 4 times, ch 1, join with slip st into top of beginning ch. End Color G. (44 sts, 44 ch sps.)

**ROUND 9:** Join Color H in corner ch-2 sp, ch 3 (counts as 1 dc), 1 dc, ch 2, 2 dc in same ch-2 sp, * [bpdc around next st, dc in next ch-1 sp] 10 times, bpdc around next st **, (2 dc, ch 2, 2 dc) in ch-2 sp; rep from * twice more, then from * to ** once more, join with slip st into top of beginning ch. End Color H. (100 sts, 4 ch sps.)

**ROUND 10:** Join Color I, ch 3 (counts as 1 dc), [dc in each dc to corner ch-2 sp, (2 dc, ch 2, 2 dc) in ch-2 sp] 4 times, dc in each st to end of round, join with slip st into top of beginning ch. End Color I. (116 sts, 4 ch sps.)

*(Continued opposite)*

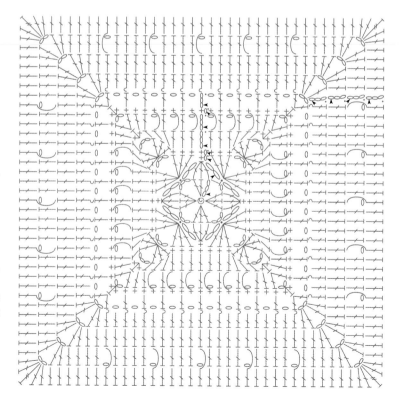

## Yarn requirement for throws

**NOTE:** *All yarn requirements are estimated using an H-size (5 mm) crochet hook and worsted/10-ply yarn. Measurements and yarn requirements do not include joining and edging.*

| Square Foot Garden | | | |
|---|---|---|---|
| | **BABY** | **LAP** | **BED** |
| A | 45 yds/41 m | 100 yds/91 m | 175 yds/160 m |
| B | 54 yds/49 m | 120 yds/110 m | 210 yds/192 m |
| C | 225 yds/206 m | 500 yds/457 m | 875 yds/800 m |
| D | 189 yds/173 m | 420 yds/384 m | 735 yds/672 m |
| E | 72 yds/66 m | 160 yds/146 m | 280 yds/256 m |
| F | 63 yds/58 m | 140 yds/128 m | 245 yds/224 m |
| G | 63 yds/58 m | 140 yds/128 m | 245 yds/224 m |
| H | 117 yds/107 m | 260 yds/238 m | 455 yds/416 m |
| I | 126 yds/115 m | 280 yds/256 m | 490 yds/448 m |

**Baby (36 x 36 in./91.5 x 91.5 cm):** Make 9 squares and join 3 rows of 3 squares.

**Lap (48 x 60 in./122 x 152.5 cm):** Make 20 squares and join 5 rows of 4 squares.

**Bed (60 x 84 in./152.5 x 213.5 cm):** Make 35 squares and join 7 rows of 5 squares.

**ROUND 11:** Join Color D, ch 3 (counts as 1 dc), dc in next st, * (2 dc, ch 2, 2 dc) in ch-2 sp, [dc in next 4 sts, ch 1, skip 1 st] 5 times **, dc in next 4 sts; rep from * twice more, then from * to ** once more, join with slip st into top of beginning ch. End Color D. (112 sts, 24 ch sps.)

**ROUND 12:** Join Color C, ch 3 (counts as 1 dc), dc in next 5 sts, * (2 dc, tr, 2 dc) in ch-2 sp, dc in next 6 sts **, [dc over ch-1 sp into st of Round 10, dc in next 4 sts] 5 times, dc in next 2 sts; rep from * twice more, then from * to ** once more, [dc over ch-1 sp into st of Round 10, dc in next 4 sts] 4 times, dc over ch-1 sp into st of Round 10, join with slip st into top of beginning ch. End Color C. (152 sts.)

# Index

# Cascade Yarns List

Every effort has been made to list the correct color number from the Cascade 220 range of yarns, but please use the following list as a guide only and be sure to check exact colors with your yarn supplier before purchasing.

**KEY**
Page number/name of square/color code in book/ Cascade 220 range (where relevant)/Cascade color number

**p36 Daisy** A Heathers 2439, B 8505, C 8910, D 9603; **2** A 8910, B 8505, C 9603, D Heathers 2439

**p37 Daisy Chain** A Heathers 2439, B 8505, C 8910

**p38 Spiked Lines** A 8908, B 7830, C 9496; **2** A 8891, B 8505, C 8908

**p39 V-spiked Lines** (all from Superwash range) A 1911, B 820, C 826

**p40 My Heart** A 8910, B 9469, C 8912; **2** A 9469, B 8910

**p41 Cross My Heart** A 8912, B 9469, C 8910

**p42 Carnival** (all from Superwash range) A 820, B 8913, C 840, D 810, E 804, F 1973; **2** (all from Superwash range) A 820, B 804, C 810, D 840, E 8913, F 1973

**p43 Parade** (all from Superwash range) A 820, B 810, C 840, D 804, E 8913, F 1973

**p44 Flame Flower** A 2439, B 8414, C 8908; **2** A 8414, B 2439, C 8891

**p45 Fire Star** A Heathers 2439, B 8895

**p46 Darts** A 8555, B 8505, C 8891, D 7824; **2** A 9548, B 9496, C 7825, D 8905

**p47 Lines** A 7824, B 8505, C 8555, D 8891

**p48 Popcorn** A 7825, B 8910, C 8913, D 9496, E 7815; **2** A 7815, B 7825, C 9496, D 8913, E 8910

**p49 Popcorn Kernel** A 9496, B 7825, C 8910, D 7816, E 8913

**p50 Tutti Frutti** A 7825, B 8903, C 8895; **2** A 8903, B 7828, C 8906

**p51 Fruit Salad** A 8895, B 8903, C 7828, D 7825, E 8906

**p52 Flower in Web** A 9469, B 7808, C 8910, D 7814; **2** A 7814, B Heathers 2439, C 8910, D 9469, E 7808

**p53 Webbed Flower** A 8910, B 9469, C 7814, D Heathers 2439, E 7808

**p54 Bobble Heart square** A Superwash 851, B Superwash 871

**p55 Bobble Heart project** (all from Superwash range) A 897, B 1921, C 820, D 851, E 1973, F 836, G 871, H 802, I 826, J 840, K 903, L 814, M 804, N 824

**p56 Traditional Granny** A 8895, B Heathers 2439, C 8903, D 9605, E 8908; **2** A 8908, B Heathers 2439, C 9605, D 8903, E 8895

**p57 Treble Granny** A Heathers 2439, B 9605, C 8908

**p58 Miter Box** A Heathers 2439, B 7825, C 7816, D 9484; **2** A 8505, B 9565, C Heathers 2439, D 9484

**p59 Stars and Stripes** A 9484, B 8505, C 9565

**p60 Bobble Row** A 8905, B 9469, C 8910, D Heathers 2439; **2** A 9469, B Heathers 2439, C 8905, D 8910

**p61 Double Bobble Row** A 8905, B Heathers 2439, C 9469, D 8910

**p62 Octagon Tile** A Heathers 2439, B 8414, C 8010, D 9478, E 8905; **2** A 9478, B Heathers 2439, C 8905, D 8505, E 8414

**p63 Octagon Ridged Tile** A 8905, B 9478, C 8010, D 8414, E 2439

**p64 Simple Waves** A Superwash 810, B Superwash 820; **2** A Superwash 807, B Superwash 820

**p65 Simple Ridged Waves** A Superwash 807, B Superwash 820

**p66 Back Post** A 8912, B 8910, C 7803, D 8903, E 7808; **2** A 8910, B 7808, C 8912, D 7803, E 8903

**p67 Back and Front** A 9496, B 8912, C 8910, D 7808

**p68 Mitered Flower** A 7830, B 9492, C 8010, D 9076; **2** A 9076, B 8010, C 9492, D 7830

**p69 Mighty Mitered Flower** A 8010, B 9492, C 7830, D 9076

**p70 Home** A 8908, B 9565, C 8910, D 8505; **2** A 9565, B 8505, C 8910, D 8908

**p71 Sweet** A 8910, B 9484, C 8505, D 9565, E 8908

**p72 Eye-popping Popcorn** A 7816, B Heathers 2439, C 8414; **2** A Heathers 2439, B 7824, C 7816

**p73 Eye-popping Lace** A 8414, B Heathers 2439, C 7816

**p74–75 Platinum, Purple, and Pink square & project** A Sierra 18, B Sierra 29, C Sierra 30, D Sierra 01, E Sierra 417

**p76 Pretty in Pink** A 8010, B 8908, C 9469; **2** A 8010, B 8906, C 8913

**p77 Pretty Pink Popcorn Flower** A 8908, B 8010, C 8906, D 8913

**p78 She Sells Sea Shells** A 9492, B Heathers 9561, C 8910, D 7830, E 8505, F 9076; **2** A 7830, B Heathers 9561, C 9492

**p79 By the Seashore** A 7830, B Heathers 9561, C 8910

**p80 Fluffy Flower** A 8010, B 8905, C 9484, D 9605; **2** A 8905, B 8010, C 9605, D 9484

**p81 Dutch Flower** A 9605, B 8905, C 9484, D 8010

**p82 Pink Lavender** A 8912, B Heathers 9561, C 8913, D 8906; **2** A 7803, B 9561, C 7808, D 8906

**p83 Lavender Haze** A 8912, B 7808

**p84 Love** (all from Superwash range) A 851, B 838, C 826, D 1973, E 817; **2** (all from Superwash range) A 887, B 1921, C 903, D 914, E 824

**p85 Love Heart** A 9076, B 9492, C 7830, D 8908

**p86 Framed Primrose** A 8910, B 8505, C Heathers 2439, D 8905; **2** A 9496, B 9477, C 8505, D 8910

**p87 Pretty Primrose** A 9477, B 9478, C 9496, D 8910, E 8905

**p88 Wildfire** A 9496, B 9605, C 7825, D 7827, E 8414; **2** A 9605, B 9496, C 7825, D 8414, E 7827

**p89 Embers** A 7825, B 9496, C 8414, D 7827, E 9605

**p90 Rainbow Ripple** (all from Superwash range) A 894, B 851, C 820, D 1952, E 1921; **2** (all from Superwash range) A 1921, B 1952, C 820, D 851, E 894

**p91 Rainbow Stripes** (all from Superwash range) A 851, B 820, C 1952, D 1921, E 804

**p92 Frilly Circle** A 8010, B 9470, C 8913, D 9477, E Heathers 9561; **2** A 8010, B Heathers 9561, C 8907, D 9470

## Cascade Yarns List (continued)

**p93 Frilly Granny Circle** A 9477, B Heathers 9561, C 9470, D 8907, E 8913

**p94 Big Bloom square** A 8903, B 8505, C 8912

**p95 Big Bloom project** A 8913, B 8505, C 8903, D 8912, E 7803, F 8909, G 7808, H 9469, I 8901

**p96 Spiky Square** (all from Superwash range) A 804, B 820, C 914, D 851; **2** (all from Superwash range) A 851, B 820, C 804

**p97 Side Spikes** (all from Superwash range) A 820, B 914, C 804, D 851

**p98 Bright Flower** (all from Superwash range) A 851, B 1952, C 820, D 903, E 897; **2** (all from Superwash range) A 897, B 1952, C 851, D 820, E 903

**p99 Cartwheel Flower** (all from Superwash range) A 903, B 851, C 897, D 1952, E 820

**p100 Simple Ripple** A 7808, B 8910, C 8912; **2** A 2409, B 7803, C 7814, D 7808

**p101 Simple Bobble Ripple** A 7803, B 7814, C 7808, D 8910

**p102 Orange Slices Flower** A 9496, B 9605, C 8903; **2** A 9496, B 7825, C 8910

**p103 Lemon Slices Flower** A 9605, B 7825, C 9496, D 8910, E 8903

**p104 Pastel Diamonds** A 8505, B 8912, C 9478, D 9076; **2** A 9076, B 9478, C 8505, D 8912

**p105 3D Pastel Diamonds** A 9478, B 9076, C 8912, D 8505

**p106 Circle Square** (all from Superwash range) A 815, B 851, C 826, D 1911, E 1921, F 817; **2** (all from Superwash range) A 815, B 817, C 1921, D 851, E 1911, F 826

**p107 Circle Granny** (all from Superwash range) A 1921, B 851, C 826, D 1911, E 815, F 817

**p108 Baltic Sea** A 9076, B 8905, C 8908, D 7816, E 8907; **2** A 8906, B 8509, C 8908, D 8891, E 9548

**p109 Baltic Coast** A 8908, B 7827, C 9548, D 7816

**p110 Blueberry Patch** A 9603, B 9470, C 8505, D 7808; **2** A 7808, B 9470, C 9603, D 8505

**p111 Winter Blueberry Patch** A 9603, B 8505, C 9470, D 7808

**p112 Target** A Heathers 2439, B 9603, C 8505, D 8414, E 8910, F 2409; **2** A 8910, B 8906, C Heathers 2439, D 8414

**p113 Appliqué Posy** A 9603, B 8910, C 8414, D Heathers 2439, E 8505, F 2409

**p114 Aztec Sun** A 8414, B 7825, C 9496, D 8906, E (project only) 9573

**p116 Puffy Flower** A 9496, B 9477, C 9469; **2** A 9496, B 8908, C 7816

**p117 Puffy Picot Flower** A 9496, B 8912, C 7808

**p118 Connect Four** A 7808, B 7828, C 8903, D 7824, E 7816; **2** A 7808, B 7816, C 8903, D 7824, E 7828

**p119 Square of Four** A 7808, B 7828, C 8903, D 7824, E 7816

**p120 Magic Carpet** (all from Superwash range) A 887, B 820, C 1952, D 1921, E 897, F 814, G 914, H 807, I 804; **2** (all from Superwash range) A 804, B 914, C 897, D 1921, E 820, F 807, G 814, H 1952, I 887

**p121 Flying Carpet** (all from Superwash range) A 820, B 804, C 914, D 887, E 807

**p122 Octagon-framed Flower** A 8010, B 4146A, C 8509, D 9492, E Heathers 9561, F 8907; **2** A Heathers 9561 B 8907, C 8010, D 4146, E 8509, F 9492

**p123 Octagon Flower** A 8010, B 4146A, C 9548, D Heathers 9561, E 8509, F 9492

**p124 Diagonal Bobbles** A 8910, B 8912, C 7825, D 8908, E 9478, F 9496, G 9605; **2** A 9605, B 8910, C 8912, D 9478

**p125 Multi Diagonal Bobbles** A 8908, B 9478, C 9496, D 7825

**p126 Savannah Sunrise** A 9605, B 2439, C 2409, D 8505, E 8555; **2** A 9605, B 2409, C 8505, D 8555, E 2439

**p127 Savannah Sunset** A 8555, B 8505, C 2409, D 2439, E 9605

**p128 Candy** A Heathers 2439, B 9477, C 9478, D 8908; **2** A 9478, B 8505, C 9477, D 2439, E 8908

**p129 Candy Frills** A Heathers 2439, B 9478, C 8505, D 8908, E 9477

**p130 Lace Ripple** A 9470, B 9603, C Heathers 9561, D 9477; **2** A 9484, B 7808, C 9469, D 8912

**p131 Lace Waves** A 9484, B 9603, C Heathers 9561, D 8505

**p132 Woodland Web** A 7830, B 8910; **2** A 8010, B 7814

**p133 Woodland Rose** A 8910, B 8010, C 7830

**p134–135 Bold Block square & project** A Sierra 26, B Sierra 409, C Sierra 55

**p136 Swirly** A Superwash 851, B Superwash 826

**p136 Circles** (all from Superwash range) A 820, B 903, C 1973, D 804, E 851

**p137 Little Squares** (all from Superwash range) A 814, B 897, C 887, D 807, E 804

**p138–139 Ferris Wheel** (all from Superwash range) A 824, B 807, C 1911, D 914, E 804, F 887

**p140–141 Square Foot Garden** (all from Superwash range) A 820, B 914A, C 887, D 845, E 824, F 802, G 804, H 910A, I 807

## Credits

I'd like to say a huge thank you to my man, Sean Hall, who has had to listen to me rabbit on about wool, colors, and patterns, and a thank you to everyone at Quarto who has worked on the book, and for finding me.

References:
*75 Floral Blocks to Crochet* Betty Barnden
*200 Crochet Blocks* Jan Eaton
*Easy Crocheted Accessories* Carol Meldrum

With special thanks to Cascade Yarns for providing the yarns used in this book. All yarns are from the Cascade 220 range and are detailed on pages 143–144.
www.cascadeyarns.com